D0731339

We Came
to Santa Fe

WE CAME TO SANTA FE © 2009; edited by Victor di Suvero

FIRST EDITION 2009

10   9   8   7   6   5   4   3   2   1

LIBRARY OF CONGRESS CONTROL NUMBER: 2008939088

ISBN: 978-0-938631-39-2

DESIGN/PRODUCTION: SunFlower Designs of Santa Fe

Printed in China

PUBLISHED BY:

PENNYWHISTLE PRESS, INC.
P. O. Box 734, Tesuque, NM 87574 USA
EMAIL: pennywhistle@newmexico.com
WEBSITE: www.pennywhistlepress.org

We Came to Santa Fe

A number of stories describing the
backgrounds, reasons, trials, troubles and excitements
that brought this group of outstanding individuals
to make their homes in Santa Fe and its surroundings,
with an introduction by Victor di Suvero.

A Pennywhistle Press Anthology

Contents

Dedication

THIS BOOK, OR RATHER THIS COLLECTION of stories, memories, disclosures, background data, reasons, and troubles that brought us to Santa Fe is dedicated to all those that came before in terms of the reasons for the existence of the City of Santa Fe as we know it today.

It is an accumulation of dreams, desires, needs, appetites and disasters that have happened to people over the past four hundred years, beginning with Santa Fe's founding by Don Juan Oñate. It is also dedicated particularly to the memory of Juan Perez de Villagra, the poet and historian of Oñate's entry into this land whose *Historia de la Conquista de la Nueva Mexico* is an exciting but generally forgotten masterpiece which led to the establishment of the *Villa Real de la Santa Fe de San Francisco de Asis* in 1607.

This dedication will only list a few of the names that include all those adventurers, mystics, believers, warriors, politicians and ordinary people that have woven the fabric of this place over the centuries. This fabric was woven from the indigenous Pueblo traditions and the Pueblo Revolt, otherwise known as the First American Revolution, led by the charismatic leader Po'pay, who was responsible for the only action that succeeded in throwing the Spanish out of their conquered lands. Po'pay's statue represents the state of New Mexico in the Statuary Hall in the U.S. Capitol. Yes, the book is dedicated to Po'pay, to Peralta and the "Reconquesta," Kit Carson and General Kearney, to Fray Martinez and

Marble statue of Po'pay by sculptor Cliff Fragua of Jemez Pueblo, stands in the National Statuary Hall in Washington, D.C.

Photograph © Marcia Keegan

Bishop Lamy as well as to the Jewish traders and bankers who put up the money for the construction of the Cathedral of St. Francis when Bishop Lamy came to town to clean up the dilapidated state of the Catholic Church after the Treaty of Guadalupe Hidalgo in 1848. Yes, again, it is dedicated to the painter and architect William Penhallow Henderson and his wife, the poet Alice Corbin, who made the City a Mecca for their friends from Chicago, as well as Carl Sandburg, George Steighty, Georgia O'Keeffe, Mary Austin, and Mabel Dodge Lujan among the others who have all contributed to making Santa Fe the cultural center it is today.

This book is also dedicated to the continuity that has managed to survive all these years—a continuity that built the Cross of the Martyrs on the hilltop overlooking the city with a walkway studded with bronze plaques detailing the City's history. Dedicated also to those generous people who, having made fortunes in other parts of the world, having come to know Santa Fe and its history, have shared pieces of their goods and riches to maintain the history, culture and atmosphere of this City.

Santa Fe is unlike any other city I have known. One where three distinct cultures are alive and well, managing to meld and work together for the common good most of the time, an example to the rest of the world...dedicated also to all of its citizens who work and pray and help to feed others less fortunate than themselves as well as those of us whose public service keeps the City alive and functioning. In addition it is dedicated to those who serve to keep music, the dance and learning alive in this corner of the desert that has become home to those of us fortunate enough to have found our way here to live and breathe and sleep and sing in this unusual marvel, this curiosity and jewel among the smaller cities of the world... And, finally, dedicated to those whose stories are to be found within these covers and whose generosity in sharing their lives will serve to record who we are in this time and place, this City of Santa Fe at the beginning of its fifth century.

VICTOR DI SUVERO, Editor

Introduction

THERE ARE SO MANY WAYS in which the City of Santa Fe can be described that no single viewpoint ever is sufficient to properly take in the multiplicity of the City's ethnic, historical and cultural history. This City whose original and proper name given to it by its Spanish Conquistador and Founder Don Juan de Oñate was "La Villa Real de la Santa Fe de San Francisco de Asis." This name represented more than a mouthful particularly to the flood of Americans whose appetite for land had driven them westward from their original Atlantic bordering states that had become the United States of America in those early days.

It was that appetite, that hunger for land that had driven Fremont, Kearney, Kit Carson and the Lewis and Clark expeditions with the repeated cry of "Go West, Young Man" to reach out into what we now know as the Southwest and after the Mexican War and the Treaty of Guadalupe Hidalgo access to this Southwest by way of the Santa Fe Trail became possible if not exactly easy.

Traders and ranchers along with their families and institutions arrived to confront and deal with the local indigenous American Indian populations and cultures as well as the Hispanic traditions that had taken root in the fertile valleys and the rugged highlands of the area. This layering of culture and tradition still exists today. It is this vibrant and vital coexistence of differing attitudes and values that has made Santa Fe the unusual and exciting capital city of New Mexico that it is today.

Unlike metropolitan multicultural centers such as New York, Los Angeles and San Francisco, each one of which contains a multiplicity of cultural and racial elements that certainly characterize various parts of those large cities, Santa Fe is still small enough to permit the different individual cultures to express themselves in ways that are not dominant or contradictory.

This difference and the general availability of a wide variety of cultural and artistic differences has been one of Santa Fe's major attractions along with its location in one of the most picturesque corners of the world.

Given all of the above the fact that the City and its surrounding areas have attracted artists and writers, sculptors and poets as well as creative people of other disciplines that include music and dance as well as others interested in the histories and cultural treasures of the areas it is not surprising that one of the first questions asked of a new comer at any social gathering in the area happens to be the title of this book.

So that happens to be the origin of this collection of autobiographical answers to the standard questions. These answers by no claim to be absolute and all inclusive but may serve to introduce the Reader to the pleasures and surprises that have served to bring so many interesting people with their own interesting lives to this city in its corner of the Southwest.

Looking west from the hill above Santa Fe where the Martyrs Cross stands today.

HOW DID WE COME HERE?

by Victor di Suvero

How did we come here and to what end?
What was it that drew us here?
Was it the land calling, the piñon?
The great shaped clouds blessing the blue of the sky?
Was it the dawn's quiet or the other one,
The one that comes after the day of work, at dusk
In summer, promising rest and respite and all
The other good things we dreamed of when we let ourselves do so?

How did we come here? Was it the wind?
Or was it the star that moved us, all of us?
Tell me about the Anasazi, how they came here,
Out of the Earth's navel, the Sipapu, the hole
In the ground made by Coyote when Lightning
Came after him—tell me about the Old Ones,
The ones who came from over the edge
By starlight, riding the wind, driven
By hope as well as by terror—tell me!

How is it that we came here, to this place
Where the cottonwood grows? We brought
Our cooking pots and histories and prayers,
We brought our hopes to make a place
Where the children's children not yet
Born may come to tell each other stories
Of how it is that we came here
And why—and they may end up
Knowing more about it than we do now.
I have come to give
Thanks to wind and star and call of land
And all that served
To bring us here.

How I Came to Santa Fe

Babette Alfieri

Babette Alfieri is founder of Africa Calls Ltd., a Santa Fe based boutique safari design company that she co-owns with her daughter and business partner Christina. Babette spends half the year in Santa Fe, and the other half in the wilds of Africa in Zambia's South Luangwa National Park.

I N 1986, I SOLD MY BRONXVILLE, NY TOWNHOUSE to move to Zambia in Southern Africa. I was working for the prestigious tour operator, Abercrombie and Kent in charge of Sales and Marketing for the eastern half of the US, and managed to persuade them that I would be more useful to them in deepest Africa, (where back then we did not even have electricity or telephone lines!) than in New York. My motivation had been an unending love affair with Africa itself since my first exposure 12 years earlier, as well as a wonderful man, Phil Berry, with whom I still live.

Because I moved out of the country, I was allowed four years in addition to the normal two, to reinvest in a primary U.S. residence without penalty of capital gains assessment. This brought me to 1992, when I had no idea where to establish residency other than I wanted something different from New York. My daughter Christina had long since graduated from University and was well established in a banking career in Boston. I was thinking that a small condo unit on the California coast might provide a sufficiently suitable contrast to the east where I had been all my life.

With no anticipation of the outcome, I casually requested a stopover in Albuquerque on a mileage ticket to San Francisco, planning only to spend a few days to see Santa Fe before beginning my real estate search in earnest on the California coast. I had always been fascinated by Santa Fe, but knew nothing about it, other than that married friends had many years before sold their

Manhattan loft and taken a year off to travel the entire U.S. in search of where they most wanted to relocate. Their choice after a year of discovery across America was Santa Fe, a decision that had intrigued me. After a few days on my own there, I could understand the tremendous attraction they had immediately experienced, and determined to focus my energies on a real estate search of my own. Within a week, I had successfully bid on a condo villa at Rancho Encantado, and was the proud and happy owner of my own patch of enchantment. I closed on the precise day of my IRS deadline, six years after the closing in Bronxville.

By now my Abercrombie and Kent relationship had phased out and I had formed and incorporated **Africa Calls** with my sister in 1989. It presented a unique program to offer a five week American summer camp experience in Africa for teens, living on working coffee and tobacco farms, hiking and camping in wild national parks with highly qualified naturalists, experiencing meaningful cultural exchange with their African counterparts, and learning first-hand about Africa's conservation challenges. It had been a great success that first year with five adventurous teens, two guides, and myself as chaperone and I enthusiastically set about marketing the subsequent year's program. At this precise time the Gulf War erupted, and the last place any American parent would consider sending their teenage children alone was to Africa!

I had also been arranging safaris on my own by word of mouth through previous clients who knew I was actively involved with the emerging and exciting tourism potential of the South African region. Although I knew virtually no one when I arrived, I soon began meeting adventure-minded Santa Feans in early 1993, and hosted slide presentation evenings, on my own or with visiting professional safari operators and guides at Rancho Encantado when it was a

Babette and daughter Christina in Costa Rica in 1976.

vibrant and wonderful retreat. It was only a matter of time before a steady flow of travelers evolved who wished to experience the unspoiled and more remote regions of Zambia, Zimbabwe and Botswana. As a result, I then began spending half my year in Santa Fe, and the other half in Zambia where I had been living with Phil since 1986. The annual combination of Santa Fe with its unique blend of charm, sophistication, and old-world appeal, and the magnificent Luangwa Valley enriched with the most exciting of Africa's big game was quite intoxicating, and I always considered myself so utterly fortunate to have discovered them both, and to have them equally in my life.

Amongst my African adventures are many memorable and thrilling moments, including three "unscheduled" aircraft landings in such interesting locales as the middle of the Namib Desert at twilight with four other friends when our light aircraft hit a substantial boulder, collapsing the nose wheel and subsequently breaking both the wing and propeller. On another occasion I had been invited to accompany an elephant radar-tracking flight in a two seater Piper Super Cub in what was then Rhodesia before the end of their guerilla war. Faulty brakes caused us to swerve uncontrolled into a large tree stump in an isolated dry sand riverbed on takeoff resulting in a broken wing strut and bent propeller. The third incident occurred when traveling with 12 intrepid adventurers in a marvelous old PBY converted flying boat, the Catalina, that was recreating the magical flying journeys of Imperial Airways that traversed the length of Africa in the 1930's and 40's. We developed engine trouble enroute between Lake Malawi and Botswana, but ultimately through brilliant piloting, made a successful forced landing in an abandoned cotton field in the remote northeast corner of Zimbabwe. Thankfully each occasion resulted in no injuries, but the adrenalin level in such rugged and inaccessible places certainly remained high until we managed to be rescued.

Upended Super-Cub on takeoff from a remote sand river in Rhodesia, 1980 (now Zimbabwe).

Other encounters amongst many I recall, were on extended foot safaris with Phil in the wilds of the North and South Luangwa parks, camping out and following his old patrol routes where we waded waist-high through a crocodile and hippo-infested river with 25 scouts and porters, and a determined group of five young American lawyers. On another occasion we had to back off anxiously from sleeping lions we had almost stumbled upon in long grass that growled, snarled, and threatened ferociously with lashing tails and bared fangs until we were out of their immediate range. We have dealt with fire that in moments destroyed our grass and reed bush hut and all our belongings at our walking safari camp; and more recently record-breaking floods that flowed knee-high through our 30 year old house on the Luangwa River and swept away most of the beautiful wooded grove around us, leaving us in an exposed and tenuous position on the riverbank as we face the on-coming rainy season. We have had encounters with a familiar and persistent bull elephant who eventually nearly demolished our bush camp kitchen once he tasted such tempting treats as home-made carrot cake and cornflakes; and been awakened in the middle of the night to find a leopard with his fresh kill in the low branches only a few feet above our heads as we watched from our open-air bathroom. Most frightening was a medical air evacuation I had to arrange for Phil to South Africa with a life-threatening bout of malaria, during the unfortunate simultaneous occurrence of an attempted but failed Zambian *coup d'etat* that grounded all aircraft including those of the Flying Doctors. It was with huge relief that we were granted an exception the following day by special Zambian Air Force clearance.

Babette and daughter, Christina, in front of a single-engine Cessna elephant research aircraft in Kenya, 1980.

In 1995, my daughter Christina told me she would much rather design safaris with me than remain in banking which, although offering a far more lucrative and secure future, was certainly a less gratifying and exciting career choice than Africa presented. I felt incredibly blessed and at the same time flattered to know that she wanted to work with me, and happily taught her all I knew about the African safari business that I had by now been involved in for more than two decades. She had been traveling to Africa since our first adventure when she was only seven and had returned dozens of times over the years. Her practical experience was invaluable, coupled with her fine administrative, financial, and organizational skills. Her strengths, combined with my marketing expertise were a wining combination that has withstood many challenges in the travel industry, not the least of which were the events of 9/11 and thereafter.

Three years later, Christina moved from Boston, having felt the same undeniable attraction to Santa Fe that had so profoundly affected me. We have been fortunate and rewarded in the intervening years to meet hundreds of like-minded adventurous lovers of Africa, many from Santa Fe, whose lives have been enriched and forever changed by their African travels we have arranged. To be able to ignite the spark of a dream safari so far away in the U.S., and then be in Africa to see those expectations fulfilled and surpassed in most cases, is truly a unique privilege that I have been given.

Babette's self-portrait on safari in Zambia, 2004.

The Great Welcome of Toads
Page Allen

Page Allen is an artist whose paintings, writings, publications and advisory art activities have achieved recognition in many areas not only in Santa Fe but also in New York and in Ireland.

WHEN I WAS SIXTEEN, in the fervor and effervescence of the 60's, an article appeared in *LIFE Magazine* that featured Georgia O'Keeffe and New Mexico. I pored over the photographs and paintings, entranced that a place could be so deepened, so manifest, through an artist. The purity of the light, the eccentric and lyrical profiles of the land and the vivid hues of the exposed earth were all distilled by O'Keeffe's eye and hand. They became her *Black Place; Black Cross, New Mexico; Summer Days…* Nothing was described only for description's sake, and yet it was accurate, as evident in the photographs. The paintings inhabited the place, intensely, and transcended it. I could see that New Mexico, in the hands of an artist of O'Keeffe's power, lent itself to this paradox: physical, spiritual, visible, invisible. I kept the article for a long time.

I married very young. My beautiful carpenter husband and I had moved west from New England to St. Louis, when the inevitable time came to part. After our twilight year by the Mississippi, I left for New York, to try myself in the place for serious painters. He came to New Mexico for a healing summer, and stayed. Scott Morris chose the Southwest as his home then, and spent the rest of his years building, inventing and exploring the river rapids of his beloved desert.

In New York, I made my camp of independence in an old sail maker's loft, on cobble-stoned Water Street, beneath the Brooklyn Bridge. New York Harbor was my far horizon, the Fulton Fish Market my fish-scaled, pungent, mosquito flown neighborhood, as organic and spacious as New York could offer.

After the years of apprenticeship with Scott, his hammer-wielding mate, I proudly put up the walls of my loft myself, carrying the heavy sheetrock panels up four flights. And yet, having driven my point of self-sufficiency, I yearned for home. Where was home now? I was twenty four; I had been with a man for five years and had grown in his sheltering embrace. He was in New Mexico. I loved New York, was fiercely proud of my steam-vent clouded, dragon-fuming street, my friends in SoHo, my subway savvy and my pilgrimages to MoMA with my own Artist's Pass. And yet I was pining, unsure.

And so I planned my first trip to Santa Fe. I went to the jewelry district along 42nd Street and sold my Great-grandmother's broche. Her portrait, Ann Page Wilder at nineteen, painted in Florence, hangs in my studio now. I bought a plane ticket to Albuquerque. It was March of 1976. I went to La Guardia, wearing my Grandmother's Pendleton jacket, woven in a striking black and white Navajo pattern. As I waited to board, a man came up to me and asked about the jacket. He said he was from Santa Fe and had a gallery there—Forrest Fenn. He contrived to sit next to me and I began to take in the flavor of the West in his words. When we landed in Albuquerque, at the old airport, there was Scott—and the light.

I hope one day to sense New Mexico as keenly as I did in that first week: the piñon smoke; the vast, pink luminance of morning; the color of the earth and the size of the sky. I bought moccasins to better walk on the dirt. I made many solo days' journeys: up to the Puerto Nambe, through the aspen groves; out to the land that Forrest Fenn told me of, where I saw petroglyphs for the first time. The marks were so simply and intently made,

Photo by
Alice Bissel

Water Street Loft, 1976.

upon the stone canyon walls. Such eloquent, mysterious symbols, they showed me the ancient capacity of our human hands to form and transform, to evoke and to pray. Nearby, I found a grinding stone and a scraper, both perfectly fitted hand tools, which returned to New York with me, as talismans.

I must have been thinking of O'Keeffe, because I drove up to Ghost Ranch one day. Like many, I simply looked around and began to walk. Finally I sat down to eat my lunch and discovered that my hard-boiled egg was less than hard. Dismayed, I stared at the soft yolk—and then at the earth pigments all around me. Slowly I began to mix them in my palm—ochre, violet, dark red—and the golden yolk. Slowly I smeared the paste on my face. Seeking an initiation that would join me to this place and even transform me, this seemed a clumsy gesture, and yet it was eloquent. Marking my face committed me in the most basic way to the sight and insight of becoming an artist. It also joined me to the land with a touch as tender and as primitive as making love.

When I returned to New York, my work changed. I drew on sheets of paper that seemed to me like rock surfaces, or like skins stretched on my loft walls. I was more aware of the power in making a mark. I drew with pastels that remembered their earth pigment nature. The shapes I drew were organic and geologic, as though I were exploring valleys, dry river beds, hills, feeling the imagined topography under my smudged fingers.

Oh so much later, in my late twenties, I decided to return to Santa Fe for the summer. I had been teaching art near Chicago, showing my work in the city, finishing graduate school out in the cornfields at NIU. But again I had run aground against my loneliness. I decided to seek work with a different kind of intimacy and intensity, to stop painting and begin further graduate work in psychology and art therapy. But before the new fall semester, I had the summer, my teacher's pay and the promise of part-time jobs with Eleanor Caponigro and with Fenn Galleries. My family friend, Susan Herter, promised to welcome me. My uncle, Dave Allen, an architect with Skidmore, Owings and Merrill, would introduce me to his old friend, Emily Barnes. I rented a room in the Casa Solana neighborhood and drove from Illinois in my rusted Datsun. I had no thought of painting; I just wanted to be in New Mexico again.

It was very hot the summer of 1980. I often borrowed a bike and sweated my way out to Tesuque, up and down the hill of Bishop's Lodge Road, passing the house where I now paint and live. My friend, Maggie, was out at

Myrtle Steadman's house, working as cook for an Opera director lodged there. I ate with them some evenings—sumptuous steaks from the Tesuque Market butcher, fresh guacamole, pitchers of iced coffee with cream, chocolate cake. Maggie kept a generous kitchen. At dusk, I loved to see the fat New Mexico toads emerge, hopping ponderously across the cooling flagstones.

I called Emily Barnes, a gracious, refined soul. She said, please come for a drink—and then, please come for dinner when my son is visiting. On July 26th, I met Nat Owings on Emily's patio. The next day, we picnicked and swam with Maggie and Nat's friend, Peter, near to Otowi Crossing on the Rio Grande. Later in that hot, hot week, we hiked in the Barranca, across the Pojuaque Wash from the Owings home in Jacona. When I drove away, Nat filled my lap with apricots from the trees and overgrown zucchini from the garden. I laughed and laughed. New Mexico was abundant!

I went east to my graduate program with a joyfully aching heart. All that year we trekked between Philadelphia and Montana, where Nat was professor at MSU in Bozeman. Gradually I realized that I could be a good therapist or, with luck, a good artist, not both. With Nat, now I could choose. We were married in Yellowstone Park. I returned to painting, to teaching art and began learning the Northern Rockies. Their scale and beauty gave new freedom to my painting. I had been bitten by the deconstructive bug, felt compelled to dissect the process of art and to doubt its power. Now, held in the power of the landscape, I could believe once more in art's aspiration and celebration.

Bishop's Lodge Studio, 2007.

Photo by Mark Mulholland

My confidence in painting as an act of reverence, not an ornament but truly potent, grew as my life re-approached Santa Fe. Often Nat and I returned, driving down to see Emily in the summers. Nat would help out at Ray Dewey's gallery during Indian Market, and enjoyed it so much that one day in 1985 Ray said, "Why don't we do this full time? The space upstairs is for rent." For three years we commuted between his brand new gallery, Owings-Dewey Fine Art, and the University in Bozeman. I drove down the Rockies, with the pets, the clothes and even the television. Descending the canyon from Taos, there was always a thrill of homecoming, as I tasted the air of the Rio Grande mixed with its red earth, black rock walls.

Now, twenty years later, I am still at home here. This land holds the human spirit in the earth colors, the pottery shards, the petroglyphs, the adobe mud churches, kivas and ever present mountains. The devout role of art in the Hispanic and Indian cultures gives me ballast. Here I can believe that art is not futile or merely commercial, though I have come to respect the natural intertwining of pilgrimage town with market town.

I may be filled with doubts, always, but here my questions may become fruitful ones, not withering. I can affirm and have faith. In the past years, I have been able to reach through painting into mythic storytelling. I invent books through painting, then writing, that explore who we are and who we may be. The first two books are tales of children on their way to be born, hero's journeys on The Great River of Stars. A third book, in progress, describes an imagined path through death and a return to the River. The mythic and spiritual aspects of this land again help me to persist and see, beyond what I see.

On this adventure I have discovered another place long at home with imagination in the service of devotion. I often go to Ireland now, where I collaborate in adapting my first journey book for theater, and where a resident workplace for artists has proved a good counterpoint to my Santa Fe studio. I visit ancient stones on the island of Eire, returning to the sky islands of New Mexico. And always the welcome of the clouds, the bare earth, the ravens and the toads.

Why I Came to New Mexico

Patrizia Antonicelli

Patrizia Antonicelli is the owner and operator of Seven Directions, a touring company offering special tours of Native American historic, art and cultural sites to individuals and groups coming from Europe. Her many contacts in Italy and France give an international flare to her various activities.

BECAUSE I BELONG HERE. This is why I moved to Santa Fe after visiting year after year since 1989. In late October of that year, after landing at Albuquerque Sunport, I rented a car and started my way up without the faintest idea of where I was and what I could expect. No more than five minutes went by and I was hooked. The initial emotions I had are difficult to relate simply in words because of how I was struck and amazed by all that surrounded me and that still today stirs my being.

The land is beautiful and the atmosphere invigorating; its rich history creates interesting contrasts that become a part of everyday life; the diverse culture is all around us; the people create an incredible community that is visible through its generosity in a way that is unseen elsewhere.

I then quickly realized that I was not the only person to experience love at first sight for this land: many famous and worldly people have described this place with passages that are more inspiring than I can imagine. But this is not the point. It's about the connection I immediately felt: a new and unexpected experience and an extraordinary one that, 14 years later, gave me the courage to leave my beautiful country—Italy—my work, my friends and the houses I loved. The world I left behind created a very special life for me, surrounded by parents that helped my country successfully get out of the dark years of fascism and the war and build bridges to other countries; by a cultural, intellectual and business milieu from which I received incredible stimulations and teachings and by many dear friends with a big heart. But New Mexico was inevitably in my life! Here I was welcomed by people who over the years guided me in the discovery of the Land of Enchantment and helped me understand all the different angles one must consider in order to get the right picture. Those people are still my best friends today and my exciting new extended family.

Back in the late 80's I was living in London where, after many years in the corporate world as manager and consultant in communications and Public Affairs international companies—a very intense world indeed—I opened my gallery of American Native and Folk Art—P&A Collection—and Santa Fe was the obvious destination. My library became unmanageable for the too many books I kept adding hoping to learn and understand a world that completely absorbed and fascinated me. My interest for Native American art and cultures brought me here but the journey continued to other spaces that I believe only the land, the sky, the people, and the unique and diversified cultural environment of New Mexico can offer. However, after living here for some time, I also came to the conclusion that, no matter what, even today this is still the Farwest! The inspiring book *Blood and Thunder,* by Hampton Sides, helped me understand that 150 years are not enough to overcome the incredibly intricate history that shaped, for better or for worse, this unusual State. A unique place indeed!

Patrizia at the time of her first arrival in Santa Fe, 1992.

*Patrizia presenting a
cultural discussion at
Santa Fe Baking Company
literary gathering in 2007.*

It is not always easy to live here. But when things seem to be too difficult and one gets to the stage of throwing in the towel it is enough to drive
for ten minutes out of town: once again you feel life couldn't be better.

Regrets? None, so far…I strongly believe that changes make life interesting and worth living. I hate monotony! Although I have to admit that there
is one thing I do miss: Italian food! Particularly the simple dishes one can
find in the countryside, where vegetable and fruit have a taste, where simple
ingredients make your soul and heart rejoice. Unfortunately no win-win situation really exists, we are humans and this is not Heaven, although for me
it is the closest place to it.

When I first arrived I was immediately told that one needs to live here
for at least three or four years in order to become, and feel, comfortable and
settled in. I made it!

I feel fortunate to have succeeded in realizing a dream and truly discovering where I feel at home.

Why I Came to Santa Fe

Stuart Ashman

Stuart Ashman *is a recognized artist in many media as well as a musician. His many talents and his excellent administrative abilities have earned him the position of Cabinet Secretary, Department of Cultural Affairs, State of New Mexico appointed by Governor Richardson.*

I GREW UP ALONG A BEAUTIFUL HARBOR in Matanzas, Cuba. We lived in a big house that my parents and I shared with my cousin and his parents who were holocaust survivors. My mother and father had been in Cuba since the 1920's and were well established there. It was a house full of affection and the security of family. We had an old Renault. We would all pack into it on weekends to go to nearby Varadero beach.

I was twelve years old when my family left Cuba. In the summer of 1960 the United States declared that Cuban citizens could emigrate. My parents had always wanted the economic opportunities that life in "America" could offer, and this was like a dream come true for them. We landed in New York on a Friday, I was in junior high school in Bensonhurst, Brooklyn on Monday, and my dad was in Manhattan looking for work as a correspondent—he could write and speak in six languages.

I completed high school and college in New York, and after working as an art therapist in Rome, New York for two years, I decided to go to graduate school in Rochester, New York.

In the winter of 1974, I had had enough of Rochester winters and moved to Hawaii. Why Hawaii? Perhaps I was looking for the island paradise where I grew up.

I lived in Honolulu, and spent some time in Maui, Molokai and the Big Island. It was the summer of 1977 and I was living on Kauai.

In those days, life seemed carefree and almost anything was possible. I was working at the Lomi Farm, a papaya farm that had been converted to a retreat center. We had organized a tai-chi workshop by renowned master Al Huang.

One of the workshop participants was a woman named Zoë Sheckman. She lived on 160 acres in Alto, New Mexico and wanted to start an artist in residence program there. She asked me to help her organize it, along with Lynn Blake, who was my assistant and John, the cook. John had been the cook at the Esalen Institute in Big Sur.

Lynn and I booked flights to San Francisco where she had left her old Volvo 144. We arrived after midnight, took a taxi to her car and left for New Mexico. We spent the first night overlooking San Francisco Bay in the old Volvo. I named the old car "Sherman" after the venerable World War II tank.

We drove to San Diego, Tucson and finally made our way to Alto, New Mexico. I still remember the way the air felt, the smell of the piñon trees and the beauty of New Mexico. It was so different than what I had expected.

I had been in graduate school for an MFA in photography at the Rochester Institute of Technology before I left for Hawaii, and had continued to work in photography and drawing for the years I was there. I resumed my work as an artist in Alto making primitive frames for my drawings out of old wood I found.

Stuart Ashman with a friend on his arrival to Santa Fe.

Life in Alto was slow and there was not much to stimulate me artistically. I had been told that Santa Fe was a good place for artists and I had always wanted to visit there.

I borrowed a Ford Bronco from Zoë's ranch and headed for Santa Fe. Now, there was a town I could relate to! I spent the weekend in town and noticed there was a small gallery that was looking for new artists.

It was the Artist's Co-op on Palace Avenue—where the Llewellyn Gallery is today. I came back a few weeks later and presented a group of pastel drawings I had made in Hawaii and framed up in Alto. The reception was positive beyond my expectations. They accepted me into the gallery and offered me an exhibition opening on December 18th, right before Christmas!

I left my works there and when I came back after the New Year, the show was sold out and there was a story in the *Santa Fe Reporter* about my work that included reproductions of my drawings. That and the fact that you could get an espresso coffee in Santa Fe (at the French Pastry Shop) made this little city a formidable candidate for my new residence. Six weeks later I had moved here.

Part of the arrangement of being a member of the Artist's Co-op was that you had to gallery sit two days a month—in addition to paying your $30 a month rent (the storefront was $360 a month and there were 12 artists). I really looked forward to sitting the gallery because many of the artists in the community would come by.

I had long conversations with Gene Newman and Eli Levin. Gene told me about a juried show that was coming up at a place called the Armory for the Arts. I entered and got a piece in the show—not only that, but I was given a job to work in the gallery installing the show. I worked there for several years and it was there that I met most, if not all of the artists working in Santa Fe. I also had opportunity to meet and work with the curatorial staff at the Museum of Fine Arts. The Museum was closed for renovations and they used the Armory Gallery to mount an exhibition of the work of Chuzo Tamotzu, an eccentric Japanese painter that lived in Santa Fe.

When the Museum reopened I was hired to install the inaugural exhibition in the new wing designed by Edward Larrabee Barnes and Antoine Predock. I had the privilege of installing Georgia O'Keeffe's "Spring 1948"—coincidentally, the season and year I was born in.

When I lived in Hawaii, the locals always talked about how the islands opened their arms to you and invited you to stay. I felt that Santa Fe had opened its arms wide and welcomed me. It was a place where I could do my work, socialize with my peers and, once again, speak to people on a daily basis in my native language, Spanish.

I worked at many jobs over the years to support my time in the studio. I was a waiter, a maitre'd, a construction worker. It was in the early 80's I decided that I had all this experience with art, and perhaps I should develop a parallel career using these skills.

So I worked as an artist in residence for the New Mexico Arts Division, traveling around the state to schools, community centers, senior centers, even the State Hospital in Las Vegas. Later I became the art teacher at the New Mexico State Penitentiary.

One day, some good friends, photographers David Scheinbaum and Janet Russek, invited me to their house for a bridge game. I didn't know how to play bridge, but they said to come over and meet a nice group of their friends. The most important of these people was a lovely woman, a potter, who had studied in Mexico and spoke Spanish—Peggy Gaustad. It didn't take too long to realize that New Mexico was giving me my soul mate.

A year later we were sharing a house, and another year later we were married in the gardens of the Randall Davey Audubon Center. In 1986 we moved to our little "schoolhouse" in Tesuque. In 1988 we were blessed with our daughter Liliana and two years later with our son Sam.

By this time, I really had to make some sales of my art and work at my "parallel" career. The curatorial staff of the Museum of Fine Arts, with whom I had worked with a decade earlier, asked me to come and work at the Museum, as the curator of the Governor's Gallery.

I was hesitant to take on such a job, because I thought it would interfere too much with my career as an artist. But, I seized the opportunity. A little more than three years later, I found myself as the Director of the Museum of Fine Arts. After eight years with the Museum, some good friends, who were on the Board of the Spanish Colonial Arts Society asked me if I would consider becoming their executive director and help them in the building and opening of a museum dedicated to their collection.

The appreciation I have for the Spanish people of New Mexico, and the economics made the opportunity irresistible, so I accepted. We built and opened the Museum and it was a big success.

Stuart Ashman today.

Over the years, I had befriended Congressman Richardson, and when I was at the Museum of Spanish Colonial Art, I asked him if he would be willing to serve on our Board. Our Board members were thrilled that he agreed, as there had been some talk that he would run for Governor. He ran and easily defeated his opponent.

About eight months after the Governor took office in 2003, I was named Secretary of Cultural Affairs—in Governor Richardson's Cabinet! New Mexico had opened its arms even wider.

We still live in our little schoolhouse in Tesuque. Liliana just completed her freshman year at Drew University and Sam is a senior at Monte del Sol Charter School.

Santa Fe welcomed me and continues to nourish me and my family. I feel so fortunate that New Mexico embraced me so clearly and warmly.

I could not have written a better story if I had planned it.

Why I Came to Santa Fe
as seen through the eyes of a 10-year-old
BrandyWine Avila

BrandyWine Avila pursues her career as a personal assistant, office manager, and general facilitator for a number of small businesses in Santa Fe; is "Mom" to many, young and old; and lives with her 12-year-old daughter Alejandra. She found a new talent during the production of this book: she was recognized as one of three winners in an amateur photo contest held in celebration of the 50th Anniversary of the Santa Fe Historic Ordinance.

I T WAS 30 YEARS AGO. I WAS 10. My soul searching, eccentric parents chose to uproot me from my comfort zone, leaving the conventional troughs of Salt Lake City, Utah, for more rugged, diverse and unknown "elsewhere's." They didn't know exactly where they were going; they just knew they had to go! So away we went, leaving my huge 4'x2' teddy bear behind because he wouldn't fit into our '54 Chevy Panel Truck (named Sally), amongst the jungle of plants and other belongings, with promises he would be sent for as soon as we found our roots! I threatened to stay behind until they found their roots, but angrily, I obeyed and joined them on the quest for better horizons. That horizon, I recall, being "someplace between here and somewhere in Oklahoma." Oklahoma?! Or was it Tennessee? Or was it Hawaii?

The first curiosity and consideration for a new location was Moab, Utah; every Spring we would go on an adventurous backpacking vacation somewhere in Southern Utah which had always been so much fun, so I was somewhat comfortable with the idea. We arrived in Moab after what seemed to a 10-year-old as hours upon hours of driving! Curious little place, I thought. Not much here but small town, strange colored dirt and peculiarly created landscapes!

We purchased some supplies and settled for the night at Arches National Monument. Wow, this place was what I imagined Mars would look like! What an interesting place to live. I wondered what I'd learn here! Martian?

After a week or so of burning sun, sleeping with the sand and the decision that this just wasn't the place, my parents decided to move on. But which direction—toward the West Coast or toward the East? The final evening of our stay at Arches we met a couple and their son. The man turned out to be the Australian Ambassador to the UN at the time and had been traveling from the East Coast to the West Coast on an extended vacation. My parents asked that evening as we all visited around the campfire, (by the way I was ecstatic to have someone to play with besides my invisible friends!) where they had been that was mild in winter and summer and would be a great place to grow plants. This is my 10-year-old recollection. I'm sure they asked very different questions but in my minds eye my parents seemed to have jungle fever when it came to having plants in their home! (Couldn't they get rid of just a couple of plants so my teddy bear could come with us?) The couple replied out of all the diverse and different places they had enjoyed the most was…you guessed it…Santa Fe! So away we went. To find Santa Fe, somewhere between here and….

FULL MOON
HOT SUN

We camped out at Mesa Verde—both beautiful green and desery too. Loved it! How about we just live here, the Indians did, how come we can't? But off we went once again away from the tremendous landscaping and childlike daydreaming, to continue our trek to Santa Fe.

BrandyWine, aged 7, with her parents at Lake Powell, Utah, 1974.

Hours upon hours of driving, watching the scenery go by, potty breaks, tire blow outs, hot sun, rain storms, tensions mounting, music turned up so as to drown out tension, we drove and drove and drove and drove and crawled up this hill, I later learned, was called La Bajada. As we reached the top and picked up some speed we rounded the corner and it hit us like a bucket of ice-cold water during a heat wave…gasp…Santa Fe! Charming little town nestled amongst the foothills of the Sangre de Cristo's, sunset was approaching, and the tension subsided, the music was turned off and a burst of excitement fell over all of us. This looked as though it could be the place! There were big-toothed grins on both my parents' faces as we entered the city limits and drove toward downtown.

"Um, excuse me, did the roofs get cut off the houses? Look Ma…there's Indians! And Cowboys, real ones!" I stated as we drove around the Plaza. We located a grocery store and after loading up for the night headed up the mountain to Black's Canyon in the Santa Fe National Forest to set up what would be our homebase while we scouted out the City Different (boy was it different to me!) in the days to come.

It was Halloween time and not knowing the neighborhoods I was not allowed to Trick or Treat but was allowed a caramel apple for dessert and was told a chilling ghost story by the fire late at night that still haunts me to this day! That was a great replacement for the disappointment felt when I was told I couldn't trick or treat. And what a beginning to a new adventure in life!

My dad soon had a job interview and being November now, it began to get too cold

BrandyWine in Santa Fe, 1989.

BrandyWine with her daughter, Alejandra, in Santa Fe 2006.

up in the mountains so my parents decided to visit the College of Santa Fe to see if we could get a shower. We met Ted, the Student Body President at the time, who lived on-campus and his friend Ed, who had a house off-campus. Ted was somehow able to get permission to allow us to use a dorm room for the time being and later we lived with Ed until we found our home. We found it difficult to find a place. Unfortunately, many rentals wouldn't allow children or pets…and get this…no plants! Finally, we found a quaint little adobe near downtown and set down our roots! My 4'x2' teddy bear now had a place to call home! Still to this day when I dream of going home, I go to that house on Granada Street.

It was now time to enroll at the neighborhood school, Wood Gormley, and I could walk to school! Neat! I would be enrolling in fifth grade. However, the only class that had room for me was a bilingual one! Oh boy, I thought, I was going to learn Spanish instead of settling for Martian…much better! And that is how we came to Santa Fe….

The infamous parents in this story still live in Santa Fe with their jungle of plants, birds, raccoons and other assorted creatures who have "adopted" them. Russell Elliott is a specialty carpenter making art with wood as well as building custom homes and other creations. For recreation, he blows one-of-a-kind glass sculptures at Prairie Dog Glass in Jackalope. Sunflower has a free-lance business designing books (and other material) for assorted publishers throughout Santa Fe, enjoys creating kirigami, pop-up cards and displays, as well as photo collages for family and clients.

How We Came to Santa Fe
Mikaela & Craig Barnes

Craig Barnes is an author, playwright, political commentator on public radio, formerly a civil rights lawyer and mediator in international disputes in Russia, the Caucuses and Central Asia. His books include Growing Up True, *(2001),* In Search of the Lost Feminine, *(2006), and* Democracy at the Crossroads *(2008) and his plays include "A Nation Deceived," (2006), "King's Yellow," (2004), and "Elizabeth I," (2001). He runs a website on impeachment at ANationDeceived.org.*

IT WAS NOT REALLY FAIR. We would have gone anywhere. Mikaela and I were in Leningrad, in 1990, sleeping in a musky room in which the ratio of mosquitoes to humans was about twenty-to-one. Leningrad was not only an example of decaying communism but also a city on a swamp. We attempted to sleep hiding under sheets, totally covered, and slept on separate, hard couches in a room that had previously been occupied by the aunt of our friend, Boris. A year before the aunt, an old lady, had been crossing the street and had been hit by a car. Boris had not yet gotten around to removing her clothes from the closet so we hung our shirts next to his aunts faded old pink dresses. Mikaela observed that we were sleeping in a room with a ghost and blood-sucking mosquitoes.

I was in Leningrad to get some stories about the birth of democracy and the first representative elections in over 70 years. Some days I left Mikaela in the apartment and went to the old, gilded palace where the newly elected Lensoviet, "the city council," met and I tried to understand all the shouting and posturing and recrimination that had built up in the pent-up passions of 70 years. Communists were shouting at liberals who were shouting at leaders trying to start personality cults and journalists were grumbling in the corners that chaos would not be a good basis for a new government.

Russia in 1990 was not a happy place. When Mikaela and I went out along the crowded Nevsky Prospeckt in search of a chicken, or milk, or some small sweet cakes to feed to dinner guests, we had to be quite careful. Not just to avoid getting run over "like Boris poor-departed aunt," but not to get pummeled in some street-corner fight. The sound of fists smacking chins and roars of rage and pain were a regular encounter whenever we went out foraging for a chicken or a cloth bag or even to get a letter at the post office. Stores were largely empty and our most constant activity was searching for food. We were apt to walk and ride buses from one store after the next, criss crossing the city.

Mikaela did not much care for the crush along the sidewalks. One time we were on a bus to somewhere and I was squeezed in the aisle between two very large women. More and more large people kept pushing into the aisle until I was partially lifted off my feet, wedged sideways in the air. Mikaela was somewhere dangling from a strap and I was in a close encounter that was very awkward.

Finally, out the window of the bus I could see the Eighteenth Century bridge and then the grey block of communist-era shops where we might find a chicken. I pushed my feet to the floor and began most urgently to squeeze through the grey wool human barriers between us and the door. Mikaela got there first and popped out onto the sidewalk. I was then crushed by a sea of incoming passengers, closing over me like the Red Sea. For a moment I was afraid that I might be swept away, never to see Mikaela again, leaving her on the side-

Craig and Mikaela Barnes on their first visit to the Pink Adobe, August, 1990.

walk like Lara in Zhivago. Desperately, I squeezed through and fell trembling onto the sidewalk, eyeglasses dangling from one ear. My pants were also sliding down. The crush had undone my glasses, my belt, and my shirt was out. I seized Mikaela's hand and we held to each other for awhile.

One day in April we had to go to Moscow because Mikaela had a broken tooth. All our friends advised us not to go to a Soviet dentist. I found my way to the local monitor of foreigners and asked for permission to take my wife to Helsinki, Finland. The lady was embedded behind a desk in the back of a dark office at the head of some dark stairs in a dark part of the city. She heard my appeals and replied that we could go to Helsinki, yes, but we could not return. Our visas allowed for only one entry, and we had already used that one entry since, obviously, I was standing there in Leningrad, in her office, inside the Soviet Union.

I had been advised to offer the lady some cosmetic supplies, the which I did. She said thank you and accepted them. But I had not guessed the right price. She said that she was still sorry, Craig and Mikaela Barnes could leave the country, all right, but could not return. It would take more than cosmetics.

Desperate, because Mikaela was in real pain, I then searched about and learned of a Swiss-trained dentist in Moscow, a city which was, of course, still in the country and would not require a re-entry. The travel would be by overnight train on the famous Leningrad to Moscow run. Unfortunately, however, I could not just go to the station and buy a ticket. If a person like me went to the railway station the answer was routinely, *Nyet*. All sold out. So I asked our friend Boris how to get a ticket to Moscow.

"Take the bus on the Nevsky Prospeckt to the Moscovsky Hotel," he said. "Go around the corner to a big grey building. Go up the steps and when you are inside turn right to room 104. When you get into the office, ask for Natalia Andreevna. Tell her that her good friend Boris Galperin sent you. Tell her you need two tickets on the train to Moscow. She will help you because we are friends."

I did as I was told: Took the bus; found the hotel; went round the corner and found room 104. There were signs on the door that read, "Do Not Enter." "Enter Only Upon Request." "Break Between 11:45 and 1:30." None of these was very inviting.

Waiting in the hallway for approximately an hour, I studied a Russian newspaper to improve my vocabulary for the challenge that was ahead. Eventually, I was the last person standing and a voice through a loud speaker above my head scratched out the single word: "Next."

I turned the handle went in and approached a forbidding counter, wondering who to talk to. A woman on the other side of the counter scrutinized me. I asked for Natalia Andreevna.

"I am Natalia Andreevna," said the woman.

"Your friend Boris Galperin sent me," I said.

"Who?" She looked empty, like a clean white plate.

"Boris Galperin," I said again very distinctly.

"I do not know any Galperin," she said just as distinctly.

This was life in the Soviet Union: No friends, no contacts, no tickets.

"My wife has a broken tooth." I spoke the words slowly and in some obvious despair. "We have to go to Moscow to find a dentist. The pain is quite bad."

Natalia Andreevna looked at me for some time. Maybe she thought I was telling the truth or maybe she could see the fear in my eyes or maybe she thought it the best story she had ever heard from a capitalist. Slowly, I could see a smile creep around her eyes. "I will help you," she said.

"Thank you," I said, and never meant it more.

Andreevna took from me a handful of bills, left the room to go to some secret place and was gone for about ten minutes. When she came back she smiled as if, of course, she always knew everything would be all right.

I felt like crying.

Soon thereafter Mikaela and I rode the legendary overnight train to Moscow, the same route that Lenin had taken in 1917 to bring the proletarian revolution to Russia. That night, just before we left Boris' apartment we had a call from Santa Fe. Our son Will and his wife Julia were expecting their first child and Julia had just gone into labor.

Mikaela and I rode through that long night bouncing along through the Russian woods very aware that we would not be good grandparents so far away in Leningrad. We arrived in Moscow the next morning cold and stiff and then found a place to stay with our friends, Sergei and Anna. Then we found the dentist, and then that night when we were already asleep the phone rang. It had to be a call from someone in a different time zone. It had to be our son Will. Sergei brought me the phone. A thin, tired voice shouted all the way from New Mexico: "We have a son!"

After that, there was no doubt. Enough of chicken shopping and mosquitoes and Boris' aunt's clothes. We were headed home. At the end of June we left Leningrad for the last time and by July were in Santa Fe to visit our new grandson, Elisha T. Barnes. Mikaela and I drove to see him in their house on Otero Street where they still live. Then we wandered out to Albertsons and gazed in awe at all the chickens and butters, soaps, aspirins, cloth bags and jams that just anyone could buy. The next day we went house hunting.

Craig and Mikaela at home in Santa Fe, 2004.

Why and How We Came to Santa Fe
John & Barbara Berkenfield

*Barbara and **John Berkenfield** moved from the suburbs of New York to Santa Fe in 1989. John is Director of Planning at El Rancho de Las Golondrinas, an active participant in the local arts community and hospitality industry, and serves on the County Lodger's Tax Advisory Board. He won the Mayor's Award for Excellence in the Arts for community involvement in 2003. Barbara is a free-lance writer, poet, gallery associate and a docent at Las Golondrinas. Her book of poetry* Driving Toward the Moon *was published by Sunstone Press in 2006.*

IT'S USUAL TO ASK PEOPLE WHOM you have just met why...and how...they happened to come to Santa Fe and we have answered these questions often over the last 18 years. However, when our friend Victor di Suvero asked us to answer these questions for this book, we had to reflect a bit more deeply about the road that brought us to this wonderful city.

At one time in our lives we were tried and true Easterners with no connection to New Mexico, or even the West. When you are raised and schooled in the East, you learned history from teachers focused on the East and the English. We heard of Coronado, but class time was given more to stalwarts like John Smith, the settlement at Jamestown, and the contributions made by the English to the New World and the colonies. Oñate? Never heard of him. Peralta? Who is he? Santa Fe? Sure, we knew about that place from old Western films, but never knew anyone who lived there...or for that matter anyone who had been there.

When we were first married and living in New York, we usually went to Europe on vacation because it was so reasonable in those days and that's where people our age went. We did travel in the U.S. from time to time: Washington,

Boston, Maine, Vermont for the autumn leaves, Florida and Pennsylvania to visit aging parents and their aging friends. Occasionally we would give up our parking space in Greenwich Village and drive to Upstate New York or the mid-Hudson Valley to visit Woodstock for the weekend.

Rare trips to California to visit our brothers and their growing families were by plane, avoiding contact with any states west of the Hudson River. San Diego, where John's brother lived, had the advantage of being close to Mexico and we loved crossing the border at Tijuana to get Mexican hand crafts, cheap tequila and great seafood.

But, when we got serious about vacations, Europe was the only real place considered. We were comfortable in Paris and in Marrakech, had friends in Copenhagen and managed very well in Spain and Portugal, Switzerland, or the Cotswolds. Then, in 1968, a landmark event occurred in our lives: we moved to San Antonio in south Texas for a one year assignment for IBM, John's employer at the time. Texas! This is no place for New York liberals! Our hero, Jack Kennedy had been killed in Texas only a few years before, and we had no idea how we would fit in this cow culture town in south Texas.

As we found out soon enough, people in rural south Texas (wasn't it all rural in Texas?) actually carried guns into restaurants and had rifle racks above the back seats of their pickups. And they had political views very different from our own, and we weren't used to paying much attention to political opinions that didn't match our own. After all, we were from New York where all the great ideas of time seemed to be formed. Good ideas certainly don't come out of south Texas. You couldn't even buy a drink in a restaurant in Behar County, where we lived.

Something remarkable happened to these two New York liberals isolated in San Antonio: we liked it. In fact, we liked it a lot. We found that we could get along with people whose politics didn't match our own. We learned to love the open spaces and how the sky seemed so low that you could almost touch the clouds. Good old Texas boys invited us to their ranches and we found them to be warm, funny, and more open to different ideas than we were.

We learned a lot and every driving trip we made in the south of this vast state a new experience. The border at Nuevo Laredo was only a few hours away and we took our young son into Mexico frequently, driving through the huge King Ranch on the way. It gradually occurred to us that, despite the famous Saul Steinberg New Yorker cover cartoon depicting the country to the west of New York, that there was life west of the Hudson River, there was something between California and New York.

Soon afterward a new IBM assignment took us to France for seven years and Paris became home. Returning to the U.S. in late 1979, we settled back into the familiar New York world but realized how little we knew about our own country. Our nephew, then a Park Ranger in the Grand Canyon, urged us to come see this great natural wonder. We took our two boys out of school in April, 1983 and hiked down to the bottom of the Grand Canyon for a few days. The much over-used word "awesome" actually applied to the amazing place.

Borrowing our nephew's old VW van, we drove to Hopi, Canyon de Chelly, the Petrified Forest and the Painted Desert and were astonished at the beauty of every day in the Southwest. Returning to our nephew's home full of enthusiasm for what we had seen in these few days, we said in chorus, "It is really a beautiful country." When we enthused to John's brother and wife, they said if we wanted to see more beauty we should meet them in Santa Fe.

We had no idea where Santa Fe was and probably could not have found New Mexico on a map without state names. But plans were made and the following April John's brother and wife joined us for our first trip to New Mexico. They were familiar with the state and planned the itinerary a bit differently, visiting Taos and Rio Arriba County first, and saving Santa Fe for last.

When we drove into Santa Fe at the end of the week and parked the car in the center of town, we walked into the Plaza on a very bright, sunny afternoon. The snow was still on the mountains, clearly visible from the Plaza and the light was extraordinary, as it is on most days, but especially in April. People were on the Plaza in shorts and some man was selling something called a "carnita" from a colorful cart at the corner. We were instantly hooked!!

We spent a few days in this old capital, enjoying every moment, seeing… and buying…unique art and crafts, eating in colorful restaurants, and meeting very friendly and charming people. The adobe architecture reminded us of villages in Spain and North Africa. For folk art collectors like us, the Museum of International Folk Art seemed like the Promised Land. Books on the history of the state and of the Southwest helped us learn that history could indeed be fascinating without the Eastern bias we were accustomed to from our school days. We were surprised to learn that the Palace of the Governors was the oldest public building in the United States. No one had taught us that in school in New York!

The decision that someday we would like to move to Santa Fe was actually reached the minute we saw the sun-drenched Plaza that beautiful April afternoon. But John was still working for IBM and, while based in White Plains in New York, was traveling overseas frequently. We still loved going to Europe, particularly to Paris where much of our recent family life had been spent and where we felt totally at home. But increasingly we were drawn to New Mexico and began coming out to Santa Fe for vacations once or twice a year for the next five years, either together or with one or both sons.

We came to love Indian Market and began volunteering at this great event while still living back East. We got to know some people in town, including the colorful guy who made carnitas on the Plaza and many Indian Market artists. Convinced now that we could be happy living here, we looked forward to a time when that would be possible. One son was still in college, so it seemed like moving here, i.e. retiring from IBM, would have to wait until he graduated.

The year 1988 brought a wonderful surprise: IBM, in its efforts to reduce costs of a business in serious trouble, of-

John and Barbara Berkenfield in France, 1982.

John and Barbara Berkenfield at El Rancho de Las Golondrinas, 2005.

fered a "Golden Handshake" to employees like John with many years of service. The financial incentive to leave IBM and retire on the Frontier of the American West won the day. In the summer of 1989 we moved to Santa Fe. John happily traded in his suits and ties for jeans and bolos and settled in to a job as one of the directors of El Rancho de Las Golondrinas, and Barbara found her niche at an art gallery in town. We thought we would work for only a few years and then completely retire and do nothing but volunteer work and explore this great part of the world.

Well, we have been in Santa Fe for more than 19 years and we are both still working and enjoying every day as much as we had ever imagined. It is a long way from Greenwich Village, this dusty town in New Mexico, but we wouldn't trade places with anyone, anywhere! New York is a place we hardly ever visit now, certainly don't miss and, while we still go to France quite often, we are just as happy to get in our car and drive to the Four Corners area which we find endlessly fascinating. And to make life even better, our sons and their families now live in the West, one in California and one in Idaho. Bleecker Street seems a long time ago…and very far away!

We Came to Santa Fe
William & Marcia Berman

Marcia Berman is retired from the Heard Museum in Phoenix, Arizona and now volunteers at the Wheelwright Museum of the American Indian in Santa Fe. Bill Berman still is active in his various business ventures and plans on participating as long as possible.

S ANTA FE IS THE END (maybe) of a 50 year span of wandering from the Eastern US (Pittsburgh), where we married to the Midwest (Chicago), then Phoenix, and finally Santa Fe, absorbing and learning along the way.

Bill, the little boy from Pittsburgh always wanted to be a cowboy. Marcia, certainly not a cowgirl but a frustrated anthropologist was always drawn to the spectacular scenery and diverse ancient and contemporize cultures of the Southwest.

After we married, Bill's work took us to the Chicago area where we raised our four children and eventually sent three of them off to college and various other places. On a business trip to Phoenix, Arizona, Bill heard there was a huge snowstorm in Chicago, complete with fallen electrical wires and an ice storm. We had no phone service for two days and could not get out of the house. This was the beginning of very cold, snowy and icy winter. He called and said if I want to be cold I can go skiing. Let's get out of here and see what Phoenix holds for us. We planned a trip and off we went to start a new warm life.

Shortly after that we packed up and dragged our 16-year-old daughter crying hysterically on the plane and moved to Phoenix. When we arrived and got off the plane it was 120 degrees. She still thinks it is a nice place to visit but doesn't want to live there. She now resides in New Jersey.

We began our romance with the Southwest and golf. Golf eventually went by the wayside when we realized frustration wasn't fun or good exercise both physically or mentally. We traveled the Southwest and became enamored with the indigenous cultures both ancient and contemporary. Living in Phoenix we found the Heard Native American Museum. It excited us even more. We became very involved and eventually the deep volunteer involvement led to employment for me (Marcia) satisfying the old desire to be an anthropologist.

One Valentine's Day we came to Santa Fe to explore the area. The scenery and the art captivated us. We were hooked. We started traveling back and forth between Phoenix and Santa Fe. When we went to our first Indian Market we knew it was time to expand our horizons. We started to explore the area and really fell in love with it.

During this time, Bill took the first step to become a true Westerner. At age 65, he took horseback riding lessons. Horses have since become his second love (I hope) and a near obsession. Shortly after I (Marcia) retired, the Phoenix area became a sea of red tile roofs, impossible traffic, smog and throngs of people.

The lifestyle of Santa Fe and New Mexico became more alluring. We decided to test the waters and rent a house for the summer. When we saw a great little adobe house in Tesuque, we bought the house and when fall came, the thought of going back to 100-degree temperatures was not very appealing. So we stayed longer. We came back more and more often and within a year and a half, pulled up stakes once again and moved here where we feel comfortable and can continue to learn and explore.

We now live outside of Santa Fe on a few acres of land near the beloved horses and in the heart of New Mexico's rich Hispanic and Pueblo cultures. But in spite of our dreams of being true Southwesterners and Bill's dream of being a cowboy, we seemed to have missed the acquired gene

The young parents, Bill and Marcia, with their son Will, 1991.

for cleaning acquit and fence mending. But happily, Bill rides into the sunset a few times a week and every once in a while we climb into our newly acquired motor home and take off on a new adventure.

Bill and Marcia in Paris in 1985.

Bill and Marcia leading a Museum Trip to Chaco Canyon for Bill's birthday, May 2005.

Why We Moved to Santa Fe

Richard & Helen Brandt

Richard Brandt is the Chairman Emeritus of Translux Corporation, Chairman Emeritus of American Film Institute, Founder of Live Poets Society and enjoys skiing, his grandchildren and puzzles. Helen Brandt is very involved with the New Mexico Women's Foundation and the Desert Chorale, Chairperson of the Taos Talking Pictures Film Festival with a background in the management and design of major commercial and residential projects.

S O HERE WE ARE IN BEAUTIFUL SANTA FE, living in our splendid dream house, viewing mountains valleys and meadows just outside our windows, and waiting for summer thundershowers.

And we're also coughing, sneezing and wheezing from the thousands of junipers and other desert materials that surround us.

How did this happen?

"Let's stop off in Santa Fe," we said to one another, as Richard, Chairman of Trans-Lux Corporation based in Norwalk, Connecticut, planned a business trip from the East Coast to Los Angeles. Each of us had visited many years before, Helen as a child on a visit to Bishops Lodge in the 40s, and Richard during his first marriage with his young family.

And of course, like many people we're real-estate nicks (when that was actually fun once upon a time!). So, after a visit or two in the late 80s, we called a real estate agent and had her take us "around," once a year, as it happened, as we began to visit Santa Fe regularly. After several years she began, with some good humor, to call us her "oldest" clients, which, with time, we might actually have become.

A generation or two ago, movie theater owners as we are, "exhibitors," were friendly competitors. The businesses were owned largely by families, many of whom knew one another. So in visiting new areas, it was a natural thing to explore what theaters were around, and who owned what.

And we found this adorable little theater, the Jean Cocteau, and met it's owner, Brent Klieuver, who had the young (and yet to become famous) architect, Jeff Harner, design a one screen theater in the historic district of Sanbusco, adjacent to the Santa Fe Railyard property. Little did we know, as we got to know Brent, that one day, through a series of business deals, we would become owners of the Jean Cocteau and the building in which it resides.

We traveled in Colorado and Utah as well as other areas of New Mexico, and began to acquire properties which were added to the chain of movie theaters owned by Trans-Lux. When it became clear that Trans-Lux needed to establish a Southwest office to manage the theaters, Richard found his opportunity to relocate his office from the company's corporate headquarters in Norwalk, Connecticut to Santa Fe.

But by this time, we had purchased land in Tesuque, and, bitten by the building bug, had begun to work on a new home for ourselves. The future was swiftly becoming reality.

It was a three year process. In those times uploading plans to a site wasn't even envisioned, and we were happy to receive overnight plans mailed to our home in Connecticut via Federal Express. We began to feel very comfortable Santa Fe as a result of our monthly visits during the design and construction periods. We joined boards non-profits such as the Santa Fe Desert Chorale, The College of Santa Fe, Taos Talking Pictures, the Wheelwright and other museums, and made many friends. And we moved into our incredible home.

Planning to move to Santa Fe, 1987.

Richard and Helen in front of their home, winter, 2006.

We still love Santa Fe. Where else while enjoying our lovely seasonal climate, can you also appreciate an entire week of cloudy, misty, rainy weather— summer thunderstorms which often bring rainbows, one end of which settles on the roof of our next door neighbor's home? Nearby skiing and rafting, great restaurants, a lively art world, and wonderful people? We are happy with our move to Santa Fe, which has become a pleasant reality for some years.

The open and creative atmosphere in the Santa Fe Area that we found ourselves in made it possible for me to pursue my interest in poetry and we found a number of people who, though involved in various aspects of business had been writing poetry for years and were "closet poets." This surprised me and the discussions in this group of non-professional writers and poets led me to suggest that we band together and begin meeting on a more or less regular basis. This communality became the basis for the establishment of *The Live Poets Society* that has been functional for the past sixteen years. Its members include some thirty persons most of them in the Santa Fe area and range from retired State Superior Court Judge to teachers, publicists, artists and lawyers.

The Live Poets Society has published three anthologies of the work of its members and had been responsible for staging a number of public readings and performances in venues as different as the College of Santa Fe as well as restaurants and the Santa Fe Playhouse. Its membership is widespread and includes people in Virginia, California and Colorado as well as the core group in Santa Fe.

This development in our personal lives has given a special meaning to our involvement in the cultural life of the Santa Fe area.

We Came to Santa Fe

Doug Coffin

Doug Coffin is an internationally acclaimed artist whose career started when at the age of four he was given some clay and a few sticks by his grandmother on the reservation in Oklahoma where he grew up. He was told to do "something" with them. His development as an artist over the years has earned him recognition and appreciation not only as a recognized interpreter of American Indian themes here in the United States but in Europe and in Africa as well.

MY FIRST EXPERIENCE IN SANTA FE started when I was eight years old. My brother and I had come with our parents from Haskell Institute in Lawrence, Kansas. Haskell was a boarding school for Indians. (It is now Haskell Indian Nations University.) My father was a sports coach at Haskell, coaching football, basketball, and track.

During the month of August the school was closed for vacations. My father was assigned to contact students, encouraging them to return to school. There was a dropout problem, many of the students had never been off the reservation before and my father was assigned to Santa Fe and other places to see if he could talk some of the dropouts into coming back.

Unlike Kansas, Santa Fe was Shangri La for me, high mountains with incredible air that was cool air, that I wanted to put in glass jars and take back with me. As a child we came back several more times since Santa Fe had begun to cast its spell over us.

During the happy crazy 60's I returned as an adult. My professor at K.U. offered a two-week jewelry workshop in Cloudcroft, N.M. during August. I borrowed $600 from my Grandmother. This money would cover my travel as well as room and board for the time there. Working in the New Mexico mountains opened the door, turned on the light bulb...maybe Kansas was not the "ultimate" home for a wannabe artist. Completing the workshop gave me two more credits towards my BFA. I had declared a double major at KU, Jewelry and Sculpture. Leaving Cloudcroft, my wife and I with our son Brian, drove to Santa Fe. Wham! Driving up Canyon Road, seeing the smiling hippies and weirdo's, I felt right at home. Canyon Road had this incredible feeling of energy and openness that captured my dreams right then. We rented a lodge in the mountains somewhere and I'm still not sure of its location.

I knew then that I would do whatever it took to eventually live in Santa Fe and be one of the people with that smile on their face. My father had died but my wonderful mother and three brothers still loved living in Lawrence. I stayed and did graduate with my BFA. I was offered an excellent position at Jaccards Jewelry store in Kansas even before I graduated. I studied diamonds, colored stones, sold top of the linc watches, etc. I also bought a 1947 Bentley. At 24 life was starting. I had also served in the U.S. Marine Corps and had my Honorable Discharge. Santa Fe was still my dream. I had the opportunity to pursue an MFA at Cranbrook Academy of Art in Bloomfield Hills, Michigan. My third son Gabe was born there. My excellent son Erik was already part of the family. After graduating from Cranbrook I was offered a National teaching fellowship to start a jewelry department in Spokane, Washington. After three years of teaching there a divorce happened. My world was

Doug Coffin in one of his inspirational moments.

totally unglued. I moved to Laguna Beach, California, to work as a goldsmith for a Cranbrook friend.

After six months I thought, "Doug, maybe now is the time to do what your dream has been, move to Santa Fe." Two of my brothers were going to IAIA. I went back to Kansas to visit my mother for six months. In the spring I drove to New Mexico. My brother had arranged an interview at Shidoni, the world famous foundary in Tesuque, with Tommy Hicks. I was offered a job by him. I had also interviewed at the College of Santa Fe for the first sculpture class to be taught there. That job was offered also and I took it as well.

Santa Fe had said "It's time!" I went back to Lawrence, packed my tools and moved to Santa Fe for good in May of 1979. I arrived on a Sunday night and started at Shidoni on Monday morning. With me I had a 24 inch model of a sculpture that was to be 24 feet tall. Shidoni was going to have its fifth outdoor sculpture show. Tommy Hicks and Andy Jenkins said of course I could show my sculpture! Now I was a Santa Fe artist. The piece sold to Ann Maytag. During the run of the show 5,000–6,000 people had attended the opening. A collector from Michigan saw my 24 foot totem and flew me there so I could do a sculpture for him. I produced a 35 foot steel sculpture for him. It was on the front page of the newspaper. Next stop was Africa where I installed a 35 foot steel totem along with an earthwork of 90 feet. Since

*Karen and Doug
at home, 2007.*

then my work has continued to be recognized and I have been fortunate enough to have been commissioned to design and erect my sculptures in Italy, as well as in other states here in the United States.

I was also fortunate enough to meet Karen Ochoa, a film director and visionary, whose entire view of life dovetailed with mine and we were married last spring. With all aspects of my life now working well together I have managed to maintain a good relationship with my mother who moved here and with my extended family, while continuing to expand the horizons of my work.

The Santa Fe area has become my true home and life is so good that when I die it will be with a Santa Fe smile in my spirit.

Doug Coffin in a contemplative mood seated before his "Snake Dancer Sun/Moon," 2007.

Coming to Santa Fe
Rosé & Linda Cohen

About Rosé: *Rosé was born deep in the Bronx in 1934. He began crafting his poetry attending a number of colleges during the 50's. After a stint in the army he bounced around working as a lifeguard, masseur and astrology writer. He saw his heaviest combat duty teaching High School English in New York. In the early 60's he assiduously pursued Ancient Greek while dining on Mexican beaches, stopping in European cafés and touring Moroccan dives. Between poetry and acting, including the movie "The Edge," he published a book of drawings and launched skin diving trips throughout the Yucatan and the Florida Keys. His "School of the Night" specialized in occult classes and his "Liquid Wedge Gallery" made media history with sculptor Tony Price's first "Atomic Art Show" in NYC in 1969. In 1980 Rosé started his epic poem "The Pearl Upon the Crown," still a grand work in progress. He performs as stand-up poet in salons, homes, theaters, clubs, sushi bars, on radio and television in New York, Los Angeles, Miami and Santa Fe. Rosé now lives in Santa Fe, New Mexico. Santa Fe. Rosé now lives in Santa Fe, New Mexico with his beautiful wife and partner who is a noted graphic and installation artist in her own right.*

IN 1968 NORMA CROSS ASKED ME if I would like to join her and her son Jimmy, then about seven years old, and help drive her VW van to New Mexico. Neither of us had been there before. Many years later I wrote:

NORMA

Norma, across the states we go
From New York to New Mexico
Been five and twenty years or so
But seems like yesterday

There's a hill that we ascended
Before the Eastern mountains ended
Where Jimmy tilted half suspended
I saw him float away

And Colorado dawned supreme
House on a bridge over a stream
Saw Libre born out of a dream
Under the Milky Way

We pushed on to the Rio Grande
Where the gorge drops a mile and splits the land
We rested, then on through the sun and the sand
On the trail to Santa Fe

Where I saw you last week at a dinner
Looking just like an angelic sinner
Quite aglow with a light that is inner
And beams through your mortal clay.

Well, I loved Santa Fe. I returned to New York and in 1969 I met my wife to be, Linda:

LINDA

There is one friend among the rest who stands
Tall as a lily in a field that's rife

Rosé and Linda,
September, 1971.

With countless weeds and thorns and shifting sands
Who for some decades now has shared my life
Her name is Linda with the lovely hands
She is my daughters' mother and my wife
To honor her in hopes she won't depart
For pain I've caused, I give her here my bleeding heart.

We were married in 1971. We had a daughter born in the Yucatan in 1972, delivered by a Maya midwife in a hammock. We named her after a Maya princess, Nicte-Ha, Water Flower:

...For soon an asteroid sent reptiles down the tube
By landing in what's now the town of Chicxulub

Where after sixty million years had passed
Sweet Linda of my heart brought forth a daughter
Whom we named for a princess of high-caste
The Maya Nicte-Ha, flower of the water

Perhaps, we should have named her for the blast
That had precipitated reptile slaughter
Or for the tiny mammals who possibly foresaw
This human birth upon the Yucatecan shore...

Wind over water
Mind over matter
We've got a daughter
Mad as a hatter.

The three of us settled down in my loft resuming our New York way of life which became increasingly unbreathable and unbearable. No matter how much money you made, New York demanded you spend it all on her:

...Now, money is a funny thing
It has a way of vanishing
Before your very eyes
It turns to food, to clothes, to smoke
This morning you were flush and now you're broke
No matter what its size

Your bankroll is diminishing
It rolls away, a ball of string
That's always getting smaller
It disappears—the more you earn
The richer you become, the more you yearn
To be a social crawler

You must improve your way of life
Another mink coat for the wife
Take limos everywhere,
A better college for the kid
You have become a financial invalid
While still a millionaire

So it turns out that you have pandered
Your very soul to raise the standard
Of living to a point
That's just beyond what you can make
And now you won't eat anything but cake
You hate the lousy joint

You live in, if you had some dough
You'd move into that smart chateau
And cater to your gout
Tonight you dine on roast gazelle
While several families do very well
On just what you throw out…

We had to get out of this town that we both loved, but we loved life more. It was spring, 1975. We packed up the camper, the three of us jumped in, waved good-bye, and we never looked back. In August of 1977 our second daughter, Bella, was born in Santa Fe.

SANTA FE

You know, they ask me everywhere I go
What things are like in Mexico
"No! New Mexico," I say
How do you pass the time out there

In San Jose, does it compare…?
"No, No! It's Santa Fe!"

Well, we lie around all day in splendor
Ambrosia, nectar in the blender
On terraced mountain tops
Like Gods in pearl encrusted boots
We speak only in absolutes
And pull out all the stops

Hop in your car and drive out there
Stars swim in pools of crystal air
You're in for a surprise:
The welcome station knows your name
They're overjoyed, so glad you came
They even know your size!

Yes, spread upon the desert lawn
Your own pearl boots, your own new sawn
Off shotgun, and for luck
Old turquoise beads, a western hat
Coors beer, string tie, a lariat
And brand new pick-up truck

Linda, 2000.

They give you maps, a few stiff shots,
Some priceless Pueblo Indian pots
    And send you on your way
Along that road so charming, quaint,
Where there's no need to feel restraint
    The trail to Santa Fe

            The open skies, the endless plain
            Highway rest stops that serve champagne
                The cactus silhouette
            That dominates the distant hills
            And then without fanfare or frills
                One more perfect sunset

                    As you go roaring down the road
                    But, wait! That car ahead has slowed
                        He signals like a gent
                    He's pulling in, you'd better stop
                    A combination litter drop
                        And Historic Monument

                Is coming up—don't think I mock
                This grand affair (like Camel Rock)
                    Is something you must see
                Look! Ancient writing on the cliff
                Stop here, my friends, especially if
                    You have to take a pee

                It's Paradise, I won't be vague
                Land of the Flea, Home of the Plague
                    The cozy Great Southwest.
                Smart dinner clubs, Art without reason,
                Prison riots, the Opera Season.....

Rosé with his usual smile, 2007.

We Came to Santa Fe
Guy Cross

Guy Cross has been a professional photographer working for advertising agencies and fashion magazines in New York, Los Angeles, Austin, and London. His fine art photographs have been shown in numerous galleries and museums. He has published three magazines: The Picture Paper, Edge City, and has been publisher and creative director of THE magazine (Santa Fe's magazine on the arts) since 1993.

IT WAS THE SUMMER OF '78 WHEN I HIT IT OUT OF AUSTIN in my 1954 Plymouth station wagon…heading west in 90-degree heat…no air conditioning…I put the pedal to the metal…I headed west, towards east Texas… towards New Mexico…I did not look back…I was running…I pulled into Amarillo…checked into a $35-a-night motel, where I stopped long enough to look over my shoulder…I saw nothing…I did not then hear the Hounds of The Hell yapping at my heels…I slept well…dawn comes…I head west… dawn becomes day and day becomes late afternoon, which puts me on the outskirts of Albuquerque…the temperature is hot, brutal…I punch a tape in the tape deck…open the glove box…fish around for a Quaalude… find it… swallow it with the last of my lukewarm Dr. Pepper and settle back in the safety of my car listening to the Stones singin' "Ain't no use cryin'…I ain't never ever comin' back"…I ask myself, "Where am I going?"…I exit the Interstate…pull into a Denny's…order up a plate of crispy fries and a glass of milk…the Quaalude begins to take hold…"Where am I going? Where should I go?"…I look around…sitting at the counter is one honey of a babe with curly mouth and moist red hair (just out of the shower?)…she is wearing a frown, staring at the wet ceiling above her wet head…I stare at her until she looks down and at me…with a wave of my hand I ask her to sit…she rolls her eyes to the heavens and offers me her sigh of sighs…then she is up—off her stool and sitting opposite me…I smile…she smiles, well sorta…we talk…she is from Santa Fe…she tells me that "Santa Fe is situated in Central New Mexico at the base of the Sangre de Christo mountain range…Santa Fe is remote, obscure, and steeped in the desire to be recognized, to be adored…. no major airline comes to the Capital City, no Interstate highway cuts up, tears up, divides the City Different"…she tells me more, "Santa Fe is the End of the Trail Town, the place where the *Dead End Kids* come to meet, the place where the bottom bottoms out—the place where you stand up or where you give up, the place where you fess up or where you take up what you left behind…Santa Fe is the *Last Chance for Most*"…now I know where I am going—Santa Fe…I get in my car and head north…at the very same moment, on the Plaza in Santa Fe the Indians are gathering their handmade jewelry, their wares, having finished their day selling to the tourist, to the White Man and walk in groups of twos and threes to La Fonda Hotel, where they sit together in the lobby, like a forgotten hobby—like an old game…I check into La Fonda…lay down in my room and take a nap…I wake up and it is evening…I look out my hotel window and see the Plaza full of people…young Spanish girls in tight pants strut their stuff like flamingos fucking in the dust…I was hooked…too hot…too cool…I hit the streets…I wander around downtown… lots of laughing, drinking, flirting—I love this town…back to La Fonda to sleep…morning

Photo by Lisa Law

Guy Cross on his arrival in Santa Fe, 1972.

comes late…I wake up…drag a comb though my teeth, wash my hands and face with my socks, and take the elevator to the lobby, whispering to no-one in particular, "Don't leave me out, don't feed me to the fishes"…I waltz into the hotel coffee shop…I am floored by the aroma of coffee and croissants…I finish my breakfast with an ice water…hit the 11am streets…it's so, so hot…my eyes were seared by the heat…somehow I stumble and spin to my car in the parking garage…open the door and start the engine…the engine does not start…I try again and again and again…the engine does not start…I am confused…"Where am I going?"…I feel lost—as in a bad dream…then I remember my mother, the envelope she placed in my hands last time I saw her…written on the envelope are the words: OPEN WHEN WORRIED…I open the envelope…inside is a sheet of paper,., It says: *O Thou Whose Glory fills the Ethereal Throne and All Ye Deathless Powers, Protect My Son*…and I say to myself, "What have I got to worry about with a Mother's Blessing and her appeal to the gods that be?"…I call a mechanic…he comes to the hotel late in the afternoon…examines my car…the diagnosis is: "Blown head gasket. Gonna take a few days to fix it, chief"…okay, okay… I find myself on the prowl…ending up at 11 pm in Casablanca—the nightclub in La Fonda…and that's where I saw her…I remember her sitting alone at a table… wearing a satin jacket with the word *Reckless* emblazoned in felt script across the back of her jacket…her with her henna hair and her sassy talk that night… that night…

Guy Cross 2007.

He: "Hello."

She: "Hello you."

He: "Can I sit here?"

She: "Why Not?"

Silence

He: "Why are you here?"

She: "I was sent."

He: "By who?"

She: "Who cares?"

He: "Who cares?"

She: "Yup."…

Silence

She: "I gotta go now."

He: "Call me?"

She: "I am expensive."

He: "I can afford it."

She: "Okey dokey."

Laughter

She: "I gotta go. Trust me, I'll call you."

She called…walked past me into my hotel room…took off her jacket… sat on the couch staring at me…she laughed…reached into her purse…and the rest is (as they say) history…

THE *Magazine cover, July 2007.*

ART ON FIRE…
How I Got to New Mexico
Jane Davis

Jane Davis, LMSW has a BA in Cultural Anthropology and a Masters degree in Clinical Social Work from Washington University in St. Louis. She has studied cultures all over the world. She is the founder and director of HOPE-HOWSE Int'l. (www.hope-howse.org), an all volunteer 501c3 organization and currently employed by the New Mexico Corrections Dept. Jane has been published in the Sunday New York Times, Sporting Times, Atlanta Journal Constitution, Chicken Soup for the Prisoner's Soul *and other anthologies. She is at work on her first book.*

"WE ARE SHORT STAFFED AT THE NORTH (super maximum prison)," the voice on the other end of the phone began. "Can you come to Santa Fe and work temporarily?"

I answered without thinking, "Yes!"

I was sitting in my home office in Atlanta, Georgia. The man calling me was the Bureau Chief of Mental Health for the State of New Mexico. He was familiar with my work through HOPE-HOWSE as well as the fact that I was a Masters level social worker

I began visiting New Mexico in 1993, after witnessing an electric chair execution as media. I was a contributing writer to *Prison Life* magazine.

I never wrote about it. Instead, I had a vision called "HOPE-HOWSE" an acronym for Help Other People Evolve through Honest Open Willing Self Evaluation/Expression that includes the logo of an eye (honesty), a heart (faith) and a hand (service/action). HOPE-HOWSE International is now a 501c3 organization.

This vision, my life's purpose, essentially guided me to New Mexico where it foreshadowed me overseeing 20–40 acres of land off the grid. I didn't even know what "off-the-grid" was let alone much about New Mexico. Essentially the vision represented that we are all "One Heart," all connected. It was about service as a path to peace. About giving of ourselves. About the world as community. About accountability. About volunteering. About rescuing animals. It was also about creating a space where the land could teach and heal. It became apparent why I was lead to New Mexico.

I was introduced to Jimmy Santiago Baca, an ex-con turned poet and screenwriter *(Blood In, Blood Out),* who exemplified those who committed crimes and could make changes in their lives. My first trip to New Mexico was to meet Jimmy.

Walking off the plane at the Sunport my eyes darted all around trying to find him. I continued to baggage claim, and then stood, waiting. I had mentally prepared myself for the fact that he might not even show up. 5, 10, 15, 20 minutes passed. As _ hour approached I decided to go into Albuquerque when a rush of energy came bursting through the door. Our eyes met. There was no question it was him.

Those ten days were a whirlwind of activity from meeting his family to being introduced to others who had made changes in their lives. This included Bobby Dorado, one of the "three bad Mexicans" including Miranda and

Escobeda in Burton Wolfe's book *Pile-Up on Death Row,* and Daniel Blea, a folk artist, who was released from prison just before the infamous riot at "The Main."

I intuitively knew after this visit that I would one day live here. The scene that stands out most for me that sealed the intuition was driving down Highway 25 with a 360 degree view with rain over the Jemez, sunshine over the Sandia's and a double rainbow over the Ortiz. It was more magnificent than any painting I had ever seen in any gallery around the world. In my 54 years, I have traveled all over the world including Africa, India, Israel, the Philippines, Egypt, and Europe. New

Jane Davis at work, 2007.

Mexico, to me, was art on fire. New Mexico had an unavoidable vibration that permeated my eyes, heart and soul. One saw and felt this in the landscape. It enveloped you, if you allowed it to. I used to tell people, "Being in New Mexico, there is no question there is a G_d."

When I returned to Atlanta I was under the spell of the Land of Enchantment. Since I was working for myself I had the luxury of time and travel. I began returning to New Mexico for 3–6 months each year. While here I would housesit, work on my book, *Letters To my Master…a woman's sexual and spiritual journey,* do writing and meditation workshops in the community as well as visit prisons around the State where I would also conduct workshops and do readings from *Chicken Soup for the Prisoner's Soul,* in which I have two stories.

I arrived (officially) in Santa Fe in April 2001 after driving across the country in my red 1989 Toyota Celica convertible. Since I was planning to live and work here for a few months I had left my home, my other half of 13 years, my dogs, my cat, assuming I would return soon.

I had made arrangements to live in a 100-year-old adobe on the arroyo in Cerrillos. I was told it would be furnished. In typical New Mexico style, the casita was empty and the people renting it to me were gone for three weeks. This was Saturday and I was scheduled to begin work in a super maximum penitentiary on Monday morning at 8AM. Fortunately my neighbor had a big piece of foam in her truck, which became my bed.

After a month working at the penitentiary, I was sitting in my office in the bowels of a dark, dingy prison where the way I controlled the temperature was how many pieces of paper I used on the vents. I learned this survival skill, among others, from the inmates.

There were no windows to the outside but there was a door-sized pane of glass outside of which sat a correctional officer when I would see an inmate in a therapy session. He was there in case anyone got violent. No one ever did in my sessions.

One time I knew we were close to an inmate really dealing with his feelings, which was going to entail him getting angry. I sent a letter to my supervisor and the Unit Management Team leader asking permission to continue with this treatment because I didn't want the officer bursting in on the session when the inmate raised his voice. The next day when I came in the inmate was moved to another pod and I received my request back, "Denied."

My phone rang. It was my supervisor who was quite excited.

"We just turned your position into a permanent one!" she practically shouted with glee.

"Isn't that great? You are now a permanent employee!"

"Yes," I replied softly not wanting to poison the moment. Frankly I was not sure if I was happy or not.

Permanent? I felt like I had just been sentenced and she might as well have been the judge and jury. Did I want to be here in this dark place permanently? I felt a combination of excitement and disdain.

I loved the work with the inmates even when I would get called in at 1 or 2AM to sit with a human being who was hearing voices or was so distraught that he wanted to kill himself. I often had to pull over on the side of the road and weep with an overwhelming feeling of blessedness that I was the one who got to go into these bowels to minister to a human being that most people could care less about. I was blessed that I got to meet the human beings behind unconscionable acts.

So, as I pondered "permanent" I knew that I was exactly where I was supposed to be.

Almost seven years later, I still work for Corrections (my "day job" as I call it), and have continued growing HOPE-HOWSE to the point where we bring in volunteers from the community—artists, musicians, business people and authors—to bring light to the darkness. We may even be contributing to lower recidivism rates.

The number of animals rescued has grown. Two of the dogs, Hogan and Magic, are now therapy dogs and also come into the prison. The 30 acres of land is a recent reality with incredible potential.

The challenges and sacrifices have been plentiful but there are reasons why New Mexico is called "The Land of Enchantment" and suffice it say I am enchanted and planted.

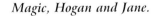

Magic, Hogan and Jane.

Always Looking Forward

Victor di Suvero

Victor di Suvero *is a poet, publisher and has been involved in a variety of businesses and projects in New Mexico as well as in Nevada and California. Arriving in America as a political refugee from China at the age of 13 early in 1941, he served in the Merchant Marine as a deck hand in World War II in the Pacific. He then graduated from UC Berkeley in 1949 with a BA in Political Science. Based in the San Francisco Bay Area for almost 40 years where he had owned and managed his own Real Estate firm while continuing to write the poetry that has been part of his life since he first went to sea. He continues to do so in his new life in Santa Fe and Alcalde where he lives and helps Barbara Windom in the raising and training of her Peruvian Paso horses.*

LIVING IN SAUSALITO, CALIFORNIA IN 1969 with my wife Henrietta and our two children Romana and Alexander we heard that a pending reorganization of the nation's railroads would most probably eliminate the continuation of traditional passenger rail service. I had just returned from Europe and felt it would be an interesting thing to have the children, who were six and four years old at the time, to have the experience of at least one night in a sleeper on a train before the sleeping cars disappeared. In those Vietnam days anything of that sort seemed possible. Easter was coming and I asked Henrietta if she would find a place which we could reach by overnight train where we could spend our Easter vacation with the children.

When I returned from my office in San Francisco that evening, Henrietta was pleased to tell me that she had in fact found the ideal destination and it did call for an overnight sleeper train ride while taking us to Lamy. "Lamy?" I said, "where in the name of heaven is that?" "It's the station on the Atchison, Topeka and Santa Fe closest to Santa Fe. You know where Santa Fe is," was the answer. Yes, of course. We had friends who had been there and raved about the place and its various charms and cultural aspects. After leaving from the station in Berkeley, going south to Bakersfield we woke early, had breakfast in the diner, and landed in Lamy where Avis had a car waiting for us. Venturing into the unknown we headed north and found our way to Bishop's Lodge that Maundy Thursday afternoon.

Yes, we had followed the map's directions and driven through downtown Santa Fe, around the Plaza, past the Palace of the Governors and out Bishop's Lodge Road to the hotel we were staying at, with the children pointing out the "funny looking houses," while trying to find my way. I remembered all the stories I had read and heard about D.H. Lawrence having been here and other writers and painters who had discovered this "City Different" earlier in the century. So many things crowding into my head as we checked in and found our rooms.

Yes, there were stories I had heard about the Pueblo Indians and their Revolt, and about the Penitentes and the crypto Jews of New Mexico. I really did not know anything about them, only that Bill Merwin was living in Taos, and Charles Bell was a tutor at St. John's. It became a question of how we were going to spend this Easter week—around the pool with the children or on a voyage of discovery. A bit of both was the verdict. On Good Friday after having had a bit of pool and suntime we got into the car to drive up to Taos on the highroad by Truchas and Dixon. Overlooking a cemetery on the way there was a group of people re-enacting the Way of the Cross, the children wondering what those people were doing. Two older men were sitting on chairs in

Victor di Suvero on the trail above Bishop's Lodge, April 1969.

the middle of the road with rifles on their laps. I stopped, of course, and one of them came over and said we looked like nice people but did not belong there and should turn around and go back to where we came from. Which we did without any argument, finding our way down through Dixon to the highway. We learned later that they most probably were a part of the Tijerina group of followers who were land grant activists still staking out the old Hispanic claims that have yet to be resolved today, some 40 years after the Tijerina's raid on the courthouse at Tierra Amarilla.

Yes, there were horseback rides and visits to museums, finding poets who were friends of friends, and continuously discovering curious, interesting and amazing facts about this town and its various histories in those few days that went by as if it had been only one afternoon. We took the train back to Berkeley and then home to Sausalito knowing I would be back at some time in the future.

Some 20 years later, with the children grown and my marriage dissolved, I found myself in a new life with Barbara Windom, the new love of my new life. We realized that neither Southern California (which had been her home), nor Northern California (which had been mine), would work for either one of us because of the respective ghosts in those places that would have haunted our future together. So we decided to go to Santa Fe for Thanksgiving that year and found it so much to our liking that we decided to begin our new lives together in this City so full of color, history, excitement, art and life, and we began to look for THE house in which to spend the rest of our lives together.

We did not find THE house but we did find land in Tesuque with a small house on it that we could start with. We remodeled the small house and a studio building next door, got to know the neighbors, and worked our way up the hill building a pool and a pool house. Eventually, with the help of Betty Stewart, we built the Main House just under the brow of the hill that overlooked the Valley. Tesuque, Santa Fe's first outlying area, with stories about William Penhallow Henderson, the painter and architect and his wife Alice Corbin, the poet, who had settled there in 1914 and all the artists and poets and musicians who had come to the Tesuque Valley to find their pieces of peace and inspiration.

The village consisted of the Tesuque Market and Restaurant, the Elementary School, the Post Office and the important Bar and Restaurant still known as El Nido, with an early painting of Zozobra by Will Shuster in one of its many rooms. This village became the home place.

It's there that we met Linda Strong who had her Peruvian Paso Horses in a pasture on the other side of Tesuque Creek reviving Barbara's interest in the horse world which had lain dormant for all the years her daughters were growing up. We began to build corrals and then the Barn and an Arena until we finally needed to have more land and facilities. Horses can only add and multiply, but don't know how to subtract or divide, so we ended up with more horses than the zoning permitted.

During those years of discovery and delight I kept on with my writing and still remained involved in a number of projects that I carried with me from my previous life in California. I learned that Tesuque, whose original Tewa name was Taytsoongay, the "Place where the Cottonwoods Grow" had been christened Tesuque because the Spaniards who came there, the Romeros, Trujillos, Montoyas, and Gonzales could not manage the Indian language in its original way.

Later, the horses needing more land led us up the Rio Grande all the way into the Española Valley and into the Village of La Villita which had been the Stagecoach stop halfway between Taos and Santa Fe. We began again to build and weave our lives into a fabric that is made of the dawns and sunsets, the clouds and mountains and the Springs and Autumns of a life enriched by the history, the arts and the spirit of this place in time. Here is a poem that tells this part of the story in its own way. It was written for all of us which is why it is simply that statement.

Victor and Barbara at the entrance of the home they were building in Tesuque, 1990.

FOR ALL OF US

This was the sea once
And I walked across the hills,
Down to the arroyo and up again
With my eyes swimming across the face
Of a blind escarpment, across red and
Ochre bluffs as some strange finned
Creature must have eyed them
When all was water here instead of air
And another way of being was the way.

I think of that reptilian ancestor
Whose appetite for light drove him and his kind
To breathe air, instead of water.
They took possession of the land
Wondering if there was another way to be.

I know that when my children first saw the light
They came out of that same sea
And their children too in turn will rise
From there into the air with perhaps
A better chance of finding
Still another way.

This was the sea once
And the sun rests, on solstice night
While the autumnal dark is forked by lightning
That charges down the draw, driving
The huge and crackling thunder into the ground
Reminding us once more that all things change
Some slowly, and others in a flash
As happens whenever we happily discover
Another way to be.

While finding my way into this new life in New Mexico, opportunities to help in the literary world came my way. PEN, the international writer's organization did not have a branch in New Mexico and Rudolfo Anaya and

I managed to get one started. Then when New Mexico was invited to participate in the International Book Fair in Guadalajara, Mexico as the *Invitado de Onor,* Richard Polese and I and a number of other writers and publishers established the New Mexico Book Association in 1996 which is still functioning and growing today. Richard Brandt's Live Poets' Society also joined and have helped in structuring and publishing their anthologies.

Our own small Pennywhistle Press, published *¡Saludos!* the first and still only bilingual collection of the poetry of New Mexico to celebrate the event. Since then the Press has published a few volumes of poetry and sponsored readings at the College of Santa Fe, St. John's, and the Española Public Library among other venues in a continuing campaign to integrate Poetry into the life we live each and every day. The recognition of this Upper Rio Grande Area as one of the 24 National Heritage Areas in the entire country underscores the multicultural and widely diverse elements that can be found in the immediate area around Santa Fe, from the nuclear facilities at Los Alamos to the petroglyphs in the Black Mesa Area and from the tourist serving facilities of downtown Santa Fe to the ancestral ruins of Chaco Canyon, this city and its environs continue to speak their messages of generosity and welcome to all of us.

In closing, I feel that with all the cultural and historical riches, pleasing days and nights and seasons that enrich the lives of us fortunate enough to call this place our home, we should all think of what we can give back to the country, the environment, and the people with whom we share our lives so that future generations will also have the opportunity of being as pleased as we are in this corner of our world today.

Victor with his son, Alexander and daughter, Romana on a visit to Jersey City, 2007.

How I Came to Santa Fe
Mary-Charlotte Domandi

Mary-Charlotte Domandi is producer and host of The Santa Fe Radio Cafe on KSFR 101.1 FM, a program of interviews on subjects including politics, science, the arts, and issues ranging from local to international. She is a Latin music DJ, has studied social and folkloric dance in Cuba, and has interviewed many distinguished Latin musicians. She is originally from New York State and holds degrees from Yale University and St. John's College; she also attended the Institute of American Indian Arts.

The **DRIVING FORCE** was of course Love, but the vehicle was the Intellect.

The moment I graduated from college, I sensed the possibility of true freedom for the first time. I had gotten into, and out of, an Ivy League school, and felt that I no longer owed anybody anything (except a manageable monthly payment to a bank). I abandoned the idea of an academic career, despite my multi-professor family, and decided to try my hand in the Real World (which in college we called the RW). My first job was as a marketing assistant in a startup high tech firm. It was the '80s in Boston, and optimism, energy, and money abounded. On the first day of work I looked into the eyes of one of my new colleagues, and she looked back, and neither of us looked away—for months.

She had sultry dark eyes and played the guitar and talked about New Mexico. We made plans to take our vacation there. All I knew about New Mexico was that it was a state. It didn't matter, I would have followed her to Mongolia. We arrived in April. The dry wind, clear sun and thin air somehow brought a feeling of simplicity. I felt that I knew the hills, even as they were magically foreign to my New England sensibilities. She and I read aloud to one another from Carlos Castañeda, climbed up Chimney Rock at Ghost Ranch, walked around dusty flea markets and rock shops, ate honey-soaked sopapillas, beheld the astonishing sky, listened to a quality of silence I'd never known. Driving through Santa Fe a thought came to me: Some day I am going to live here and make ceramic tiles and paint watercolors.

Back in Boston. I lost my beloved Woman, quit my job, and muddled around for a while, fretting about my place in the RW. One day I went to the dentist, an old, sweet man with a Polish accent and tattooed numbers on his arm. He exuded an infinitely kind, observant acceptance that made me feel humble and calm, and I thought about the word "enlightenment" when I was in his presence. He asked me to fill out a form, and under "profession" I had nothing to write. He asked, "What would you do if you could do anything at all?" I said, "Move to Santa Fe, New Mexico, and paint watercolors." On the form he wrote, "Artist: aquarelle."

Across the street from my old high tech job, a new job materialized. I became the manger of an experimental art space, and there I met a Man. He had sharp features and played the acoustic bass and talked about Noam Chomsky. I lived and breathed to be with him. I loved everything about him — his way of speaking English as clearly as it could be spoken, his easy knowledge of everything in the world from Balkan rhythms to experimental film to mathematics, his ability to draw like a Renaissance painter, his deep voice, his thin, soft lips, his quick movements, his glorious cooking.

Mary-Charlotte Domandi in Boston, 1988.

I wanted to love him until the end of time, to bear his children, breathe his breath. But he didn't even want a "full-time relationship." I tried to content myself with part-time; I wept, twisted myself into inapt identities, turned desperately to Buddhist meditation, poured my soul into art and photography, and generally grew in ways that one grows when Love is too painful to bear.

I joined a Support Group (the successor to the previous decade's Consciousness Raising Groups) at the Cambridge Women's Center, and there I met a woman about 15 years my senior, a hilarious, irreverent student of Divinity at Harvard. At 40 she had never married, and instead had lived life as a series of adventures. She was studying to be a Unitarian minister, as that religion was sufficiently open-ended to encompass her wide-ranging intellect. She read a book a day, saw about four movies a week, did her coursework, and still seemed to have plenty of time to hang out with me, as well as with an adoring cadre of young men of dubious sexuality. We became instant, life-long friends.

She had gotten her Masters degree in the '70s at St. John's College in Santa Fe, where she had lived and worked as a schoolteacher. She had fallen in love with a boy just barely out of high school and gotten her heart broken—the one and only time in her life. I liked the idea that heartbreak could be a thing of the past, an anomaly within a life of adventure. Meanwhile, after years of working in the arts—scrambling to meet grant deadlines, to satisfy the demands of needy artists, to get programs to the printer, to make a small budget last for an entire year—I had gotten tired and stressed. I couldn't remember when I'd last had a thought, read a book, or had a leisurely, contemplative conversation. I took an eight-week leave of absence and signed up to go to St. John's for the summer.

It was five years after my vacation with the Woman, but now I was alone. I was assigned a little, white room in a dormitory named after a Greek Muse, and the sky and red earth outside my window somehow suggested both tranquility and infinite possibility. The first night before I went to sleep I looked at the list of names of my classmates, read each one, and thought; At least one of these is going to be my friend by the end of the summer.

I made friends slowly. I said little, felt shy, retreated into the hills with Aristotle and Heidegger. I tried to hear the sounds of the insects and lizards instead of the music in my head that sounded a defense against the noise of car metal and rage in Boston. I tried out acupuncture for the first time, for

Mary-Charlotte Domandi, 2007.

no other reason than to relax. I thought about my Man and wrote him post cards, but email hadn't yet been invented and there were no phones in the rooms so we had little contact. By the end of the summer a door in my soul opened that the pollution and hierarchy and concrete of the East Coast had kept blocked shut.

I returned to my Boston apartment and to my job with a sense of renewal, of calm energy and focus. That lasted two days, after which I was stressed again. On day three I decided to move to Santa Fe. I gave eight months notice to my job and to my Man. The Job was more upset, though on my last night the Man cried and told me no one had ever loved him as I had and that he would miss me terribly. His heart, which had felt like stinging acid in the past, now felt like a warm, leafy forest. But it was too late. I sold most of my belongings, packed the rest into my mother's attic and my Honda hatchback, and drove west.

The Desert Taught Me to See

Linda Durham

Linda Durham *is one of the principal art gallery owners and managers in Santa Fe. Her vision and understanding of the artist's function in our society today is mainifest in the range and quality of the exhibitions she has and continues to sponsor not only in her gallery but also by encouraging and supporting the work of artists in the community.*

A T FIRST, EVERYTHING LOOKED BROWN TO ME: *the rocks, the dirt, the houses, the faces. Even the trees looked more brown than green. And then, one day, while hiking through the sandstone rocks and arroyos, I noticed, to my complete surprise, the pinks and yellows and purples in the rocks. I was amazed! When did that color appear, I wondered! Was it always there? It was. I just didn't see it.*

The desert taught me to see.

During my superficially glamorous Playboy Bunny years in Manhattan, I used my vision to **look** (wide-eyed and bushy-tailed) at buildings and people and traffic and more people and at art and fashion…but I didn't use it to **see.** Not really. In those days, I was only interested in being seen. To see was a concept beyond my ken. It wasn't until I moved to the windy and water-less quarter section south of Santa Fe on the Turquoise Trail that the desert shared its remarkable secrets with me. At twenty-two, I was an impatient, shallow and self-conscious young woman who was persuaded by love to abandon one dream (money, adulation) in search of another (inspiration, adventure). The New Mexico desert revealed its depths to me and gave me some critical direction for my Life.

With my new husband Bart, my old cat Big and a trunk full of books (including all sorts of inappropriate clothes for the desert), I traded my dreams of fame and fortune in favor of love and discovery in the Land of Enchantment.

For the first few months of 1966, Bart and I lived in the Palace Hotel in Cerrillos while we put a roof on an abandoned rock sheepherder's house in the middle of our newly purchased land. My husband had an extensive collection of Hopi Kachina dolls that he had collected during his undergraduate days at the University of New Mexico. He attached them to the beams of the roof that we had added to the rock ruin. Along with some Navajo rugs, a pot-bellied stove and a few pieces of hand me down furniture, we settled in to newlywed life in the desert.

We were pioneers. We were young, happy and free. We were "off the grid." We had no telephone, no electricity and no water. We hauled our water from Cerrillos in the trunk of our car—in two twenty-gallon garbage cans.

Photo by MILO, Photographer

The desert taught me not to waste water.

I would take a sponge bath in a basin of clean water. Then I'd wash the floor with the same water. Then I'd pour the twice-

Linda in NY Playboy bunny costume at Tiffany Saloon in Cerrillos, 1966.

used water on the few plants that struggled to survive my "gangrene thumb." Once a week, I would check in to La Fonda Hotel for the day. I'd take a luxurious bubble bath, have lunch with some of the regulars at the hotel restaurant, go back to my room and take a second bath before returning to "the ranch."

One afternoon, after six months of no rain, I glanced out the window towards the Ortiz Mountains. They had disappeared! In their place, I saw a wall of russet red dirt moving towards the house. In an instant, the awesome red wind blew the roof off our house—much like a Madison Avenue gust might blow a fedora off a pedestrian! One minute I was standing in the combination living room-bedroom; a second later I was in a roofless rock pen. And then the rain began! Warped two by fours and splintered tongue-in-groove boards were strewn across acres of rocks and arroyos. Pieces of painted Kachina bodies lay broken and scattered across acres of sagebrush and sandstone. I remember Bart's eyes, full of tears, holding a tiny painted fist clutching a tiny rattle and feather. When I related this event to a Hopi friend of mine, he smiled knowingly. The Kachinas did not want to hang on the rafters of some Hippie Homesteaders!

Linda Durham at the entrance to her gallery, 2007.

Opening at Linda Durham's Gallery, 2007.

The desert wind taught me the difference between that which is sacred and that which is profane...the difference between that which can be captured or owned and that which must go free.

In time, the majestic western sky replaced the ocean as my favorite feature of Nature. It informed my days then as it does now. My eyes and mind embrace sundogs and dust devils. I marvel at the ways in which the wind plays with the vultures and ravens. I love seeing the wind engage the clouds...Vast desert vistas have given me the treasured key to focusing on distances—both inner and outer. For the profound gift of appreciation of Nature—of space, power, vulnerability, beauty, mystery, vision—I am most thankful for this desert land, this New Mexico.

Every cell in my body celebrates my connection with this rich and remarkable desert. For more than forty years, it has been and continues to be my most important teacher.

In Search of Wild Beauty:
Why I Came to Santa Fe

Jennifer Ferraro

Jennifer Ferraro, now 33, currently lives in Santa Fe with her twin sister Heather, who moved here in 2006. She teaches writing at the University of New Mexico part-time and works part-time as a professional writer. She has written a book of illustrated poetry called Divine Nostalgia *and has co-translated a book of Turkish mystical poetry with Latif Bolat titled* Quarreling with God: Mystic Rebel Poems of the Dervishes of Turkey *(White Cloud Press). She presents readings and workshops in Santa Fe and elsewhere, combining dance, music and poetry. She has been a student of the Sufi path for the past seven years and in 2007 completed a four-year Sufi Studies program called Suluk Academy under Pir Zia Inayat Khan. To see her art and find out more visit* www.jenniferferraro.com *or* www.turkishsufipoetry.com.

NOW THAT I HAVE LIVED IN SANTA FE FOR TEN YEARS, I am starting to clearly see how this place has shaped me, bequeathed particular gifts to me, and answered some of the deepest longings of my soul. I came to Santa Fe after completing college at the New School for Social Research in New York City in 1996. Before that I grew up on the suburban New Jersey shore, but I never felt a kinship to that place...I see now that the blandness and bleakness of the consumer culture I saw there and the domestication of the landscape created a powerful thirst in me for that which is beautiful, wild and true.

Ever since I saw pictures of it in high school, New Mexico exerted an incredible pull on my imagination. The openness and mysteriousness of the landscape seemed full of promise, new beginnings. The first few years I lived in Santa Fe, in my early twenties, I actually tasted what it meant to be truly alive for the first time in my life. Looking back, I can say it was a kind of peak experience—I felt the bliss of potentiality, youth and the thrill of newness in my veins. Everything felt possible. New and unknown beauties lay around every corner. I remember hiking to the top of a high hill behind the old Ojo Caliente hot springs, seeing expanses of brown rolling hills in all directions and the beginnings of the snow covered Rockies, and thinking, *Holy hell.* This is it.

Within the first six months of moving here, I became strongly connected to art again, and even began selling my work. One day I was in Hobby Lobby and I noticed a particular craft tool I had never seen before—a woodburner. I had always drawn with charcoal and sketched and even painted a little, having a particular aptitude for drawing the human face, but it had been some time since I had taken my artistic abilities seriously. On a whim, I bought the woodburner and immediately began burning images into wood. I specialized in portraits, spiritual icons and old-world style renderings. My first job was working at a Mexican import store off the plaza. Though I made barely enough to survive those days, the owner of the store became a friend and let me sell my pieces in the store. He even let me create art pieces while on the job! What a thrill it was to actually sell my art work. One time I had several icons of Christ stolen in broad daylight from the display in the doorway of the store. Several weeks afterward I happened to be talking to a gallery owner from down the block… He was telling me about this talented local ex-con who made these beautiful wood-burned icons…learned to do it in prison, he said. Unfortunately, this thief had taken my stolen pieces just a block away and sold them

to the gallery, who in turn sold them for a pretty penny!! On the bright side, my art was selling, and worthy of stealing.

Jennifer on the Santa Fe Plaza selling her art at an art show in 1997.

Some of my experiences over the past ten years have certainly felt touched by some cosmic principle. It was in Santa Fe that I met and got involved with a well-known Turkish musician who happened to perform here. For four years I toured internationally with him playing Sufi music, drumming and reciting the poetry of Rumi, Yunus Emre and the Turkish mystics in hundreds of theatres, universities, churches, museums and spiritual gatherings. I performed devotional Persian style dance with poetry embedded in it. I traveled more widely than I ever had hoped, spending several summers in Turkey on the Mediterranean translating the poetry of the Turkish Sufis — a fulfillment of my heart's desire. I even spent six weeks in Hawaii once, and performed devotional dance in a fairy tale palace owned by Doris Duke called Shangri-La. As a culmination, in 2007 our book, *Quarreling with God: Mystic Rebel Poems of the Dervishes of Turkey* (White Cloud Press) was published, featuring poems we had translated by Turkey's ancient Sufi dervish poets. I have never ceased to be amazed at the twists and turns of destiny and the power of a soul-wish. I know that somehow being in Santa Fe brought these things to my life, made it possible for such things to find me and for me to find them. I am filled with gratitude when I think of these rich gifts of experience I've been given.

This is not to say it's been all roses here… There has been struggle and some truly terrible things have happened here as well. But I do know that Santa Fe has nurtured me spiritually and artistically and given me permission to be myself…to feel nurtured among other kindred souls who understand this impulse to live a life of devotion to beauty and soulfulness, to reclaim the wildness intrinsic to the spirit and the natural world.

Jennifer reading a poem during a Turkish Music Performance—Houston, 2006.

Lately I think a lot about longing and belonging—and what home means. While the journey westward has been personal and spiritual, it also takes place at a particular moment in time, in a culture whose overarching theme, in my opinion, is exile.

New Mexico is my chosen home, but not my ancestral home. I grew up a mile from the Atlantic ocean, in a landscape dramatically different from this one. The smells were different. The trees were different. I wanted that difference when I came here, in order to begin a new life, to leave the past behind. But what is the cost of such leave-taking ultimately?

Lately, I notice that when I travel somewhere wet, to a place of green grass and trees, or by the sea, I will smell something in the air that makes me feel like weeping. I've begun to wonder if perhaps there are memories locked up in those sensations that I will only access when I live in a place more similar to my childhood environment. I left home at age 14 and never really had a home after that, a place of real belonging. Santa Fe is the closest thing to home for me. In truth, I feel that we are all driven by a poignant nostalgia for home—which in most people informs the spiritual search unconsciously, like a thorn long-embedded but still aching. I've begun to wonder if it is important to return to the water sometime soon, to feel the soft grass under my feet. I've wondered if having my own family will affect this longing for home. I became an artist here, and learned that I could live passionately and creatively. The place and its expansive dramatic beauty has nurtured me and freed me in many ways. Yet do I ultimately belong here?

Jennifer Ferraro performing with
Latif Bolat in Houston in 2005.

If I place myself in the stream of free-spirits and artists and spiritual seekers who came here to start a new kind of life, I feel that I belong. But sometimes as I'm driving around and the sun is beating down relentlessly and everywhere I look is rocky, dry and brown, I look down at the blond hairs on my freckle-prone arm and wonder how it is that I came to live in such a place, where there is so little water and shade. It is a harsh place in many ways. This is also why it is such a spiritual place. But lately I'm longing for enclosure, for softness and coolness and a smaller scale of things perhaps. I try to go to Ireland each year—which feels like the perfect antidote and balance to here, and which now feeds my inspiration. I do know that for some reason, now when I see a stand of cottonwoods graceful and canopy-like in the middle the dry brown fields, it is more poignant than if there were an entire forest of green trees. You know there is a river there, running between those trees, however small. It is more miraculous here for its rarity and seeming fragility.

My gratitude to this place and love for it are endless…I've driven back and forth to the East coast from here many times, and always when I'm crossing back over from Texas on I-40, leaving Amarillo…there's that moment when the landscape changes and you're met with rolling hills dotted with piñon and juniper…The land dips and swells intoxicatingly and all the varied hues seem more vivid. I often have the desire to kiss the ground, knowing viscerally that I have crossed into New Mexico again. To me, New Mexico and Santa Fe will always signify freedom, and I will always say a quiet *thank you* upon entering back into the safe arms of this land where life for me became much more full, magical and *possible* than I could have imagined.

Jennifer Ferraro, 2007.

We Came to Santa Fe
Sandy & Jim Fitzpatrick

Sandy is a former U.S. history and government teacher, author of The Guide to Black Washington, *an art gallery owner, and now a struggling student of Spanish.* **Jim** *is a long-term partner of Arnold and Porter law firm in Washington, DC, specializing in public policy and legislative issues. Presently he teaches a Georgetown Law School course entitled, "Indiana Jones and the Elgin Marbles," considering the international trade in antiquities, as well as chairing the Board of Global Rights, an international human rights organization.*

AUGUST 1974: THE FITZES arrived at Santa Fe's La Posada with two young boys on our Western Swing Trip. The end of the bed, however, touched the opposite wall requiring all of us to walk over the bed to reach the bathroom. Even on a budget, we knew we had to move. We drove to Rancho Encantado and realized immediately that this was heaven…the horses, the tiled patio overlooking the Jemez Mountains and the great food. The frosting was the helicopter that flew over us landing at the Rancho dispatching Princess Grace, also showing her children the Great American West.

MARCH 1989: THE FITZES arrived in Santa Fe bringing the youngest son, eighth grader Benjamin, to ski with his Dad over Spring Break. Mama Fitz of the very bad knees does not ski and was armed with novels and a "What to Do in Santa Fe" book. On Monday, Mr. Fitz was not able to navigate a mogul and spent many hours in St. Vincent's Hospital. Mama Fitz called Victoria Ryan of Santa Fe Properties to "see what all of this charm really looked like behind the adobe walls." By Friday and after several margaritas at P.C.'s Lounge on Cerrillos, we decided to purchase a sweet "just being built" adobe on Berger Street.

JULY 1989: WE BLITZED all of Santa Fe's wonderful tiendas and furnished the home. Victoria invited us to her house for cocktails. There were three couples attending. She toasted all of us and said that in her ten years of selling real estate we were the only couples she wished for lifelong friends…all the rest of her clients were all "assholes!" We all looked at each other, stunned, and became instant Best Friends.

1994: WE SOLD OUR beloved home and moved to 644 Canyon Road, a delightful casita renovated by Doug Atwell 20 years earlier. We actually had a true Back Yard deep in grass, with four of the Historic District's venerable apple trees.

Jim and Sandy on their arrival in Santa Fe, 1989.

Jim and Sandy at home in Santa Fe, 2007.

2003: YEARNING FOR NEW MEXICO openness, we found a lot on Palo Duro Road in the Village of Tesuque overlooking the Sangres. The mega-talented Steve Robinson helped us design our New Mexico home, hopefully respecting the classical and serene Territorial Style with its roots in the Federal Style of the East and Georgetown, Washington, D.C., our other home.

WE ARE HERE FOR THE LONG RIDE.

We Came to Santa Fe
Thomas & Karen Fitzsimmons

Thomas Fitzsimmons *went into World War II as an underage merchant seaman just after Pearl Harbor and came out of the USAAF just after Hiroshima. He was born in Lowell, Mass., October 1926. Formerly writer/editor,* **The New Republic** *(Washington, DC) feature writer,* **The Asahi Daily News** *(Tokyo, Japan), he is author, translator or editor of some 60 books. At present he is editor of two book series from University of Hawaii Press: Asian Poetry in Translation: Japan; and Reflections. Professor Emeritus of Literature, Oakland University, he has received a number of honors, including three National Endowment for the Arts fellowships (poetry, translation and belles letters) and several Fulbrights to countries in Europe and Asia. In the mid-1970s he and* **Karen Hargreaves-Fitzimmons** *did a 16-month, 18 nation poetry-reading tour through the Pacific, South Asia, the Middle East and Europe under the auspices of USIS. They live just south of Santa Fe, where they publish Katydid Books, distributed by University of Hawaii Press.*

W E CAME TO SANTA FE IN 1990 by way of Japan and France. When I retired from university teaching in the late '80s we went directly to Japan, on a Fulbright grant, to compile an anthology of the most challenging modern poets there. I had first gone to Japan in 1962–64 on a teaching Fulbright, and shortly after that began editing and publishing the first of two series of books for the University of Hawaii Press *Asian Poetry in Translation: Japan.* The anthology, not finished and published until we had settled here, became the #15 in that series: *The New Poetry of Japan: the 70s and 80s.*

While in Japan I was awarded my third National Endowment for the Arts award (in *Belle Lettres;* the previous two had been in *Poetry and Translation*). We had lived some ten years, off and on, in Japan by then and had decided not to, as we thought we might, stay there. The other country we had strong feelings about and had lived in a lot is France (the homeland of my mother's people). So we used the grant to settle in France and do a book of poems, prose and (Karen's) paintings about our experiences in Japan: *Water Ground Stone* (#4 in the series *Reflections*).

We hoped to become permanent residents of France.

I had first left the US as an underage Merchant Seaman at the start of WWII, and both Karen and I have spent much of life in other countries, so we wanted a place outside of mainstream American culture.

We settled happily in a village in the Alps Maritimes in the south of France (country not unlike the northern New Mexico highlands), and we were moving through all the steps required for permanent status, when the Gulf War and a plunging exchange rate made it clear how vulnerable we were. So — where to live in the States?

We'd become acquainted with Santa Fe on camping and hiking trips while crossing the country going to or coming from Japan. We had a few friends here. Karen was clear from the beginning that it would be the right place for us, but I had some doubts because of a kind of cafeteria mysticism (a little Zen, a little Taoism, a little Hinduism, a little Native American...) we'd often run into when here to read poetry.

The traveling Fitzsimmons, in France making up their minds to come to Santa Fe, 1990.

Karen and Thomas Fitzsimmons at home in Eldorado, 2006.

So we explored the Allegheny Mountains and the Rockies from north to south (we already know California well enough) and ended up, as Karen had foreseen, here, the most "other" of American cities.

We've been here 17 years, and we will stay.

After some 35 titles, we're closing down our series of books for Hawaii.

I write modern American haiku (as well as long forms). Karen, who studied for many years with a Sumié (Oriental Ink Brush painting) master in Japan, now paints mostly in that tradition (and teaches it in her studio). These approaches seem to fit the northern New Mexico highland reality very well. Our latest book is a celebration: *High Desert. High Country: Seeds (modern American haiku and modern American Sumié;* available at Collected Works bookstore near the Plaza.

And there are all the Santa Fe friends for another celebration…

> *skeleton trees reach*
> *into a wild northwest gale*
> *twist it into song*

Home Sweet Santa Fe

Ted & Barbara Flicker

Ted Flicker was one of the founders of Improvisational Theatre in this country and subsequently had a distinguished career in both film and television. He and his wife Barbara left the West Coast to avoid the continuing frenzy that life in the movie world required.

LEMME TELL YOU ABOUT MY PALS Ted and Barbara Flicker. The Flickers. There are a few versions of how they got to Santa Fe. They're all real. About as real as Santa Fe is.

One is: Ted woke Barbara up at three in the morning and said, "Sweetheart, if I don't get out of L.A., my heart is going to attack me. Pick any place in the world and I'll go there with you." Barbara said, "Okay. Rome, London, New York, or Santa Fe?" and Ted said "Why don't we get in the car." That's true.

They'd first seen Santa Fe in 1970. Ted was checking it out for a movie location. It turned out Santa Fe wasn't right for the film; Las Cruces was. But they were hooked. They kept coming back to Santa Fe for another hit of green.

Another story is: they came here for their twentieth anniversary to buy a Houser sculpture, which they did, and then they needed a house to put it in. Barbara wanted an existing house. Ted wanted to build a house. They checked into the Eldorado for what turned out to be for five months and started looking at land.

I don't know what it is with the Flickers, but as long as I've known them the first thing they do when they go someplace new is to get a real estate agent to show them around. Actually it's not too stupid. They get a good look and a lot of gossip which some people call local lore. Over the years that's included a meadow overlooking a lake in Switzerland, a small palazzo on the only quiet street in Rome, and an Elizabethen manor in the Cotswalds. On the Santa Fe search, in spite of Ted's insistence on building, their broker consulted his psychic and became adamant about showing them, "just this one house." The psychic scored. They bought it on the spot. That's more or less true too.

Still another version is they bought this house and Barbara thought it was a second home. They moved in, opened a bottle of wine, lit two candles, and Ted said, "I'm never going back to California." Barbara's thought was, oh no. I'm too old to share a bathroom and a closet with anyone, no matter how wonderful. (She adored their 1920s California chicken-wire and plaster Hollywood mansion. The one with eleven bathrooms and a ballroom.) Ted said don't worry, it'll be fine. He got his wish too, he's been building ever since. That's true, too.

Why Santa Fe? It was exotic. It was like a foreign city without ever getting on a damned airplane. The natives were fun and bright and welcoming. The first year they went to everything that had music, food or an art auction in order to figure out how and with whom they wanted to spend their time. They didn't stay home more than two nights a month. And House Guests! Everyone wants to come to Santa Fe. Their little guest house had a higher occupancy rate than the La Fonda in their best year. There were so many places to take friends: opera, gallery openings, trips to the old turquoise mine, Tent Rock Canyon, ROSWELL. Now that's exotic.

A painting by Bill Schenck of Ted and Barbara Flicker and their Series E 1970 Jaguar done on or about the time of their arrival in Santa Fe.

**Ted and Barbara Flicker in a sculpture
done by Ted himself in his studio.**

And....and....instead of movie people there were *artists,* and *poets* and *music makers.* At the coffee houses there was actual conversation! Paradise!

Barbara learned to garden here. A real challenge. In California her major tool was a machete. Everything grows. Too much. In New Mexico it's tough. Improve the land. Don't use chemicals. Throw away the garden books. It's learn by doing. Put out a drip line. Plant a seed where it drips so you don't waste a drop of water. Learn to tell the snakes apart and be good to the ones who eat mice. And the tomatoes Barbara grows. Amazing. Maybe that's why they call it the *City Different.* You've never eaten tomatoes like those from Barbara's garden.

Ted, meanwhile, wrote some books and then decided he'd like to learn about sculpture. He'd always wanted to try it and now was the time. He went to study with Paul Moore. God, the stuff that started falling out of his fingers! Portraits and naked women. The most sensual, interesting, mythical, big bronze sculptures. All those years in Hollywood it was there on the MGM logo ***ars gratia aris*** and he never got to do it. What does *ars gratia aris* mean? **Art for Art's sake.** That's what Santa Fe has for Ted.

Ted had been a writer and director for his entire adult life. And he liked it. He liked doing theater and making films. But with sculpting, Ted found the real joy, and fulfillment he never experienced in Hollywood. *Ars gratia aris.*

They're having a very good life in Santa Fe, thank you. Thank you, Santa Fe. Barbara thanks you. Ted thanks you, and I thank you. Me? In 1970 when Ted decided Santa Fe wasn't right for his film and went to Las Cruces, I quit the movie racket and stayed in Santa Fe. I knew they'd be back.

A former Assistant *Asistant*

We Came to Santa Fe
Richard Gaddes

Richard Gaddes, the General Director of the Santa Fe Opera since October 2000 has had a colorful corner in the world of music. Born in Northumberlandshire in England his work and travels bought him to the United States in 1968. Since his arrival his organizational and management skills have brought him an international reputation as one of the most powerful persons in the Opera world.

I N 1967 I HAD COMPLETED MY music degree at Trinity College of Music in London, and rather than becoming a school teacher had opted for a career in arts administration. I took a job working for a small artist management company and was mainly responsible for the instrumentalists whom we represented. One day the owner of the company announced that in future we would concentrate exclusively on opera singers, conductors, stage directors and designers. Suddenly I was in the opera business. We happened to represent the music director Glyndebourne Festival Opera at the time, John Pritchard, and so very soon I was immersed in a world that I came to love and which has taken up just about all of my career.

Late the following year, in 1968, John Crosby, founder and General Director of The Santa Fe Opera, advised us that he was coming to London and wanted to hear some of the singers we represented. I was assigned the task of taking care of him and arranging the auditions. John Crosby was very shy and I spent a whole weekend going to opera performances with him, arranging auditions, and rounding up a few singers who were going to be at the Santa Fe Opera during the coming summer to say hello to him. On the day he returned to New York, John thanked me for my kindness to him and said that when he returned the following year, we would meet again. At that point I was thinking of making a career change, perhaps to work for a symphony orchestra, but told him that we could at least have a drink together when he returned. John, the master of understatement, suggest that perhaps there might be a job for me at The Santa Fe Opera. I was twenty-six and enjoying the goings-on in London of the sixties, and paid little attention to his comment.

The following February 1969, a few of the staff in the artists management company and I went out for a drink after work. Arriving home quite late, one of my roommates was up on a ladder plastering a crack in the ceiling of the house we all shared and he greeted me with, "There has been a man named John Crosby calling you from New York. There is his number—call him back." When I reached John he asked me if I remembered our conversation when he was in London. "Which conversation?" I asked. It turned out that the position of Artistic Administrator of The Santa Fe Opera had become vacant and John wondered if I would be interested.

I agreed to fly to Santa Fe to see the theatre, then to New York to see the company's New York offices where I would be working for a good part of the year. I had never been to America before, and my trans-Atlantic journey was complicated because PanAm was on strike, resulting in my flights being rearranged and requiring me to spend—unexpectedly—a night in New York en route for Albuquerque. I found a hotel on Eighth Avenue, gave the cab driver a fifty-dollar bill, thinking it was a one-dollar bill, and checked into my room.

Photo by Ken Howard

Richard Gaddes and John Crosby, the founder and first General Director of The Santa Fe Opera. The photo was taken at a reception for the apprentice artists in 1975.

I was nervous being on my own in a strange city, but excited all the same. I remember opening the curtains in my room and seeing the lights of Times Square. It was an unforgettable moment for a twenty-six year old on a wild adventure. I turned on the television. President Eisenhower's funeral had been held on that very day and as it was being shown I remember a brass band playing "Onward Christian Soldiers…"

The next day I flew on to New Mexico and was introduced to a landscape that was a far cry from the pastoral scenery of England. It was March, the sun wasn't shining, and everything seemed grey and cheerless. I remember looking out of my window at La Fonda Hotel wondering if I really could imagine spending part of my life in Santa Fe. The next day, however, John showed me the magnificent opera house with its unsurpassed setting and even though Santa Fe itself had not yet captured my imagination, I was bowled over by the facility and was able to imagine how it must be during the summer. That evening, John, Eleanor Winfield Scott, and I had dinner at The

Compound. The Compound looks very much today as it did then, and I still look at the *banco* where we sat whenever I go there. It's almost hallowed ground for me.

We flew to New York to see Opera's offices there and John by that time had persuaded me to accept the position. I flew back to England, packed my things, said good-bye to all my friends, and returned on June 12, 1969. Santa Fe has changed. Suddenly it was green and lush; the sun was shining and the sky was blue. I was smitten, and even though coming to Santa Fe was a huge cultural shock, I soon looked upon it as home. Little did I think that almost forty years later I would

Photo by Robert Godwin

Richard Gaddes, 2004.

still be here.... thinking about retiring but grateful for the wide range of support the Opera has managed to attract not only local but national and internationally as well.

❖   ❖   ❖

Photo by Robert Reck, 1998

A view of the interior of the magnificent structure housing the Santa Fe Opera showing elements of its soaring architecture as well as a scene from "The Magic Flute".

We Came to Santa Fe

Charles Gallenkamp & Karen L. Wright

Charles Gallenkamp was born in Texas and educated at the Universities of Texas and New Mexico. He has conducted Archaeological research in the Southwest USA, Mexico and Central America. He has written articles that have appeared in national magazines and newspapers. He is the author of Maya; the Riddle and Rediscovery of the Lost Civilization, Dragon Hunter, Roy Chapman Andrews and the Central Asiatic Expedition. *His wife* **Karen** *flew for years with Braniff International airlines and had a successful career in Radio and Television advertising. She was the Editor and Illustrator for the Dragon Hunter book. They have recently finished working on "Dinosaurs Alive" an Imax film and are currently working on various other projects.*

I FIRST DISCOVERED SANTA FE in the winter of 1949–50 while studying anthropology at the University of New Mexico. Having found my way here after spending my early years in Texas, California, and New York City, I was instantly attracted, like so many visitors, to the town's natural setting, architecture, and ambience, which drew me back many times—indeed somewhat relentlessly. It was, I think, the sunsets and the pungent smell of piñon smoke on cold winter evenings that most captivated me, and after my first visit to Bandelier National Monument one November day, I vowed to someday live here. I roamed everywhere: to all the Rio Grande Pueblos, to Chaco Canyon, Navajo National Monument, Acoma, and Zuni. Three times I accompanied my good friend, Valentino Montoya from Santa Ana Pueblo, to the Hopi Snake Dance and the Shalako at Zuni. In those days one could still trade used clothing for museum-quality pottery, which I did on many occasions. And for two summers I was a member of the archaeological field school operated by the University of New Mexico in the Gallina River Valley between Cuba and El Vado Lake.

In 1953 I met one of Santa Fe's most colorful residents, the late John Skolle, a performer in his family's circus and a brilliant translator, writer and painter whose imaginative creations have been acquired by the Museum of New Mexico, the Raymond Johnson Gallery in Albuquerque, and many other museums and collectors. A native of Czechoslovakia, John spoke five languages, had lived in France and Germany, was involved in the Spanish Civil War with ties to anti-Franco forces and had traveled extensively in Africa and the Middle East. He lived for long periods with the Taureg, journeyed with them by camel caravan from Timbuctoo to the salt mines at Taoudeni and acquired, albeit briefly, a Taureg wife.

John was a marvelous raconteur and enjoyed a wide circle of friends in Santa Fe and Taos. Through him I came to know such storied individuals as Louise Ribak and Beatrice Mandelman, Andrew Dasburg, Leon Gaspard, Dorothy Brett, Frieda Lawrence, Witter Bynner, Alfred Morang, and Helen Wurlitzer, whose foundation in Taos provided support to many writers and painters. John and I traveled a great deal in Mexico and Central America, and he contributed superb illustrations to my first book, *Maya: The Riddle and Rediscovery of a Lost Civilization.*

By 1954 I was spending every summer in Santa Fe, at a time when it was possible to rent charming guest houses or apartments for $75 to $150 a month, especially if one knew, as I did, a wildly alcoholic but efficient real estate agent who took me to look at properties only

Karen Wright with her grandmother Lee Wright on her right in 1957 on the Taos Plaza at the time of the Taos Fiesta.

after a long stint at La Fonda Bar. Given my idyllic surroundings, ample time to write, and a heady social life—punctuated by an extraordinarily cast of characters and numerous parties—these summers in Santa Fe were magical. So much so that by 1960 I decided to settle here year around, though with frequent breaks for travel on writing assignments. Being something of a nomad by nature, I never owned property in Santa Fe until 1972 when I co-founded the original Janus Gallery near the Plaza, now no longer in existence.

For years my passion as an archaeologist and writer had been the ancient Maya, whose culture once flourished in the Yucatan Peninsula, Guatemala and Belize. Interestingly, Santa Fe had a long tradition of scholarship in this field, having been home at various times to several Mayanists, including Sylvanus G. Morley, regarded as the founder of modern Maya archaeology. Because I had published a series of articles and books on the subject, the Albuquerque Museum of Art and History approached me about organizing a major exhibition of Mayan art—a proposal that would have far-reaching effects on my life. Eventually known as *Maya: Treasures of an Ancient Civilization,* the show—one of the so-called "blockbuster" exhibitions of the 1970s and 80s—traveled to New York, Los Angeles, Dallas, Kansas City, Toronto, and Albuquerque attracting overflow crowds at each location. And midway through its itinerary I met my wife, Karen L. Wright, who happened to be handling advertising for the project at KHFM radio in Albuquerque.

Charles Gallenkamp as the younger archeologist in 1950.

Born in Boston and raised in Connecticut, she first came to new Mexico at age eleven to visit her grandmother, Lee Wright, who had gravitated to Santa Fe from Massachusetts and California and build several houses with the help of Taos Indians. Famous for her charm, superb cooking and gatherings of colorful characters, Lee resided here for the remainder of her long life. During the summer of 1957, Karen stayed with her on Canyon Road and spent several weeks on the Taos Pueblo living with the family of Lee's close friend Augustine Mirabal. "After the dark and humid woods of New England where I grew up," Karen relates, "I was overwhelmed by northern New Mexico's light, dramatic mountains and limitless sense of space. I instantly identified with everything about it."

After attending the Hartford Conservatory of Music and graduating from the Oakwood School, Karen enrolled for two years at the University of New Mexico. On weekends she worked at the Santa Fe Ski Basin, helping to clear new trails. Eager to travel, however, she eventually joined Braniff International Airways as a flight attendant, serving in northern Europe, the United States, South America and the Pacific Theater, including Medivac flights from Vietnam during the war. Following several years in England she ended up back in New Mexico, living in a house high in the mountains of Cedar Crest just east of Albuquerque.

Karen Wright in 1990 still smiling her way to Santa Fe.

Why Karen and I did not meet sooner is a mystery we often ponder. We knew many of the same people, frequented the same restaurants and even preferred the same tables. Ironically, I was a guest in her parents house in Santa Fe on two or three occasions without knowing she existed. We both regularly attended the Santa Fe Opera. She tells of hearing a performance of Wuthering Heights in the original theater (before it burned) while the Russian spacecraft Sputnik soared overhead. A few days earlier I had met Igor Stravinsky as he stood under a street light in front of the old Capital Pharmacy on the Plaza.

But meet we finally did and it marked the beginning of what for us has been a fascinating odyssey. Shortly thereafter we collaborated on a biography of the celebrated explorer of Mongolia, Roy Chapman Andrews, entitled *Dragon Hunter.* In 1995 we traveled to China and the Gobi Desert to retrace some of Andrews' routes. Next we worked on a film about Andrews for the Discovery Channel, which was shot entirely in Santa Fe and at Ghost Ranch. And most recently we acted as consultants for an IMAX production, *Dinosaurs Alive* that is partly based on Andrews' explorations and was filmed in Mongolia and again at Ghost Ranch.

What comes next is uncertain. But there is not doubt that Santa Fe will continue to play a major role in our lives.

Charles Gallenkamp at the Maya Ruins 1986.

We Came to Santa Fe

Charles Greeley & Bunny Tobias

Bunny Tobias *and* **Charles Greeley,** *both artists and 36 year residents of Santa Fe, as well as the owners/directors of Gallery ZIPP, discuss their long time involvement in the local art scene—and the beauty of the environment in which they work and live.*

W E MET AT THE NEW YORK SCHOOL of Visual Arts. I was 18. He had just turned 19. It was 1960. We were raised and educated in the Big City, and yet both of us had a dream of living the artist's life in a remote mountain setting.

Our interest in surrealist subject matter—dreams, reversals of meaning, ancestral memories, and the world of the unconscious—may have begun in 1964 after seeing Max Ernst's retrospective at MOMA, and meeting the artist himself. In 1934, after painting the largest of his forest pictures, Ernst wrote: "What will be the death of the forests? The day will come when a forest, until then a friend of dissipation, will decide to frequent only sober places, tarred roads, and Sunday strollers. She will live on pickled newspapers. Affected by the virtue, she will correct these bad habits contracted in her youth. She will become geometrical, judicial, pastoral, ecclesiastical, constructivist and republican..... It will be a bore."

Four years after Charles and I met we were married. That began an adventure of sharing the love of art, the challenges of survival for two artists, and the realization of our dream of a high mountain lifestyle, isolated, surrounded by nature, independent. On the way we made a few stops.

We left New York in 1966 to live and paint in San Miguel de Allende, Mexico, a mountainous artists colony not unlike Santa Fe. This diversion from NYC made a lasting impression on us. Eventually, we ended up in San Francisco as 60's peace and freedom hippies, painting psychedelic visions in altered states and exploring the collective unconscious. This was a vital time for developing new ideas in art and learning how to be open to change. In 1970, after vacationing in Santa Fe, then a hippie-dippie little town, we fell in love with the place, and in 1972, after finding our mountain retreat, we made New Mexico our home. During this time, we allowed the influences of the various Southwest cultures, very foreign to our NY upbringing, to affect our art. Thus begun our 35 year involvement in the then budding Santa Fe contemporary art scene. We were both represented by major local galleries, took part in all the museum biennials and Santa Fe Art Festivals, while at the same time enjoying our

Photo by Mark Miller

Bunny and Charles Greeley at Coyote Cafe, 1986, after their opening at Sloan-Horowitch Gallery.

*Bunny and Charles,
2000 at their ZIPP Gallery.*

peaceful country lifestyle, nestled in the Glorieta Pass, affording us the seclusion of the Sangre de Cristo Mountains.

However, this remote lifestyle did not prevent us from being involved in art related projects out of New Mexico. In 1979 we were invited to have a two person, 10 years retrospective of our paintings at the Contemporary Arts Museum in Houston, Texas. Also, we were both contracted to Walt Disney Corp. to do original art for their Disneyanna convention for four consecutive years.

In the summer of 1996, Gallery ZIPP was born. Being "Zen Inspired Professional Pagans," we created an alternative venue offering invitational theme shows in our 250 year old adobe hacienda with the intention of exhibiting emerging, cutting edge, provocative artists from the community for the purpose of variety, greater interest and pure pleasure. Eleven years later our goal of creating a winning situation for ourselves, other artists, and the public has become quite a success.

Our life together, as artists and partners, has been inspired and blessed as a result of following the direction of our dreams.

Knitting Dreams into Reality

Sharon Greenleaf La Pierre

Dr. Sharon Greenleaf La Pierre lives and works currently in Boulder, Colorado. She is the Director of Administration for Look Dynamics, Inc, an optical computer company owned by her husband, David A. Bruce, and other investors. Her career started in the education field, beginning with teaching at the community college and university levels in design and fiber design. Later, her Ph.D. focused on the nature of artistic intelligence and its measurement, leading to a Kellogg Post-doctoral Research Fellowship at Montana State University and the running of a graduate program at Northern Arizona University. Dr. La Pierre has published extensively in her field and served as president of several national professional organizations, as well as editor for peer reviewed publications. At present, she is active in animal rescue issues and travels to Santa Fe regularly where some of her horses are being trained and where she has established her second home. She and her husband founded the Wildlife Legacy Trust, a not-for-profit committed to the support of wildlife rehabilitation. She is a licensed fawn rehabilitator for the Colorado Division of Wildlife.

I GREW UP IN ST. HELENA, NAPA VALLEY, CALIFORNIA. My father's ancestors came originally from Iowa and South Dakota and were of Santee-Yankton Sioux heritage. Before coming to California, my father's family worked in the fields of Washington picking fruits and vegetables. Later, they did the same in California. My Dad had a third grade education because his family migrated from town to town, always on the move. He became the town barber in St. Helena, a craft his father learned in an Industrial Indian School in Montana at the turn of the century.

It was my dream to go to college (especially Stanford University), but my family did not have the money for such an expense, and I was not expected to reach such a lofty goal because of my class and gender (or so I thought). From the age of eight years, I picked prunes along with my brothers and migrant workers. We organized many farmers' fields during the summers, and

I saved all of this money for college, as well as paid for my own school clothes. We were paid twenty-five cents a box for our labor, which included box stacking and the shaking of the prune trees.

I was fortunate to have had a mother and grandmother who valued education and spiritual knowledge. My mother taught me it was acceptable to be different and to succeed differently from others. She used to say, "True education is being able to sit on a curb with a transient and hold a conversation (common sense knowledge) or to eat dinner with a king or queen (learned knowledge)." This meant being aware of my own talents and strengths and having the courage to reach for the stars with the spirit of a warrior.

Upon graduation from high school, I received an anonymous and surprise scholarship during the graduation ceremony to pay for books and tuition for a four year college of my choice. This was the first time such a scholarship had been offered, and I learned 40 years later at a class reunion that a committee discussed who would benefit the most and achieve the most success as the criteria for the award. They wanted to give it to someone in need, but I was not their first choice. My advisor, Ralph Ingles, fought for me to receive this award. Because I had good grades, but did not test well, it was thought that I could not succeed, especially in a college setting. This very issue of not testing well became the basis of my doctoral dissertation and a Kellogg Post Doctoral Fellowship in Adult Learning Research at Montana State University, emphasizing research on the topic of artistic spatial intelligence and its definition and measurement.

My talent as a visual artist allowed me to be successful. I started in interior design and music and later got a masters degree in fiber design, creating whimsical basketry and weavings that were exhibited all over the U.S. But, my heart was in exploring how to determine the patterns of thought and measurement in regard

Sharon Greenleaf La Pierre, fiber artist, 1979, in front of her woven whimsical tapestry.

to artistic spatial thinking or intelligence. This took me to the University of Denver with special classes from Stanford University to study research methods and methodologies in art education curriculum. As a poor, little girl in the days of picking fruit I had fulfilled my dream of attending Stanford University and received my Ph.D. in 1987 thanks to an anonymous donor from high school. I was the first in my family to graduate from college or to even finish high school. My brothers followed later with the help of the Service. Through all of this growing, I learned that I was good in mathematics and language, something I thought impossible at an earlier age.

I settled in Colorado from California in 1969, where I taught at the community college and university levels, giving workshops and lectures, and later running a graduate program at the University of Northern Arizona in Art Education. I published extensively on the topics of artistic spatial reasoning and artistic research methods and methodologies, serving as president of several national professional organizations and editor of peer-reviewed publications.

David A. Bruce and Sharon Greenleaf La Pierre, December 1980, on their honeymoon, riding the Taos Reservation, New Mexico.

David A. Bruce and Sharon Greenleaf La Pierre, December 1980, Honeymoon on Taos Plaza, New Mexico.

In 1980, I married David A. Bruce, nine years my junior, and we spent our honeymoon in Taos horse back riding and enjoying the crisp December air on the Plaza. We still enjoy each other's company after 27 years of marriage. From Taos on, I continued to come to New Mexico and Santa Fe regularly until I discovered La Estancia Alegre in Alcalde. Because I rescued a Peruvian Paso filly from starvation (my pleasure is to rescue and place animals in need), I wanted to help this horse become the best she could be. So, I searched for the right place to train her and to learn to ride this breed. How ironic that New Mexico would be the place.

The conclusion brings me to the reason of why I agreed to author this chapter for this book; what is the draw, the lure, the need to return and live in Santa Fe? It all has to do with the variety of experiences, textures, patterns, beauty, colors, ideas, and beliefs…a "bigger than life" kind of thing tied to our own personal historical roots. We are not all alike, and more than any other place I have been, Santa Fe represents the rich flavors of many unique personalities. Education can be formal here, or it can be learned through common sense or hard knocks. Beauty can be colorfully harmonious, or it can be as textured as an adobe wall with its stark reality. Spirituality can be religious and mystical, or it can be the innate expression of the person's desire to find peace. Art can be personal, or it can be public. Human faces can be brown, black, or white. The fact is, no one seems to care about what things might be. What Santa Fe does demand of the individual is a zest for life and a desire to qualify the elements of daily experiences. Humankind seems to thrive on this need to ebb and flow.

David A. Bruce and Sharon Greenleaf La Pierre, 1993, Boulder, Colorado.

At first I thought the pull of Santa Fe was of a spiritual nature. In my search I have discovered that it is like an onion when pealed away displays the layers of variety and interest…dark, light, smooth, textured, colored, etc. It makes me reach for my roots in comfort because it inspires and stimulates me to think and act, feeling no age or limitations.

It is important to determine for oneself what makes a successful and joyful life. The hardships of my youth taught me to work and think with my hands and gave me strength and knowledge about life, other than book learning. On the other hand, formal education led the way to make dreams become reality. The integration of spiritual beliefs allowed me to master daily challenges and to ultimately succeed in a world filled with seeming facts and realities contrary to my intuitive, native thought patterns.

In a sense, I live the life my mother and grandmother could not have achieved because of family obligations, the era, and gender. I learned through discipline to forge ahead for other women by changing laws in the 60's and 70's in regard to credit, the legal use of my given name (federal and state), and modeling behaviors which altered the course of applied feminine creativity. Where else could I go to live but a place like Santa Fe that allows me to flourish?

Sharon Greenleaf La Pierre in 2007 at La Estancia Alegre, Alcalde, New Mexico with her "LEA Esplendor," Peruvian Paso Horse.

Orange to Green
Rob Hager

Rob Hager, a graduate of Brown and Harvard Law School has worked as a public interest lawyer handling a number of high profile civil rights and environmental cases and also as an international legal consultant for the United Nations and other international organizations in such countries as Afghanistan, Bosnia, Guyana, the Central Asian republics and elsewhere.

BLAME IT ON AGENT ORANGE, the chemical poured on Vietnam by the United States to destroy that country's verdant jungles. No, I wasn't exposed to Agent Orange. Though I flirted with the idea of military service as a teenager, by the time I was in college and my draft board acquired interest in greeting me, my perspective changed. Working on Great Lakes ore boats in the summer of '65, when I had time to study the situation, I decided this war was one I would take no part in. I danced through the exits available at the time to students and others. By the time the U.S. was ejected from Vietnam, I had graduated from law school and spent several years working as a development lawyer in Afghanistan, learning about a country that would become the site of a botched colonial war for another generation.

Twenty years later I was doing public interest lawyering in Washington, D.C. Most of my generation who had danced to that different drummer into Vietnam, and were exposed there to damaging doses of Agent Orange, were by this time starting to suffer from its effects: cancer, lymphomas, neurapathies and other nervous system disorders, to name a few.

Taking the case of a widow of a Vietnam veteran, dead from such diseases, and of other affected veterans, seemed an appropriate way to "support the troops" of my generation unfortunate enough to get inveigled in that misadventure. The Agent Orange veterans' story raised two important issues: one of the human cost of war and the penchant of warmongers in every generation to discard those they force, persuade or hire to fight them. If this were better known, it might be harder to raise a volunteer army to fight the wars of empire, such as the current ones. The other issue was the destruction that chemical pollutants—here in the form of dioxin—does to lives and families over a long term.

Having already worked on big cases involving nuclear and chemical pollution, such as from the Three Mile Island disaster and the Bhopal (India) disaster, I was aware of the political struggles required to obtain large-scale justice from the U.S. courts, particularly after they became dominated by Reagan/Bush appointees (and Clinton's were no match for Brennan and Marshall the last of the great justices on the Court). I was intrigued by the possibility that veterans might better sustain the political struggle necessary to obtain any significant justice from the U.S. courts. The potential transfer of wealth from the Monsanto's of the world to their victims that simple justice would entail in such cases is what the contemporary Supreme Court is there to prevent, except when the cost to the Court's prestige might be too great. But the larger the injustice, the less likely the Court will correct it, and the Agent Orange case threatened to become one the largest injustices in the Court's history.

I proceeded to spend more years of my life trying to get justice for these Agent Orange-exposed veterans than most of them had spent in Vietnam, and I found from other lawyers that I was not the only one that found it an emotionally draining experience.

The case was like this: A Brooklyn federal judge had in the early 80's supervised a collusive class action settlement between the several chemical companies who produced dioxin-contaminated Agent Orange and the lawyers he appointed to handle the class action suit for some of the early injured veterans. The judge approved a bizarre and unprecedented settlement of all future possible injury claims that might arise over time from exposures to Agent Orange. In this settlement the lawyers he appointed to represent the veterans got paid off, while the veterans got next to nothing. In return for allowing this miscarriage of justice, letting big chemical corporations off the hook for their negligence, the judge got a stash of millions deposited in a foundation he ran out of the court. This in itself was a violation of judicial conflict of interest law. But every case filed by Agent Orange veterans in any court any-where in the country was sent to this judge, who was allowed by the appeals court to keep his monopoly over his corrupt deal.

The case I brought (the *Ivy* case) sought to challenge this bad deal on behalf of the large majority of exposed veterans who had no discoverable injury when the settlement was made, and could not in any ordinary sense have "settled" their nonexistent "case" without their knowledge. Since *Ivy* was destined for the Supreme Court, I immediately started courting lawyers who were well known for winning cases in the Supreme Court to join me in per-suading the Supreme Court to take the case up when it reached them. One of these was a friend from Law School named Joel Klein, to whom I gave the various legal filings as the case worked its way toward the Supreme Court.

By the time the *Ivy* case reached the Court, Joel had already been re-cruited for a more prestigious job: President Clinton appointed him to replace his White House legal counsel who had suddenly left the position under a cloud of corruption. Meanwhile I had recruited Professor Laurence Tribe of Harvard Law School—the most prominent constitutional scholar and Su-preme Court practitioner of the time—to join the *Ivy* case for the Supreme Court appeal.

With help from several other accomplished lawyers interested in Viet-nam veterans or chemical pollution we put together an unprecedented assault on the Supreme Court. The legal issue was whether the federal courts could interfere with the state court's powers to try the veterans' cases by shipping them all off to a single federal judge in Brooklyn. This was a "state's rights" issue that normally appealed to the more conservative judges on the court as I had learned when handling the Karen Silkwood case in the Supreme Court several years before. The Supreme Court normally would hear a case if sev-eral states stood up for their rights by filing briefs before the court.

In a broad campaign to demonstrate to the Supreme Court how flagrantly the Brooklyn court had violated the law, not just several but all fifty state attorneys general were persuaded to file briefs in the court claiming that the veterans were entitled to their day in a state court to try their injury claims. This was totally unprecedented. No case had ever attracted all of the states before.

Veterans organizations established by Congress to represent veterans' legal interests, many of which had never worked together before, or participated in litigation, also filed briefs in the case. With this strong support I decided to approach the Clinton administration to support the veterans' appeal—a cheap way for Clinton to make political gains with veterans otherwise inclined to think of the Commander in Chief as a draft dodger. The request went from a couple dozen members of Congress, including Senator John Kerry. The reply refusing to have Clinton's solicitor general file a simple piece of paper asking the Supreme Court to review the veterans' case came from Joel Klein. I was certain that if this paper had instead been filed, the Supreme Court could not have defied an historic joint request of the federal government and all fifty states to hear a state's rights case. Without it, Clinton became in my view personally responsible for the Supreme Court's refusal to hear the case, which at the time was seen by me and other lawyers as the largest single injustice inflicted by the judiciary in American history.

This was the last straw for me with what I perceived as the corrupt and careless Clinton administration—and the increasingly pro-corporate Democrats—who deserved to hear about it at the polls. If, with all his other flaws, Clinton was unable to make such a simple gesture of support for veterans who risked their lives supposedly to defend the constitutional system that they now sought to use, he did not deserve a second term. It was time to build an alternative to the Democrats who had become a sorry excuse for an opposition party to the right-wing Republicans. I approached the one person I thought capable of tackling the nearly insuperable task of making a third party run, Ralph Nader. The concept was for him to get experience and put some fear into the Democrats in 1996 without spending much money, and then to make a real run for it in 2000 if the Democrats did not get the message. Ralph

Passport photo taken in Afghanistan ca. 1975.

agreed to test the waters by placing his name on the ballot in California, which was at the time considered a decisive state for Clinton, on condition that he would not need to raise money and get involved with the regulatory burdens imposed by the Federal Election Commission. The Green Party was willing to give Nader their ballot line on this condition, and a spontaneous grass roots effort proceeded to place Nader's name on many other state ballots as well. For the type of campaign he ran Nader both did reasonably well by third party standards, and acquired a taste for campaigning. He got many more votes per dollar spent than the other candidates in 1996, and if he qualified for federal funding in 2000, the future for a future opposition party to replace the lackluster Democrats looked promising.

Since taking a job abroad in the midst of the 1996 effort, I agreed to get more deeply involved in the 2000 campaign. I returned from working in Central Asia in early 1998 to help organize the campaign. But when Ralph held back from starting an early campaign, and I attended a Green Party conference in Santa Fe, I decided it might be more useful to move from Washington, D.C. to Santa Fe, then the epicenter of Green Party politics, to work within the context of a state campaign rather than wait in D.C. until Ralph decided to run. Within weeks I realized I made one of my better decisions, and I've remained in Santa Fe ever since. Though work has taken me back to Afghanistan for several years, and elsewhere, the land of entrapment has no difficulty drawing me back.

❖   ❖   ❖

Hiking near Abiqui, July, 2007.

We Came to Santa Fe

Joanna Hess

Joanna Hess is a noted figure in the international art world. She was a board member of the Hess Collection Winery and the president of N.A.C.A. (Napa Contemporary Art Foundation). She now serves on the foundation council of Site Santa Fe, N.M. Her wide range of interests in Europe and America brought her into contact with Native Americans interested in perpetuating their endangered languages. As a result she became founder of the organization now known as the Indigenous Languages Institute which has become international. Currently based in Santa Fe, Joanna travels the world and remains in contact with her friends in the art and humanitarian fields. Her passion is still language preservation and she facilitates connecting I.L.I. with important sources whenever possible.

My DAUGHTER'S CURIOSITY AND A QUESTION I asked in the spring of 1991 changed my life and brought me to Santa Fe. But before I tell you about that question and its consequences, I need to share a little of the life that preceded it.

I was born and raised in Boston. After college, I moved to London when I was twenty-three and became a photographic fashion model. It was the swinging 60's. Remember the miniskirt, Mary Quant and Twiggy? Each day was like one big party, not to mention the nights. The Beetles sang, Mic Jagger strutted his stuff, and oh, we felt so free as we all worked together. Flower power filled the air.

One day, unexpectedly, a friend asked if I would like to work for *Vogue Magazine* as an editor. She exclaimed, "I am getting married and leaving *Vogue* and I know you can do this job." The Editor-In-Chief interviewed me, and, *voila,* I was "in." For five amusing years I worked in a "Devil Wears Prada" environment. In my free time, I painted nudes in a beautiful studio next to the Chelsea art club. To my surprise, I sold quite a few of my paintings.

I left *Vogue* to work for DHI, an international fabric design studio, the largest of its kind in the world. Our studio spaces were so large that we roller-skated up and down the corridors to save time. Great fun!

Just before I was to leave for Soweto in South Africa to study fabric trends, I met Donald Hess. Donald was a Swiss industrialist who lived in Bern, Switzerland. Our attraction was immediate. In a short time, he enticed me to leave my beloved London. We married in Bern in 1972. My new life began with much travel. There was a business in Morocco, trips back and forth to London, and new friends all over Europe and in America.

In 1973, our daughter, Alexandra, was born. In 1978, we started the Hess Collection winery in the Napa Valley in northern California. This winery produces excellent wine of many varietals, and also houses a part of Donald's private art collection. I was involved artistically from the outset and loved working on the labels and other aspects of marketing.

When Alexandra was studying at Aiglon College in Aigle, Switzerland, Donald and I lived most of the year in Bern. Alexandra decided to do her art A level thesis on the Hopi Indians. Reading about the Hopi was not enough for her. She wanted to visit the people on the Hopi Reservation to enrich her understanding of their culture, ceremonies and the landscape out of which those ceremonies arose. I knew little about Native Americans. I certainly knew nothing about the boarding schools and how they attempted to strip the children of their culture and language.

I wanted to help Alexandra with her thesis, so I spoke to my husband, Donald, and he suggested we contact the Light Artist, James Turrell, in Flagstaff, Arizona. Donald was, and still is, a collector of James' Light Installations. Donald is currently building a museum in Colomé, Argentina, specifically for Turrell's art installations.

We telephoned Turrell. He enthusiastically said he would help Alexandra. He told us a documentary was being made about his vision for the Rodin Crater Project and its relationship to the Hopi. He asked us to join him in Flagstaff to meet Eugene Secaquaptewa, a Hopi elder, who was a wellspring of information on his Hopi culture.

We immediately made plans to leave Switzerland for Flagstaff. We felt honored to have this opportunity. On the first day of our meeting, Eugene proved to be a great storyteller and a very patient man. He answered our naïve questions, gently educating us. On the second day, we visited Roden Crater but that is another story, for a later time. On the morning of the third day, Eugene came to tell us that he had to leave immediately: he had received a call from his family informing him of his mother's death. Then he turned to Alexandra and asked if she would like to join him at Hopi. We felt surprised and honored at the same time. We did not know what to say. He assured us we would be well looked-after. He added that he would arrange meetings that would be helpful to Alexandra.

Joanna Hess on her arrival in Santa Fe in 1989.

The beauty of the drive from Flagstaff to Hopi overwhelmed us. Such a different beauty from vertical Switzerland: endless vistas, a marine blue sky, hues of gold and bronze and pink—hard white light that illuminated the landscape in unique ways. I found myself squinting even while wearing sunglasses. As we drove the ninety miles from Flagstaff to Hopi, Eugene would point to a butte or mesa and tell us a story.

The Hopi live on three mesas, each an arm of Black Mesa in Northern Arizona. Looking up towards the mesas, we thought we saw large rocks on top until we realized that we were looking at rock dwellings that blended into the mesa. As we approached Second Mesa, Eugene told us that each village had its own dialect. He added that ceremonies also varied from mesa to mesa. Wishing us a good night, he left us at the Hopi Cultural Center. We knew that Eugene would be busy with burial arrangements for his mother and, strangers in a new land, we wondered what the morning would bring.

Eugene called us early the next day to say he had arranged for us to meet the Director of Secondary School Education. It was in this conversation with the Director that I asked the question that changed the course of my life and landed me in Santa Fe.

The director was a tall Hopi man in his 30's. His blue-black hair, tied-back with white yarn, framed his sharp-featured face. He looked at Alexandra and me with curiosity and then said that Eugene had informed him of Alexandra's interest. He asked Alexandra what she would like to see or know. Her response was she would like to visit a classroom to talk with students who were interested in art.

He then asked me what my interest was in being there. I answered, "Is your language taught in the schools here?" He responded, *"No, it is considered a dialect by the BIA (Bureau of Indian Affairs) and not allowed to be taught beyond Head Start Programs. For generations, the elders have passed-down the stories, ceremonies, medicine, and songs. If we don't teach our children to speak Hopi, we will loose our culture and no longer know who we are."*

I was speechless. And angry. My head and my heart raced. I found myself saying, without thinking, "Do you mind if I try to do something about this?"

Now, why on Earth would I say such a thing, living in Switzerland with no knowledge of these people? In addition, I certainly wasn't a linguist, anthropologist or historian. He looked at me in a very strange way. Then he said, *"If you are really serious about this, I suggest you arrange a visit with Emory at the University of Arizona."* Emory Secaquaptewa, Eugene's brother, is a senior research Anthropologist at the Bureau of Applied Research in Anthropology at the University of Arizona in Tucson. At that time, he was in the midst of a twenty-five year project of creating a dictionary of the Hopi language. He had already compiled close to thirty thousand words on a database. Today, that completed tome, the Hopi Dictionary, is a superb linguistic resource for the Hopi people.

Feeling many emotions, we returned to the cultural center. In the restaurant, we ate *nu'quivi,* Hopi stew, for dinner. Then, exhausted by our full day, we went to bed. We awoke early and drove to Old Oraibi on top of Third Mesa. Old Oraibi is the longest continually inhabited village in America. Standing in this ancient village, the Colorado Plateau stretched out below us like a vast ocean. As the wind howled around us, we saw a woman, wrapped in a blanket, making her way across the Plaza through the swirling dust. We

Joanna pleased on hearing the news that the Library of Congress is interested in working out a joint program with ILI, 2007.

stopped her to ask if it would be permissible for us to walk around the village. She beckoned us to follow her. We found ourselves in a small adobe structure. She smiled and said, "This is my piki house. We make piki here." She told us that piki is paper-thin bread made from blue corn and ash on a heated stone. The piki maker uses her hand to wipe the batter on the stone to form a large sheet that she then rolls into what looks like ancient papyrus. She gently places each roll in a basket. The piki stone is passed from mother to daughter. Even today, Alexandra and I visit Old Oraibi to enjoy the long friendships that we have cultivated there. We have learned so much about Hopi culture. It is an honor to be accepted as a Pahana (an Anglo) on Hopi.

During the day, the two words, "not allowed," spoken by the director, burned in my mind. Let me explain why.

In the early 1970's, I met Samra Losinger in Bern, Switzerland. She had started a non- profit organization in Daramsala, India to help Tibetan refugees begin immersion schools in the Tibetan language. She worked with Pema, the Sister of the Dahli Lama. They needed support and funding. You can imagine the exhaustion and hunger these Tibetan families felt after fleeing from the Chinese across the Himalaya. Once established in the village of Daramsala, they would send their children to school. Much to their surprise, they were informed that no Tibetan language would be taught in the public schools. All they had left was their faith, culture, courage, and language. Of course, they were made welcome by the Dhali Lama and the local Indian community, but they needed funding to begin their own Tibetan language schools. My husband and I joined other Swiss supporters to fund these schools. We also offered to sponsor four children whose parents had died from T.B.

So, this is why I reacted so strongly to the "not allowed" statement in response to my question in the Director's office.

Six months later, I returned to Hopi and Tucson, Arizona. Eugene arranged for me to meet Emory. The dictionary project was well under way. The publisher was to be University of Arizona Press. He was working with an excellent team of linguists. He told me he had been teaching Hopi at the University of Arizona in Tucson for many years. He loved teaching. He also told me that his lifetime ambition was to see that the Hopi language would be taught on the Reservation.

I asked him, "Is there anything that I can do to help?" He said there was a need for bilingual children's books. He suggested that a good place to start would be to tape elders telling coyote stories in Hopi and in English. The school that supported this, the Hotevilla-Bacavi Community School, did not have the funding to begin this project. I decided to fund it myself. Emory suggested that I work with his brother Eugene and his sister Marlene, who was involved in teaching Hopi at the school. Lee Kewaniseoma, the head of the Cultural Preservation Office for the Hopi Tribe, supported this initiative. I began working directly with a linguist, Barbara Pepper, a colleague of Emory's. She was willing to join me at the school and to work on the recordings.

I returned to Bern to talk with my husband. During my continuing visits to the Reservation, I learned that languages were disappearing all over the Americas. Hopi was one of many. I felt a deep need to support Emory in his determination to preserve his language by having Hopi taught in the Hopi schools. But, I also felt an organization needed to be formed to help the many indigenous groups that were losing their languages.

I asked Donald if he would fund a nonprofit for the preservation of Indigenous Languages. His response was enthusiastic. We both agreed I should have a base in either Tucson, Flagstaff, or Santa Fe. I favored Santa Fe. I rented the house of an English friend at Los Miradores. Through another friend, Lucielle Garfield, I met the poet, Victor di Suvero. He helped me set up my nonprofit. He also gave it its name, IPOLA, the Institute for the Preservation

Alexandra Hess with her mother Joanna when they returned to Santa Fe in 2004.

of the Original Languages of the Americas. Today, it is known as ILI, Indigenous La guage Institute—much easier to remember. Victor has been an incredible friend. At that time, he introduced me to a lawyer, a banker, and a realtor. He became one of the first board members of IPOLA. Fifteen years later, I am still grateful and honored to be his friend.

It took a few months to obtain our nonprofit status. During that time, I traveled back and forth to Hopi. It took time to achieve the objective of producing bi-lingual children's books for the Hotevilla-Bacavi Community School. Eventually, we agreed on a contract for books to be illustrated by the Hopi children. All tapes and videos would belong to the school. Royalties from the sale of these books would go into a fund to produce future books. We chose a Santa Fe publisher, Clear Light Publishing.

Even though IPOLA was initially formed to assist the Hopi in publishing bi-lingual children's books, we quickly branched out to assist other indigenous communities. Today, fifteen years later, I am proud to say that we have an excellent board of directors and a dedicated director. We are a grass-roots organization, with a small staff, but I must say we enjoy an excellent reputation with the Indigenous peoples that we serve. We are now a national center for research, technical assistance and public education assisting over 558 indigenous communities in North America. A long-term goal is to extend our programs to include South America, Central America, and eventually the world to enlarge this web.

Will I ever leave Santa Fe? I doubt it. I am hooked, like so many of us.

So, now you know how a daughter's curiosity led me to Hopi and a question asked at Hopi led me to my wonderful life in beautiful Santa Fe.

Joanna Hess standing in front of the I.L.I offices, in 2007.

We Came to Santa Fe

Constance Hughes

After traversing the world, **Constance Hughes** *has continued to explore a vast array of medium in her studio in Santa Fe. Traveling to third world countries has left indelible impressions from which to create an artistic tapestry.*

THE SAUDI ARABIAN WINDS WHISKED ME into Santa Fe in 1985. It was the coldest winter Santa Fe had experienced in years. My young daughter Jessica and I huddled together that winter in a large two story house on Don Gaspar. I had the entire upstairs of the house as my art studio, which was a cavernous space with wooden floors, a few windows and not much more. I could throw paint and watch my daughter cross the street to Wood Gormley school. It was in that studio that I received nine large canvases that I had painted in Saudi Arabia and crated to Santa Fe. I was ready to hit Canyon Road. I had arrived!

The desert days were behind me, but I could still hear the prayer calls, feel the devilish heat and recollect the aromas of the medina. The Arabian American Oil Company had issued me a work permit and I took a position as an Assistant Art Director. The project was teaching young Saudis how to extract oil by using textbooks that we created. It was the technical drawing of micrometers and pressure gauges and calibrators of all types. This greatly steadied my hand albeit a very boring task. My boss was a fun loving newspaper man from Washington D.C. His personality was enormous and he seemed like all the world's Hemmingway. He had a girlfriend, with some authority, at the U.S. Embassy and occasionally I would escort him there for parties. The sheiks were there too enjoying cocktails served on silver trays. I would have been detained for the same behavior so several times I stayed to night. It was wildly fun dressing up and dancing under the hot black sky.

There were also fond memories of all my travels. Saudi Arabia proved to be a great launch pad to places like Cypress, Bahrain, Kuwait, Istanbul, Egypt, Bangkok, Katmandu and others. It was known that I had a residence visa but was out of the country as often as I was there. My young daughter traveled with me and we became vagabonds of the world.

Santa Fe seemed always on its way to me. It was like filling a very large vessel with ideas that I would pour from at a later date. Extensive travel had left indelible impressions on me, with a wealth of material to draw from. Color studies were created and several paintings using a straight edge acrylic technique.

The art came forth in a flood of Egyptian-Deco style pieces. Greatly influenced by design, each cultural portrait was loaded with ornamental detail. It was the detail I was after, often using the portraits themselves as props. Each canvas was meticulously layered with several coats of gesso, providing a smooth surface in which to apply silver, gold, copper and bronze enamels.

Constance Hughes in Saudi Arabia in 1983—Jessica and her Mother on Abdul, their favorite camel.

The vitality of local artists permeated the Santa Fe air and I was starved for camaraderie, having lived so many years in the Middle East. I hung out and promoted myself at the Cardon Gallery on Upper Canyon Road. This proved to be dangerously close to El Farol which satiated my ever present need to be with writers, poets and artists. The El Farol logo, which I designed, is still there along with a little bit of my mind. On any given night you could observe a vast diversity of humanity. Many locals were there, holding up the bar and espousing art and poetry. They were truly the embodiment of poets: living, breathing words. It was "the roar of the greasepaint, the smell of the crowd."

Paying little attention to an already faltering marriage, life came crashing down on me with a mother lode of confusion. My newly acquired liberation had brought with it new responsibilities as well as a change of residence. I found an upstairs apartment directly across the street on Don Gaspar about the size of a shoebox. I said goodbye to my wildly strewn studio space and went to work for a local architect. The job had great hours enabling me to settle in with paints in all the cupboards and half finished canvases dangling from the walls.

I started freelancing, producing several portfolios of promotional materials all over town. These included La Fonda Hotel, Canyon Road Café, Eldorado Hotel, Bandelier Paper Company, St. Vincent's Hospital, The Evergreen Inn, LaVerada Compound, Habitat for Humanity, PBS,

Constance Hughes at the Cardon Gallery in 1985—her first gallery show in Santa Fe.

Santa Fe Youth Symphony and others. I was realizing that Santa Fe had many sculptors and painters, but few graphic designers at that time. Painting being speculative, I turned my attention to finding clients and started a company called Deco Design Studios.

In 1989 The Dewey Gallery on the Plaza did an opening called "Deco at Dewey's." It was just the impetus I needed to put acrylic on canvas again. My paintings sold, but I stayed in my comfort zone and continued with advertising and print work for several years. During this period I completed nine portraits of multi-ethnic women that I called "Women as Warriors" used for cloth covered books. These line drawings were later used as studies, producing several portrait sized paintings. I crossed cultures and layered them together with line and ornamental design elements. Egyptian art greatly influenced the color and I used plenty of gold leaf. It was a prolific time with a perpetual flow of creativity.

Arriving at the new millennium I showed at small venues, at the University of New Mexico and a show at the Jean Cocteau Theatre. Experimenting with techniques using acetate overlay and doing several large works, I was inspired by what I call *Acetate Plate Imaging.* The medium was fresh and new, building multiple overlays of the female form and painting with stains and

Constance Hughes in her studio in Santa Fe, 2005.

Symbiosis of Mother and Child — 1983, self portrait by Constance Hughes.

varnishes. Each piece was then embellished, enhancing lines and applying various iridescent design elements. Using this process greatly heightened my imagination with its visual, holographic effect.

Recently I made a month long journey to China. It was Beijing fashion week and I was able to compile a series called "China Dolls." Turning Beijing models into line drawings gave me a chance to study the characteristics of the faces of these Asian beauties: the Chinese "pout," the spectacular almond eyes and silken hair. The Chinese brocades were beguiling with the sheen cast off from the silk. As it seemed absurd to me to attempt to copy perfection, I instead used assemblage with Chinese brocades in the large areas of my line drawings. These new pieces were presented to a sell out crowd last spring, which seemed to appeal to a wide spectrum of people.

Presently I am turning color separations into fine art being careful not to drop lines carelessly on a page, but rather creating an almost stained glass effect. I discovered that all cultures cross, leaving behind a blend of humanity. The question has always been whether we chose art or art chooses us. Whatever the answer, I think that if it were not for art, we would all die of the truth.

How and Why We Came to Santa Fe:
An Interactive Chronology
Alan Hutner (AH) & Elizabeth Rose (ER)

Amongst various multi-media projects, **Alan Hutner** *and* **Elizabeth Rose** *host and produce* Transitions Radio Magazine *(TRM), now in its 24th year, a 3-hour Sunday morning program (8 to 11AM MT), blending a varied pacing of special features, guest interviews, cutting-edge information and practical resources with an eclectic mix of contemporary music. TRM is available on 98.1FM in Santa Fe, is live-streamed at* www.kbac.com, *archived at* www.transradio.com *and Podcast at* www.media21st.com.

AH

It was the summer of seventy-four. My time as a pharmaceutical industry "corporate executive" was coming to a close. Ten years of service to pills and potions had me rethinking the essential questions of life: Who am I? What is my purpose? I had not yet firmed-up an official exit plan; although my goal of "extrication" was in motion. I wanted a "Golden Parachute," (not so named yet), and to be out sometime in early 1977. By then, my age, plus years of service would vest me in the pension plan (I now gratefully receive the enormous sum of $143.79 monthly). Then, with twelve years of pharmaceutical grade service under my belt, I planned to venture forth on a contemporary vision quest to somewhere, to someplace, to find myself—Some-One.

ER

I was fifteen years old in the summer of seventy-four: Far from contemplating who I was and anything about my life purpose. I had but one focus that summer. I was a late bloomer. I hadn't started my period yet and my budding breasts were just buds. I spent a good part of my summer praying for my womanhood to greet me full on; she complied with my wishes, abundantly!

It was my second year in Mclean, Virginia. I hated it there. The stench of the CIA headquarters wafted into my neighborhood, the DC corruption of the Nixon years hung heavy in the muggy air. My Vietnam War vet father, suffering from PTSD, had been assigned to work in "top secret" operations at the Pentagon. Adding to my woes, he drank and smoked heavily while my older brother made his first suicide attempt in our Mclean household, at the tender age of sixteen. All the medication he could find in the house and swallowed, didn't work. He would later be successful in his suicide at age 40 in the bush of Australia—this time he made sure that the combination of an overdose of pills and carbon monoxide worked.

AH

My first cousin, Michele, was living in Santa Fe in seventy-four. Her brother, Robert, had visited Santa Fe a few times before. They both were in love with the Southwest and had shared stories with me and our cloistered family of "Northeasters." I finally took Michele up on her numerous offers to visit with her and her boyfriend, to explore the amazing "land of enchantment." I was returning from what was to be my last "Tax Executives Institute" annual conference. I was titled "Director of Federal and Foreign Taxes" and also a Corporate Officer of an offshore subsidiary corporation, a so-called "tax shelter." I was fulfilling my final membership duties at that year's annual conference in San Francisco. I had scheduled a flight stop in Santa Fe, on my way back to Philadelphia. My return to a middle-class, split-level, suburban lifestyle of banality, that I had so well crafted for myself, my wife and two children, would soon never be the same.

Santa Fe in seventy-four was the target of my wanderlust. I had begun reading *Be Here Now* by Ram Dass (destined to be classic for many seekers) on the flight from Philly to San Francisco. I continued to immerse myself in those radical pages of transformation during every possible respite from the daily tax seminars offered in the luxurious, recently opened Hyatt Regency San Francisco. *Be Here Now* had yanked me out of my ordinary reality. The Internal Revenue Code, discussions of treasury regulations and how to more quickly depreciate furniture and fixtures, droned imperceptibly in the background. By day, I could just not "be here now;" for anything of a taxing nature. By night, I was lost in a dream-state, out of intellect, out of mind. Taxes and Transformation were like oil and water, impossible to mix.

I was soon transformed. Like Superman emerging from a phone booth or Batman donning his tights and mask for social justice, I too took on a different persona after 5PM. I chanted "Toham Kohrah" (or something like that), to melodic drumming in a Giant Portable Pyramid run by a seeming cult of the times. All of this, believe it or not, was going on at the Hotel Plaza, for hours each night, a vestige of the sixties. I was transported into an altered state hitherto unknown by accountants of the past. Then, retiring to my room for another dose of *Be Here Now;* I cast the dye, the stone was set. My destiny was etched in mysterious marble. Santa Fe called and I would answer, born again.

ER

DC was wrought with stress and sadness for me as a teen. I desperately missed my Colorado Springs childhood home of eight years. For a military family that was a long time to be stationed. For me, the Air Force Academy was a tremendously nurturing environment for my childhood fantasy, play and kinship with nature. Thankfully, I would return to Colorado and attend Colorado State University in Fort Collins. Unbeknown to me at the time, my BS Degree in Human Development and Families Studies would provide a strong foundation for my 17 year practice as a Prenatal Massage Therapist and Instructor, Childbirth Educator, and Labor Support Doula in the great city of Santa Fe.

Radio or media as a profession was not something I anticipated. Indeed, as a teaching assistant and free from the constraints of my oppressed military upbringing, I was finding my voice for the first time in my life during college in the late seventies. The closest I came to radio was a class I took about how music shaped culture and defined an era—it stirred in me a fascination and love for music that continues to this day. When Alan and I pre-select the music for our weekly radio show, it is done with awe, reverence and respect for how music can consciously shift one's vibration and shape one's mood, intent, and even lifestyle.

I still find it a curious event that I became a radio show co-producer, co-host and "musicologist." Had it not been for the deeply engaging relationship with Alan, my current partner and beloved, particularly his devotion to raising consciousness as well as his sweet, seductive radio presence that lured me in, I doubt radio would have found it's way so intimately into my life.

AH

My first week ever in "The City Different," including a side trip to Taos, was a continuation of my San Francisco makeover. Cool desert winds fanned my emerging soul (and my Afro). The long views, majestic mountains, purple plains, great space, all ignited my eaglet vision. Dirt roads, mud houses, a density of sixties memorabilia, including the remnants of Hog Farm and New Buffalo long hairs walking the streets, kindled my own "drop out now" fantasies. My cousin's hippie boyfriend read his Zen poetry to me often. Other times he would drum into the night, practicing for his gigs at La Fonda Hotel. It all stirred the dissolution of who I thought I was into a soup of unknowns, including "could this be the place?"

Later, in that seemingly eternal week, I was temporarily liberated at the hot springs ruins outside of Taos. Imagine, men, women, children, whole families basking nude in the Southwest sun. I had never seen such a site before. I loved it. Freedom, naked freedom! My return to Santa Fe, packing my Samsonites, saying goodbye, found my newly formed attachments tearing at the seams. Later, unexplainable tears flowed down my cheeks as my flight lifted off from the then quaint Albuquerque airport. I was headed home to formulate my exit plan, but a big piece of my heart was still beating in Santa Fe. I wrote a poem, my first, on the plane. Somewhere it got lost in the archives of attempted epiphanic preservation. What I do remember are a few of the words, "I shall return."

ER

I would first visit Santa Fe for just a day during my college years. A brief but profound trip, entering Santa Fe via Albuquerque via the Turquoise

Alan Hutner in 1985.

Trail, still stands out. I remember a hot summer day; windows wide open in my girlfriend's Mercedes and mystical musings of another time and place. The smell of cedar awakened something deep in my bones. I cried when I left. I didn't know why. I never visioned returning, but six years later in a state of despair and confusion about my then seemingly pointless solitary life in a tiny Ithaca apartment, I had a dream. It would change the course of my life.

For a month before the dream, I meticulously prepared for a vision, to ask for what was next. I meditated, prayed and infused my first "healing crystal," in salt baths and moon baths with the intent of offering me an answer. I passionately wanted to know, "who am I, what is my purpose, and how do I get there?" I went to sleep that particular night clutching my crystal under the pillow. The smell of cedar again stimulated my senses as I drifted off. Then, "She" appeared; the "Spirit of Santa Fe," making a brilliant appearance in the dream. The words "Santa Fe" with a bright red star next to it (indicating it was the capital of New Mexico), lit up in flashing neon lights on a map of the U.S. I was called to return. As if that wasn't enough of a hint, a little wizard walked across the map from Ithaca to Santa Fe, with his laser pointer enthusiastically tapping on the neon flashing lights.

Within a couple of months, I packed all my belongings into the back of my Nissan truck and drove across country. The summer of eighty-five launched me into a newfound passion; to attend massage school. I had received my first professional massage in Ithaca and knew that somehow I wanted to integrate massage into my work with families. Now, two decades later, having given over 3,000 massages, attended close to 100 births,

Elizabeth Rose on her arrival in Santa Fe, 1992.

raised a daughter, now 18, and co-hosted nearly 700 radio shows, I am spiritually cooked and very well seasoned. As far as that elusive answer to "who am I and what is my purpose?" It continues to be a work in progess.

AH

It would be eight more years before my return to New Mexico: First to Albuquerque in 1982, then another year plus to begin my stint as Executive Director of The Institute of Traditional Medicine in Santa Fe. Initiations before that relocation included moving myself and my family to an ashram in Florida; meditating three hours a day to get to core; experiencing six years of celibacy and then in 1983, settling into another major chapter, or series of life chapters, that continue to include escalating "wake-up" calls. A twenty-four year career in radio, creative writing, some television and an ongoing multi-media focus have all became essential costumes, within which to dance, on the infinite road show of life.

Most significantly, I eventually met my consort, current work and life partner, Elizabeth Rose in Santa Fe. We walk separate but concurrent paths; in-service together, in our loving together, embracing Kahlil Gibran's suggestion to, "Let the winds of the heavens dance between you." In retrospect, I had to "be here now," and be there then, in Santa Fe, to fulfill a destiny that yet unfolds: A retiree of mediocrity, allowing the Divine to spin the mysterious web of life that keeps me rooted here physically, now in my third decade.

Alan Hutner and Elizabeth Rose happily looking forward to their future together in Santa Fe, 2007.

We Came to Santa Fe
McCreery Jordan

McCreery Jordan is known for her exquisitely painted, intensely lyrical art. Her style and subject matter are strictly her own, yet her constant experimentation keeps her work fresh and magical. Her work has appeared in many publications, most recently in New Mexico Millennium Collection — A Twenty-First Century Celebration of Fine Art in New Mexico. *She has received many National and regional awards most recently — an Award of Excellence at the Museum of New Mexico in 2006, and the First Award at the Toledo Museum of Arts 89th Annual Exhibition in May of 2007. Her work is represented in many distinguished collections worldwide. Her paintings can currently be seen in six galleries around the country and she has been the subject of two art videos.*

I GOOGLED MYSELF THE OTHER DAY to see what I'd been up to lately. I was surprised and delighted to see that on a Russian website named *elle belle10.livejournal.com,* my artwork was being shown and discussed.

You just never know. One day you're an eight year old catching the bus to the Toledo Museum of Art to take art classes on Saturday mornings — and a mere half century later, the young artists of Russia are discussing your work.

It was at that museum during that early period of my life that I discovered the paintings of Russian artist Nicolai Fechin and in the museum bookstore, I read about Santa Fe — the famous art colony. I decided very early on that someday I would be there — with the other artists — up in the mountains of New Mexico.

When I was around ten my Uncle Mitch (a professional sign painter) mentored me in his sign shop which allowed me to explore my creativity. He introduced me to the "grid-method" whereby a small painting can be transposed and enlarged, piece-by-piece, onto a much larger surface. He let me help him paint billboards, trucks and Cessna Airplanes. In his studio I would be assigned some of the squares that were part of the painting which was to be enlarged. Up the scaffolding we would go — up 30 feet with no nets or harnesses — next to the highway — with the cars and trucks zipping by.

To observers down on the street our painted squares would visually coalesce into a painting of a huge hand holding a bubbling mug of Budweiser beer or some other product.

I still do art that is large with some paintings up to 10 feet tall. I decided very early on that bigger is better, and that working without a net is a pretty exciting way to live.

During those early years, I felt that, as an artist, I should also be allowed to have wildly colored hair and to roll my own cigarettes on one of those little red rolling machines.

Being artistic and independent from an early age got me into some trouble in school, but for the most part it kept me too interested to commit any serious crimes. I credit art with keeping me from experimenting with drugs and, to this day, I am a "drug virgin." Most of my artist friends think it's pretty funny.

My mother raised me and my older brother John, along with my younger sister Janet, by herself. Most of the time she worked several jobs to support us, and we grew up a little bit like gypsies in that we were constantly moving — often without much warning. I was always the "new kid." There one day and gone the next. Gone but not forgotten though, what with the hair thing, the cigarette habit, and the attitude.

McCreery Jordan on her arrival in Santa Fe.

One Christmas Eve we were all tucked into bed, feeling very excited for morning because my Mother was a NUT for Christmas and would always go all out for us. As I drifted off to sleep, I could hear her in the kitchen cooking; in the living room the tree was decorated with lights and presents all around it.

The next morning I woke up in a different house. I was in the same bed, and the same tree and presents were in a new living room, and the same Mother was in the kitchen and I could smell the same turkey cooking. I think it was the same turkey.

The three of us got up and the new venue was hardly discussed. The holiday went on as usual—Mom as enthusiastic as ever. I learned that Christmas that wherever we were and for however long or short or revised, if Mom's there, it's home.

I also learned that evidently I am a very sound sleeper.

It was astonishing to me that in every house we lived, within a few weeks of moving in—our new home would be spotless, repainted, and cozy, with every weed removed from the yard and flowers planted. How she accomplished that and worked such long hours I cannot imagine even now. More astonishing was the fact that we laughed and joked so much. She taught us to see the humor in every situation. To this day, she has never lost her sense of fun.

"The Cave," a self-portrait 2006 by McCreery Jordan.

After moving from Ohio to El Paso, Texas in the early 60's, I attended Burges High School and graduated in 1965. I was 17 and seeing a man in the Air Force stationed at Fort Bliss. He was going to be stationed in Russia and was going to first drive home to Ohio to see his folks before he shipped out. He asked if I wanted to drive with him so I could visit relatives still living in Toledo. It was a week after my high school graduation, and I never returned to El Paso until my 20-year reunion.

When I was 18 I had my first studio — the only tenant on the upper floor of a run-down bar in East Toledo. My rent was $28 a month and it was my heaven. I was working as Advertising Manager for Gladieux Food Corp. by day, and drove to my studio at night to paint. I had my first one-person show at 20 down the street from my studio in the lobby of an "Adult Movie House" in Toledo.

At 20 I got married and had a son and I am very proud of him. He is a Registered Nurse and a fabulous artist living in San Diego. He is as independent as his mother and the kindest (and funniest) person in my life. He has his Grandmother's sense of humor.

While my son was growing up, I did commercial art in my home studio so I could be around for him. My earlier experience in advertising served me well and I also did many portrait commissions and started entering

McCreery Jordan at her easel painting in the garden of her studio, 1994.

regional and national juried shows. I also spent time during this period working with at-risk teenagers — sharing art skills with them and hoping to give them tools to cope with their own challenges.

In the late 80's and early 90's, after my son had gone off to college, I found myself separated, living in an apartment in Toledo and decided that it was time to reinvent myself.

It was 1993 and I had just completed a series of murals in a new restaurant called the Commodore Café in Perrysburg, Ohio. My design was satirical and poked fun at the battle of Perrysburg. The paintings were done in *trompe l'oeil* style and depicted, among other things, Commodore Perry looking through a spyglass at a topless Betsy Ross as she sewed the first flag. It caused a stir in the conservative town, which made the whole project worthwhile.

It was the start of another long, grey winter in Toledo, and I started thinking about the Santa Fe I read about at the Museum as a child and so I decided to visit and investigate. I fell in love almost immediately with the landscape, the energy and the art scene. I had brought with me some of the large paintings I was doing at the time and went into one gallery after another with them rolled up under my arm. Most of the gallery directors were kind but not interested. On the last day of the visit, I went into a gallery on Old Pecos Trail, unrolled my canvases on the floor of the gallery, and asked the gallery owner if she would be interested in showing them. She liked them and I got in the gallery with the promise of a show.

Before leaving Santa Fe that same day for the airport, I stopped into Cloud Cliff Bakery on Second Street for lunch. I discovered Second Street Studios across the street and spoke that day to the manager who said there were no vacancies, but a week after returning to Toledo, I got a call that one of the live-in studios was available if I could move in six weeks. Heck, I could move overnight!

Six weeks later I followed my heart to Santa Fe — not knowing a soul. I arrived in a blizzard and I lived at Second Street Studios for 11 years before purchasing a house and transforming it into my current studio. For those 11 years, I enjoyed the bakery every morning, and it was there that I met most of the friends I have to this day.

I had grown up at sea level on the Great Lakes. In a large city with a wonderful museum and a thriving art community, world-class opera and symphony. But I always felt that I belonged here in the High Desert and the enchantment I feel for Santa Fe has never diminished. I traded the Glass capitol for the Art Capitol, farmland for mountain vistas, and grey skies for blue.

One of the most rewarding activities since moving to Santa Fe has been to volunteer to do art projects with "Creativity for Peace." It is a yearly camp that meets just outside the city and is made up of Israeli and Palestinian girls who come together to dialogue, do art, and plant the seeds of peace in the Middle East through their association with one another.

As for my own artwork, I have found that being in a gallery in Santa Fe opened the door to other galleries around the country. I have had 20 solo shows since moving here, the most recent (June of 2007) in Taos—down the street from the house where the Russian artist, Nicolai Fechin, spent his last years.

P.S. I was communicating with Armand Hammer with the intent of going to Russia for an "Art as Diplomacy" project when he died in 1990. I would still like to follow that dream.

I gave up cigarettes on February 1, 1982, and with my husband, James, have been enjoying painting together, traveling the world but always returning to the home and haven that Santa Fe has become for us.

McCreery and James in Capri,Italy, 2000.

We Came to Santa Fe
Marcia Keegan

*Photographer/author **Marcia Keegan** has had her work reproduced in a wide variety of publications. She has also written thirteen books (six of which are currently available) featuring her photography. Her photographs have also been exhibited in various museums in the United States and Italy and are included in many private collections. Along with her husband, **Harmon Houghton**, Keegan owns and operates Clear Light Publishing in Santa Fe.*

THERE IS AN OLD SAYING THAT EVERYBODY WHO comes to Santa Fe wants to be the first person and the last person to come to Santa Fe. I must say I felt that way. I first came when I was in college at UNM. I came from Tulsa, and I loved the small town with its adobe houses surrounded by Indian Pueblos. The mountains, the sunsets, the rainbows and the changing pastel light also helped me learn to love my adopted home. My college roommate's parents, Letta and Keith Wofford, "adopted" me, giving me the use of a room in their large adobe farmhouse on Agua Fria off Siler Road, which was a dirt road at that time.

After graduating from UNM in 1961, I worked for the *Albuquerque Journal* as the "Home Living Editor," photographing and writing about the old haciendas and gardens in Santa Fe as well as in Albuquerque. As time went on, my pictures got larger and my stories smaller. Although I had graduated in journalism, I had not taken a photography course, so I learned on the job. Photography came naturally to me, and I loved "telling the story in a thousand words."

Finally I decided to go to New York City to take a photography course and ended up staying there longer than planned. I became a feature writer and photographer for Associated Press in Rockefeller Center as well as a free-lance photographer for other magazines and books. I also was an assistant to Alexey Brodovitch, the famed art director.

I was able to live in the big city because I came back regularly to Santa Fe to rejuvenate. New York to me was a black-and-white city, and I would come back to New Mexico looking forward to the thrill of seeing spectacular colors. I received many assignments to photograph the Southwest, because I was always praising the beauty of the landscape and the people. I was like a one-person chamber of commerce.

Keeping a car with friends in the Sandias, I flew between Santa Fe and New York for many years, coming back to New Mexico for Feast Days and doing articles and books about the Navajos and Pueblos with my friends and connections. I was "unusual" in New York at the time, since I had these Native friends and knew the varieties of landscape. In fact, many people thought I lived only in Santa Fe.

During this time, I went to a publisher and told him about the Blue Lake Celebration at Taos Pueblo and that it would make a good book. As a result, I received a contract to tell the story of the sixty-year struggle, and in 1971 the book, *The Taos Pueblo and Its Sacred Blue Lake,* was published by Simon & Schuster. The celebration of the Sacred Blue Lake at Taos Pueblo in 1971 was a historic time for

Photo by Laura Gilpin

Marcia Keegan as a young woman photographing Canyon de Chelly. Photo taken by good friend and fellow photographer Laura Gilpin.

the Pueblos as well as it was for me. I have continued to photograph the Pueblos through the years.

Later I was worried that the Peabody Coal Mining company mining Black Mesa at the time would ruin the Navajo landscape and cause environmental damage. After I went to a publisher and explained that I wanted to photograph the way of life that could potentially be destroyed, I received a contract for the book that became *Mother Earth Father Sky,* which is still popular.

More and more I longed to live in Santa Fe full time. In 1974 I married Harmon Houghton, who was a management consultant with a computer company, but his clients were in the New York area and he didn't think he could make a living in Santa Fe. In spite of that, I nagged him to move, but it seemed hopeless. Thankfully, Oxford University Press gave me an assignment to photograph New Mexico, and I was able to travel all over the state, making Santa Fe my base.

My only book about New York was a large black-and-white book about old Vaudevillians living in Times Square. It was called *We Can Still Hear Them Clapping.* The book's subjects, former Vaudevillians in their 80s, were forgotten people. My book gave them TV shows and many opportunities to perform. My new husband and I adopted these "grandparents," and tried to get a Broadway show starring them. They thought of us as their talent agents. Lincoln Center held an exhibit of my photographs of them in a bigger-than-life size format.

Taos Pueblo Celebration in 1971 when the Sacred Blue Lake returned to the pueblo. Photo by Marcia Keegan.

We met the Dalai Lama in 1979, when he came to New York, and I traveled with him for a while, photographing him and tape recording his teachings in America, and in 1980, in Canada. I told the Dalai Lama his words and my pictures would make a good book, and he agreed.

I had never been turned down by a publisher, but in 1981 I was—by three of them! They told me no one was interested in the Dalai Lama. I told Harmon, my husband, I had to keep my word to the Dalai Lama, so we had to start a publishing company, which is how Clear Light Publishing began.

Our first book was titled *The Dalai Lama's Historic Visit to North America.* We gave it to him on his birthday in 1981. It featured 69 photographs. This book was later revised to become a small book with 19 photographs titled *Ocean of Wisdom,* which includes a foreword by Richard Gere and is now available in eleven languages.

I continued to nag Harmon to move to Santa Fe. We went to Canyon de Chelly with friends and Harmon, watching the sunset, suddenly said, "Let's move to Santa Fe." I was so excited I came immediately and found the compound we now live in. He went back to New York, sold his computer company and made the transition to leave New York.

We make a good publishing team: Harmon handles the business end and marketing and I do the design, production and publicity. It became clear that our company could be what would allow us to live in Santa Fe, and that we could publish my books as well as those of friends who lived in New Mexico.

Over the years we have published the works of several old friends—including historian Howard Bryan, whom I

Marcia Keegan in Clear Light Publishing conference room surrounded by some of her photographs.

knew from my college days and also worked with him at the newspaper. We have also published several works by the pre-eminent Pueblo historian, Joe. S. Sando as well as my Native American artist friends including Pablita Velarde, R. C. Gorman and Jonathan Warm Day.

Another specialty of our company has been books on Native American Studies. Colleges across the country regularly order these for their classes. Authors of these books include Vine Deloria Jr., Robert Venables, Bruce Johansen, Oren Lyons, Doug George-Kanentiio, Gregory Cajete, Huston Smith, Reuben Snake, Donald Grinde, Jr., Tim Giago, Rolling Thunder, John Mohawk, Jay Fikes, Pete Catches, Thomas Cooper, Alexander Ewan and Paul Wallace. We have published 125 titles, including many other categories such as cookbooks and children's books, and we also act as a distributor for our own books and those of other publishers.

In addition to designing the covers and handling the production of our books, I have continued with my photography. My work illustrates many of the books we publish, including several for which I am the author. *Enduring Culture* features color pictures from my files matched up with photos by Edward Curtis and other early photographers to show how the Indian culture is alive and well and has continued over time. It is amazing to see how two photographers one hundred years apart would photograph the same thing.

I love Indian foods, so I asked my friends if they would give me their recipes to put together with some of my photographs for a cookbook called *Southwest Indian Cookbook*. The trickiest part of the book was listing the *amount* of the ingredients as my friends measure with their hands instead of measuring spoons or cups!

The children's books *Pueblo Boy* and *Pueblo Girls* followed the stories of typical Indian children from San Ildefonso Pueblo living in two worlds—one occupied with modern America and the other immersed in Pueblo culture. For *Pueblo Girls,* Desiree and Sonja Roybal posed for the pictures and told me what to write about. I photographed them playing basketball, working on the computer, and doing their ceremonial dance. It was fun when we later went to book signings and people would get their autographs and forget to get mine!

My life has been enriched by my friendships with the Pueblo people, and I have photographed four generations of families. I photographed Maria Martinez when she was 90 years old, and later photographed her son Adam, when he was 90.

After 35 years of taking pictures around the Pueblos, I gathered the best of my collection of images into the book *Pueblo People.* I have enjoyed the popularity of this book with my Pueblo friends, and I'm told that I am the only person who has photographed all 19 Pueblos.

My interest in Buddhism and the Dalai Lama did not end with *Ocean of Wisdom.* I created *Ancient Wisdom: Living Tradition,* a book about the Himalayas, combining my photographs with ancient prayers. Lobsang Lhalungpa, a Tibetan elder living in Santa Fe, helped with the translations, and the Dalai Lama wrote the foreword.

While driving through the Himalayas taking pictures for that book, I saw many similarities between the Tibetan culture and the traditional Navajo and Pueblo cultures. My photographs of a Tibetan deer dance, the mountains, the architecture and even the physical traits of the people reminded me of my photographs from the Southwest. I have been working on gathering images and research for a new work on the cultural similarities between these two parts of the world.

I feel blessed to live in Santa Fe when the world has so many problems. It truly is the City Different in the Land of Enchantment.

Why We Came to Santa Fe
Tom Kravitz, MD

*An individualistic, sensitive and many faceted medical practitioner, **Dr. Kravitz** cares for a wide variety of individuals and families in his private practice that has made him a member of the larger Santa Fe community as a whole. His experience in various corners of the world have broadened his vision and his ability to enhance the lives of his patients as well as his community as a whole.*

LIFE'S JOURNEY TAKES US TO MANY different lands. I was born on an island called Long Island, about 120 miles long. No mountains but a great ocean, the Atlantic Ocean, right near by. New York City was also right near by. It had a lot to offer but it wasn't my kind of town.

My early years were spent mainly in the northeastern USA and Florida. I loved the beach—Jones Beach 4—salty water and bubbly waves. The sun and sun tan. Bodysurfing. Baseball. Football. Basketball. Music and friendship. Street corner harmonizing. Late night philosophizing. Golf and bowling. Niagara Falls, Sag Harbor, Westport, Martha's Vineyard and Woodstock were also a part of my path. Real big cities I visited, Miami, Montreal, Boston, Philadelphia and Washington D.C., were just not my kind of town.

My true "travel awakening" actualized when I attended medical school at the University of Brussels in Belgium. Now I began to understand the influence America had upon me. Now I began to appreciate other cultures from a first hand point of view. But instruction was in French and I had never studied French as a language. So I taught myself French using a friend's old torn grammar book and conversations I had along the way. By the end of the first school term I was able to think in French but it was still my brain doing the thinking.

I spent most of the school year in Brussels studying and going to class. In my first year it was very difficult for myself and most Americans to understand what was being said in class. So we had to study more independently. Without formal French lessons I would have to look up almost every word I read. And there was also Medicine to learn. This process was arduous and slow, so on weekends and holidays we would travel. London, Les Ardennes. Positano. Palermo. Milos. Mykonos. Acropolis. White-washed walls. Romantic hidden coves. Green-blue seas. Brugge. Amsterdam. Monaco. Marseille. St. Tropez. Narrow winding cobblestone streets. Bicycles over canals. Rijksmuseum. Rembrandtplein. Van Gogh. Windmills and clogs before there were blogs. Warm beer and good cheer.

Then here was Paris. That most beautiful, romantic and elegant of cities. Monet at the Musee du Louvre. Strolling the Champs-Elysees. Boating the Seine. The view from the Eiffel Tower. Notre-Dame. Saint-Germain-des-Pres. Gauloises. Bordeaux and chocolate truffles at Montmartre. If I were to live in a big city Paris is my kind of town.

Eventually my travels took me through more of Europe, India, and the Middle East. Though my spirit was broadened by my experience in India, it was my volunteering in the Bedouin Field Clinics of the Sinai that changed

my perception of how a landscape could impact my existence. A friend and myself rented an apartment on the outskirts of Jerusalem and volunteered at a local hospital. Soon the opportunity arose to go to the Sinai and we set up our main camp near the convent of St. Catherine amongst mountains of granite and history. We spent many days traveling through the river valleys and mountains offering health care to the Bedouin. I felt aligned with the children of Israel's wanderings of the past. One day we ascended to the summit of Jebel Musa, where it is believed Moses received the Ten Commandments. The view, the feeling was never to be forgotten. For me every moment I spent in the Sinai

Tom Kravitz, M.D. in 1982.

charged me with an energy never before experienced. My feet would vibrate when they touched the ground. My awareness was clear and pure. I was filled with a deep sense of inner peace and exhilaration simultaneously. This was my kind of town.

My return to the United States in 1976 brought me back to the northeast. Training in an internal medicine program associated with Yale University School of Medicine was quite instructive, but I was seeking a broader, more integrative paradigm for health care delivery. Besides the mosquitoes were too aggressive and the winters too long and cold. My younger brother Murray was writing poetry and fixing VW's in Santa Fe. He invited me to visit him and instantly upon arrive I felt as though I was back in the Sinai. Exhilaration and inner peace. My body shaking at the realization of being. My visions pictured me amongst the earliest inhabitants of the region. I had been here before and now I was home again.

Some 25 years later I still regard Santa Fe as home. Green chili and desert sunsets. Healing energies and meaningful friendships. Opera. Art. Culture. Museums. Horses and hot air balloons. Softball. Pilates. Chi Quong. River rafting. Though my *raison d'etre* has been healing and service to my fellow man, I have been fortunate in my travels to find a place that effects me in a very positive way. There is still more travel left in these aging bones and many places on this planet worth the visit. Wherever life's journey should take me I know I can always return to the people and mountains of Santa Fe I call home.

❖ ❖ ❖

Tom Kravitz, M.D. in 2006.

Caution Advised on Area Lakes
Denise Kusel

Denise Kusel, a former editor and columnist for The Santa Fe New Mexican, *a working journalist for most of her life is now semi-retired and teaches at the Community College in Santa Fe.*

I COME FROM A PLACE AT THE EDGE of a continent from a time when jobs were plentiful, people hopeful, and content to sit in the shadows of the sun and dream. Money was rarely an issue and although people reveled in exposing public personas, they refused to have their names listed in the telephone directories. It was all part of the allure of Southern California.

Living was easy. College admissions were cheap. And the phrase "Surf's up" was enough to jumpstart the day with a grand promise of adventure. For me, these escapades always were played out on back roads, rambling through towns that had long out-lived their reason for being. Roads that reached into the heart of the Central Valley, emptily reflected in the eastern glare of the Sierras and leaving behind only a windbreak of tall trees to show where a town once stood. Roads that disappeared into the surf at high tide, emerging the next morning with starfish caught in rocky tide pools. Roads that stretched along the very fringe of seismic plates, offering restless attraction in the shrug of earthquakes.

To say that I came from a place where people with names like Mad Man Muntz and Gypsy Boots achieved hero status by their names alone is true. It also is true that the magnets of chance, which pulled people West searching for their own chunks of golden expectations, had begun repelling those very dreams. It left behind a land that was used hard and ruthlessly. While I never ran out of the inquisitiveness that had formed me into a journalist, I no longer cared about the answers. By the time I left L.A. in 1980, I had covered stories of murders, sometimes arriving on the scene before the cops after receiving an anonymous tip. I had reported shoot-outs and riots. Mass murders, remembered more for the parts of bodies left in trash bags along the freeway than the names of the victims. I held a young boy who died in my arms, a victim of being at the wrong place at the wrong time. I had seen L.A. burn, rimmed with fire in the midst of a Santa Ana wind and a full moon in September when the rest of the country was celebrating harvest festivals. I also found time to study writing with such teachers as John Rechy, Joan Didion and Kate Braverman, who taught me to use words raw and unfettered.

But those long beaches and restless waves weren't enough to keep me. I eventually escaped, heading east across the Colorado River. I found the kind of freedom of expression I craved when I crossed a sluggish muddy river called the Rio Grande. The first thing I did was get a fishing license, a handful of maps and headed down to the southern part of the state. From there, I worked my way up, heading north, turning left on the first small highway I came to and right on the next one. It was my way of learning about the geography of the state and, more importantly, it gave me a chance to listen to the stories of people I met along the way. It didn't take me long to draw pleasure from the unyielding red earth, and jutting mountains that pushed its fingers into colossal clouds hanging in impossibly blue skies.

I have been a listener all of my life, fueled by a hungry curiosity about people and why they do the things they do. Santa Fe provided me with sustenance and the riches of everyday people willing to share the stories of what it was that made them special. The philosophy Santa Feans embraced was one of *laissez faire* mixed with a hearty dose of humor. After all, why do battle with something you can't change when you can gracefully embrace the best life you can. In other words, when life hands you lemons, make lemonade.

I got a job at *The New Mexican,* and this time instead of covering murders and trials in a big city, I covered the arts in a modest 16-page tabloid called *Pasatiempo.* I also went fishing a lot in those first years. The early 1980s saw the Santa Fe art scene explode and embrace drugs, money and puffy egos. Forget "the City Different," life quickly was morphing into the same avarice found in other places. The more that greed turned the art scene nasty, the more *Pasatiempo* ran stories on young artists, poets, writers and local theater.

These were the people who called Santa Fe home, and as the editor of an arts supplement, which had quickly grown to 80 pages, these were the people who mattered. When the magazine won the Penny-Missouri Award for lifestyle journalism, beating out such publications as *The New York Times* and the *Washington Post,* I figured that brand of journalism was right on. I also knew it was time to stand down as editor and do something else.

I became a columnist, which usually is where a newspaper places someone when it can't think of any other job. The column was called "Only in Santa Fe." It ran three times a week and managed to put me closer to the people I enjoyed writing about: Folks like you and me who were trying to do the best they could. I never lacked for stories or the characters that peopled them.

Santa Fe kept changing, out-growing its one-way lanes and narrow, dirt roadways. Speed bumps now perched on once sleepy streets. A couple of places even have traffic circles, one of which is so narrow you have to back up before proceeding forward, proving that a necessary

Denise Kusel when she first got to Santa Fe.

sense of the absurd endures. When parking meters began popping up on side streets, I stopped shopping downtown. When businesses began posting signs proclaiming "No public restrooms," I stopped going downtown. When people no longer told stories of arriving in Santa Fe after their car broke down and ended up staying because they couldn't afford to have it fixed, I began spending more time gardening. I grieved when Spanglish was no longer spoken on the streets.

So why do I stay? I still have things to do.

This summer, I'm going to teach a young friend how to fish, thus passing down important knowledge of life survival. Besides this just may be the year I find out exactly what "Caution advised on area lakes" really means. And then, who knows: I just may be able to find the area lakes themselves.

Denise Kusel today.

Why We Came to Santa Fe

Lisa Law

Lisa Law's fame as one of the most important photographers of the "Beat" scene and careful interpreter of the changing cultural patterns in America over the past 40 years is well established. Her work has been recognized and published in more than 40 books and periodicals and continues her involvement in the cutting edge of art being developed by the younger generations in New Mexico.

THE REVOLUTION THAT TOOK PLACE in the U.S. in the mid-sixties was a reaction to the military madness, cultural conformity and corporate corruption that dominated our culture leading into the Nixon years. On the West Coast, demonstrations against the testing of the atomic bomb evolved into demonstrations against our country's immoral involvement in Vietnam. During 1967's "Summer of Love," thousands of young people descended on San Francisco's Haight-Ashburhood to join the movement. Scott MacKenzie's "If You're Coming To San Francisco, Be Sure To Wear Some Flowers In Your Hair" was a coast-to-coast clarion call. Small get-togethers in the park started becoming large public events and the mood of the times was reflected in the music. We went from "I Want To Hold Your Hand" to "Why Don't We Do It In The Road," from "Love Me Do" to "Light My Fire." That summer, the Monterey Pop Festival became the ultimate rock concert, reflecting and defining the elevated consciousness that had been spreading from across the country. And at the gathering of the tribes for the *Human Be-In* in Golden Gate Park, Timothy Leary uttered his anthem, "Turn On, Tune In and Drop Out." But the scene in San Francisco quickly became commercial and lost its center. We decided Dr. Tim was onto something and started a new search for the spritual. Many of us came to feel the land offered us a way to connect. Our tribe headed for New Mexico.

Crossing through the Southwest, from Arizona into New Mexico, I could feel the difference in the air. I could feel the vibrations of the 19 Pueblos and their people, their way of life, their dances, their connection to the earth and the land, their reverence for the creator, mother earth and father sky.

The air wasn't polluted and the skies were blue with huge white clouds. You could see when a storm was crossing the land. It would be sunny one moment, stormy the next. There is a saying: "If you want the weather to change in New Mexico, wait a few minutes."

As we drove into Santa Fe, we were blown away by the architecture. It was mostly adobe and the houses seemed to blend right into the mountains. The streets were windy. I've heard they were designed by following the trails of the burros. The Santa Fe Trail was the beginning of the trader's routes, turquoise was everywhere. The plaza reminded me of old Mexico. Why not? New Mexico was one of the last states to join the union and most of the streets had Spanish or Indian names.

Most inspiring was the river that ran through town and the acequias that flowed along canals through the streets. Santa Fe was built because of the river that was fed by the Sangre de Cristo Mountains east of town. Cottonwood trees lined the river giving much needed shade to the land. And there were four seasons here, unlike California where the seasons seemed to

Lisa Law on her arrival in New Mexico in 1967.

blend into each other. When it snows here in the spring and the snow clings lightly to the blossoming trees, the sight is truly spectacular.

Tom and I were getting ready for our first child and Santa Fe was the only place that offered Natural Child Birth—The Catholic Maternity Institute for Natural Childbirth. The Institute was in an adobe building on Palace and Don Gaspar. We signed up, had our first exam and headed to Taos to help out at the New Buffalo Commune. They were just starting to build their main house, making their own adobe bricks and pealing vigas.

We were traveling by VW bus, setting up our tipi wherever we went. Rick Kline had used his inheritance to buy the land, then he joined with friends who were into growing their own food and living together, to start a new utopia. It was one of many communes that sprouted up at that time. We thought we would create new economic and social structures—alternative cultures, based on bartering instead of money. We had all sorts of ideas about how we would do it. A lot of us went off in different directions to try. We learned a lot that has been useful since, but we were also very naive. The original group lasted for a few years before people started going off on their own to survive.

Photo by Shawn Law

We found a hand-built mobile home in Taos, which became our wheels, and we pitched our tipi on Cerro Gordo Road in the field of a forest ranger, Matias Armijo. I went into labor in that tipi and Pilar was born at the Maternity Center on September 15, 1967. We were sure we had made the right choice in the way we brought her into the world.

I became a member of the La Leche League and began to help other mothers with the natural way of breast-feeding, which at that time was not "In."

Lisa Law as the young mother with newborn Pilar, 1967.

We were soon growing our own food, making our own goat milk yogurt and cheese, and canning fruit from all the trees that are so abundant in Santa Fe and Rio Arriba counties. We felt like pioneers.

The women's liberation movement, the environmental movement, the holistic medicine movement, the natural food movement, the spiritual revolution, all came out of a fundamental re-evaluation of America and the people who were committed to their new lifestyle. We were right in the middle, experiencing it all

Our groups were not the only ones to discover Santa Fe and New Mexico. It seemed that every religious group soon followed, from Tibetan and Zen Buddhists to Sikhs and Hindus. The area became a spiritual and healing Mecca for crystal healers, psychics, astrologers, past life regressors, acupuncturists, massage therapists, raw foodists, yoga practitioners and the like.

Back in the day we used to say, "If you want to survive in New Mexico you have to know how to do most any job or it will chew you up and spit you out." We had to learn many trades to support our growing family. I sold homegrown and home prepared food door to door along with Amway and Shaklee soaps. For a short time, I was a house cleaner and then peddled silver and turquoise jewelry and Pendleton blankets. I was a waitress in the Pastry Shop at the La Fonda. The kids and I were extras in many films made in New Mexico—which was the most fun of all.

Photo by Doug Magnus

Lisa Law with her pioneering bus which brought her and her group from California to New Mexico in 1967.

As I experienced life I also documented it and soon I was doing small photographic jobs like weddings, concerts, portraits and magazine shoots. I kept all my negatives in a little box and my proof sheets in another.

We traveled around the state in our mobile home along with Wavy Gravy and the Hog Farm Commune putting on shows. We were even asked to provide security for the Woodstock Festival in Bethel, New York, the rock concert that changed everything. When asked by the press how we intended to enforce security, Wavy told them, "Cream pies and seltzer bottles."

I began to show my work and from that came my book *Flashing on the Sixties*. Soon to follow was the documentary film *Flashing on the Sixties, a Tribal Document* and then the book of all the interviews from the film in their entirety, *Interviews with Icons, Flashing on the Sixties*.

All the while I grew my gardens, providing my family and friends with the nourishment we needed for a healthy life.

Having lived in many places in northern New Mexico, I am now back in Santa Fe in an adobe house with a beautiful vegetable garden designed by my permaculturist son Solar. At the end of the little path in the garden is my tipi, which is now used as a playhouse by my two grandchildren Kunjabihari and

Asraya, offspring of my daughter Sunday Peaches. I have remodeled the adobe garage into an office where I work on my photo archives with the help of my daughter Dhana Pilar on computers, with a server managed by my son Jesse Lee Rainbow. In front of that, out on the driveway, sits Silver, the psychedelic bus that is now a museum piece that I take out for Peace Day, the Historical Hysterical Parade and other special events. My wish

Lisa Law in Santa Fe, 2004.

is that one day it will be the centerpiece for the Museum of the Sixties here in Santa Fe.

Today I share my photos and memorabilia with many museums and help provide materials for documentaries and books. I screen my film to raise money for our local teen center, W21, and continue to travel, documenting life and sharing the experience.

Santa Fe is growing up, trying to figure out what its heritage will be. There is still music on the plaza during the summer where you can find Mayor David Coss enjoying himself with his two daughters and granddaughter. Every May we celebrate All Species Day to honor all the sentient beings on the planet. During Fiesta we are into our 83rd year of burning Zozobra (Old Man Gloom) to start off the festivities. On Saturdays and Tuesdays everyone who is any-one can be seen buying fresh vegetables at the Farmer's Market. You can see and hear great performances in music and theater at the Lensic Performing Arts. Our Governor, Bill Richardson, is running for President of the United States, and our Senator, Tom Udall, is calling for the impeachment of Vice President Cheney. Yet still, you have to drink bottled spring water because we now have plutonium in our wells delivered to us from the Los Alamos arroyos to the Rio Grande. 'Twas ever thus.

Ah, life in Santa Fe!
Viva Santa Fe, que viva!

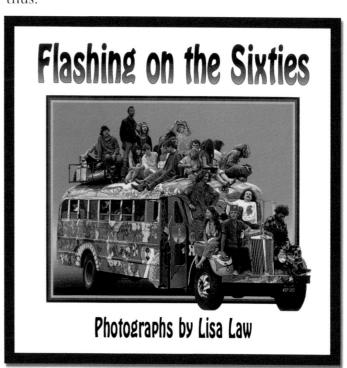

Flashing on the Sixties,
Photographs by Lisa Law.

Why I Came to Santa Fe
Joan & Michael Logghe

Joan Logghe is an award winning poet, writing teacher, and artist-in-community. She teaches at Ghost Ranch, UNM Los Alamos, and is a founder of Tres Chicas Books. Awards include a National Endowment for the Arts Fellowship in Poetry, Witter Bynner Foundation for Poetry grants, and a Mabel Dodge Luhan Internship in Taos. Books include Twenty Years in Bed with the Same Man *(La Alameda),* What Makes a Woman Beautiful? *(Pennywhistle), and* Rice *(Tres Chicas Books).*

THERE WERE TWO ARRIVALS. BUT WHERE DOES IT START? Maybe when my Hungarian ancestors boarded a boat and ended up in Western Pennsylvania. But that's too far back. It could be choosing the college that lead to Bob who led me to Chicago where in an all-black elementary school, a woman in a pea jacket with a peace button was the only white woman on campus. That would be Robin Reider, the weaver and Los Alamos native, and she is what brought me to New Mexico.

We'd commute down to the school, passing the Sherwin Williams Paint plant "We Will Cover the World" it said with paint dripping over the globe. Robin didn't notice it as she was busy lamenting the Illinois weather and talking about her New Mexico as others might Shangri-la. One day we'd commute in her black VW bug and the next in my baby blue one. Through Robin I met Michael, the intellectual and Euro looking guy who would become what some call a husband, a dairy farmer renaissance man who has consented to consort with me all these years. Robin met Jim, my college friend.

After the year of teaching, we both quit and took off with our respective men, in our respective black and blue VW's and arrived via Boulder and the Holy Man Jam to a night in Santa Fe at Hyde Park after a viewing of

Woodstock. We left the movie to our first gully washer, a foot of water running down San Francisco Street outside the old Lensic Theater, a continuation of the 60s rains on screen. Los Alamos where Robin's dad was safety director of LANL. From that first siting I remember that Cundiyo in the Spring in full blossom is otherworldly and the wood carvers of Cordova might be in a village in Spain. Robin and Jim left Michael and I in the ceremonial cave at Bandelier National Monument. We looked at each other in total nerves, with a sinking feeling in the cool kiva room and thought, "who is this person and why are we alone up here?" We had seen each other on and off for maybe four months.

This was our secret marriage, a ceremony with as much fear as joy, and we went on to a year in the Bay Area where we were legally married at the Glide Church, or as my brother refers to it, "The church of what's happening baby."

We then lived 18 months on Michael's family dairy farm, a time of chickens and heifers, the world's most delicious water carried in, no money, and two sub-zero winters. My father and brother visiting in business suits on a 20 below zero day to our wood heated, uninsulated house, illustrate the culture clash I smoothed over with good hippie spirit.

When our friends Jim and Robin said, "come on down, there's work for you here," we loaded up our belongings including two cats in a red Chevy truck, and yowled on down the highway, stopping at The Farm in Summertown, Tennessee, and breaking down in Texarkana.

When we landed in Pojoaque with Jim and Robin, they ceremonially took us to The Shed and I ate my first enchilada, red, the enchilada to which all others are compared. To be honest, we have

Joan and Michael Logghe: The Chevy in which they moved to Santa Fe packed for Farmer's Market, 1973.

Michael and Joan Logghe: Building their house in La Puebla, 1977.

never lived in Santa Fe proper, skirting the northern fringes of Santa Fe County we found Virginia and Toby Martinez, rented the house in Nambé and stayed hauling water, cooking with wood for three and a half happyish years.

I substitute taught and worked in a garden center. Mike worked construction with Jim. We had a baby 11 months later, then found six acres a bit further north, had another baby and built our house, hour-by-hour, dollar-by-dollar. We didn't know from mortgages or credit cards. How sane we were then is only now recognized in looking back. Nixon was impeached; I was breastfeeding. There was a gasoline shortage; I washed cloth diapers and hung them on the line.

Now, living since those days in the house of our young dreams and building, the cottonwood 30 years old is a giant. People can't believe we planted it.

When I graduated from college I had never been west of Cleveland. The 1971 day I stepped out of my blue VW bug onto New Mexico soil I sniffed the wide-open air and found a small bone, a pelvis. I thought, "Oh my gosh, I am going to become Georgia O'Keeffe." But I didn't become Georgia. I became the builder of a solar house, the mother of three children, and three grandchildren. I slowly became a poet with six books, teaching at UNM-Los Alamos, Santa Clara Day School, and a jillion other places. I founded Tres Chicas Books with Miriam Sagan and Renée Gregorio. I began a couple of cool projects, Write Action and Artist of the Month. When I give thanks, it is New Mexico I thank along with other forces and family.

How I Got Here

I got here by daughter and by rain.
If I weren't a mother would I be a train
or a clarinet. Today's rain while I talked
to you on the phone about your lover
and his teacher, soothes me. That rain
because I can get all knotted up in happiness.

Gentle Rain is my maiden name I don't use
except as mantra. I don't have a sign
over my beauty salon that says, GENTLE RAIN.
My mother hung out a shingle and cut hair,
let all the customers come to their 1950's beauty.
Platinums and ash blond, I knew them all.
Their stories joining the immortals.
I came to gray hair.

I used to be old and then I loved children.
I used to be gentle rain and then I lived
with flash flood. I never lived in north woods
or a trailer, but I've lived in Chicago and the like,
San Francisco three years after The Summer
of Love. I got here by cities and by dairy farm.
I lived among cows their stare and cud.

Christmas, 1991.

Joan Logghe 2007.

I got here by teaching school
and a peace sign on a woman's black coat
that led me to you and to this place,
this right now, among the other losses
and gunshots, the scar on my belly
and the one on my knee. I got here.
That was plenty. Dear Right Now,
I want to say, Dear Could Have Been
Otherwise. How the tributaries of any life
lead us to each other, this intersection.

I got here by subway and streetcar,
by atomic bomb, Los Alamos led me here
and Santa Clara Pueblo, the dancers danced
me, I rode here on an old horse named Blanco.
I was white. I fell fast in love.
I didn't love desert, I always loved people first
and the landscape came dragging its heels.

He Hated the Cold
Sue & Beryl Lovitz

Sue's passion for musical theatre is still glaringly evident when she performs in her SHOWTIME SANTA FE productions. She keeps the music of Gershwin, Berlin, Sondheim and others, alive in Santa Fe. Beryl, a retired internist/cardiologist, and former president of the Santa Fe Symphony board of directors, remains a staunch supporter of classical music organizations and performers. A self-taught violinist, he spends as much time as possible, playing his own beloved fiddle.

EACH FALL, AS THE DAYS GREW SHORTER and shorter, his face got longer and longer, anticipating another cruel Chicago winter.

I had a choice. I could continue to fight my husband's suggestion of moving to Florida and have a miserable time trying to buoy his spirits each winter — or — I could bite the bullet and move — yes, to Florida, of all places — and perhaps, then, have a happier husband.

I sprang it on him. "Honey, let's move to Ft. Lauderdale!" It startled him and scared the hell out of him. We sold our home and bought a house on a canal in Ft. Lauderdale. We knew no one and my husband walked away from a successful medical practice in Illinois, plunging into the Florida medical world with not one patient to speak of. He also plunged into a depression. Well, of course. Even though he could carry his piano on his back, so to speak, we were gambling. We had no income and the future was uncertain.

Within a short time, reading journals and worrying was replaced by a flourishing private practice which was to grow into one of the largest in town!

But what about me? I had been a professional singer all my adult life so landing roles in Florida musical theatre was an easily surmountable challenge.

Local theatre kept me busy for the first few years and then came the magic words, "How would you like to go to the opera in Santa Fe, New Mexico?" Well, sure! Why not? I really didn't know much about the Southwest. I only knew that I'd love to have some relief from the Florida humidity and, as a singer, experiencing the opera sounded good to me.

I guess our story has been told a thousand times by others who have "found" Santa Fe. Very honestly, when we got out of the rental car at Rancho Encantado, I had an overwhelming feeling of peace and belonging. This was "my" place and I knew it—instantly. Illinois, which is where I was born and raised, never felt like home. Florida certainly had a foreign feeling. But Santa Fe felt like home.

Well, if I couldn't move there I realized I would have to bring Santa Fe back to Florida. And that's exactly what I did. I spent our vacation scouting retail stores and galleries. Impulsively, I made the decision to open a gallery in Florida, combining contemporary American crafts with contemporary Native American paintings, sculpture and pottery. I had fallen in love with the art, the artists and the idea of bringing this unusual beauty and sophistication back to Florida.

My husband was totally supportive of this apparent whim and backed me 100 percent. I had never been in a business and we were not collectors. But I plunged into this new venture feet first, sliding along by the seat of my pants, turning the dream into a reality. We called it "Canyon Gallery."

Sue with Amado Peña and the Canyon Gallery "girls" 1996.

Traveling to Santa Fe several times a year was an exciting experience as we got deeper and deeper into the art, the fascinating history and natural beauty of the area. We were hooked, and the business flourished.

Eight years later, my husband decided to take a three-month sabbatical from the stresses of his practice, leaving it in the hands of his younger partners. We rented a house in Pecheco Canyon and after one month, he took a giant leap, turned to me and said, "I'm calling the office and telling them I'm not coming back." We returned to Florida only to close the doors of the gallery, sell our house and pack our bags. We then headed West—to this unbelievably varied and gorgeous landscape with its rare and wonderful collection of unique people.

And what were our challenges to be in this nurturing environment, filled with creative people? My husband latched onto the Santa Fe Symphony fulfilling his passion for exposure to classical music. The Symphony organization needed people like him. He was willing to share his enthusiasm and work tirelessly for the cause. He became President of the Board and has been instrumental in the exciting success of the Symphony. Today, that group is flying high!

After a 16 year hiatus, I returned to the theatre world—happily but with great trepidation. For many years, my focus was my gallery and interior design. And who said I would be able to recapture a singing voice? In reality, I hadn't sung in 16 years.

Backstage in Santa Fe. Sue Lovitz flanked by Mara Getz and Darcy Shean before a Showtime Santa Fe performance in 2002.

Sue and Beryl Lovitz in Florida in 2005.

We were at a dinner party in Santa Fe. The host had hired a Santa Fe Opera apprentice to entertain. Before he started singing his final selection, he asked if anyone in the large group of guests would come up and sing with him. My husband pushed me on my feet and there I was, in the arms of this handsome young man—singing—once again. Well, that was just the beginning of a wonderful new career. I created a small company called "Showtime Santa Fe," using both local talent and later, bringing in New York cabaret stars whom I had met along the way. The shows are written and directed by me and usually focus on a single Broadway composer. The story of that composer is told by a narrator and the composer's music is demonstrated by four or five singers—including me. It has been a terrific run with shows about Irving Berlin, George Gershwin, Rodgers and Hammerstein, Kander and Ebb, and many others.

Santa Fe has kept us vibrant and young in spirit and we consider ourselves blessed to be able to call it home.

I Came to Santa Fe

Jonathan Lowe

*Since 1983 **Jonathan Lowe** has been producing film and video projects in many areas of the business. Starting with "Jetfighter," a music video he co-created with the band "The 3 O'clock" in Los Angeles, which played on MTV in 1984, he has gone on to create a very successful video production company — Video Magic, in Santa Fe, NM. Also a teacher for the past 14 years, Jonathan works as an Artist-in-Residence in New Mexico schools and has taught Filmmaking at IAIA for the past three years. He is well versed with all aspects of digital film production and now has an editing studio near downtown Santa Fe. For the past two years, Jonathan has worked on many projects, most notably as cameraman for "Tangled Up in Bob," (Feido Films), a documentary which covers the early years of Bob Dylan. He is also working on an ongoing documentary about the most recent attempted to discover what really sank the Lusitania, for which he is both cameraman and producer.*

IN ENGLAND IN THE MIDDLE OF THE STANDARD public school environment, I had a vivid dream at 15 years of age of building a rock house in a hot arid climate. Thinking of America's west. (Now I plan on building a rock house at 55 years old, near El Rito.)

Moved to US in 1982 at 29, following and marrying Toni Zeto, a wild and crazy artist/musician who lived in Santa Monica who subsequently elected to choose her musical career over her marriage.

While the marriage was dissolving in 1984 and on the threshold of changing careers from the corporate world to videography, I had three identical dreams, which progressed each time.

In each dream, I was walking down a dirt road surrounded by evergreen shrubby trees (junipers and piñons as I discovered later). As I walked toward

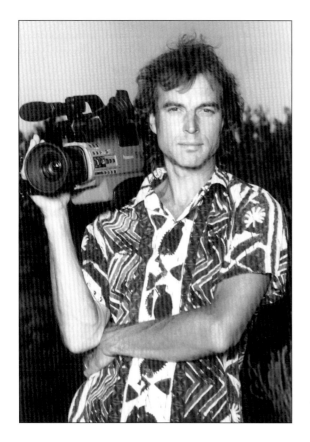

a house that I knew to be mine, a shock wave hit hard and I left my body. As my spirit flew I was directed to look down and the land below (to the West) was liquefied by a massive earthquake. I went back to my body. The earth was solid there in the high mountains. A sign showed that I was in Santa Fe. (In a later dream the words shortened to become the word SAFE and in the third dream the year was shown to be 1988.)

I did not know then where Santa Fe was. I asked an office mate who showed me a map. I knew that I would go there in 1988. (It was then 1984.) In 1987 I went to Sedona for the

Jonathan the traveling video magician on arrival in Santa Fe, 1988.

Jonathan still making video magic, 2007.

Harmonic Convergence at which I met Jennifer who lived in Santa Fe. A few months later while traveling from hot spring to hot spring I woke up on my 35th birthday in Jemez Hot Springs. I decided that it was a good day to go to Santa Fe.

I arrived early, checked out the town, kept trying to call Jennifer. By night, I decided to head back to the hot springs. On my way out of town at the Giant gas station, I tried to call her one more time. She was there! I went to visit, stayed a few days, and then went back to California to get my stuff. I've lived in Santa Fe ever since…(waiting for earthquakes), living my dreams and recording the life, the art, the poetry, and the magic of this place while teaching the up-and-coming young ones the technical side of the Video Magic I practice. My delight in having had the opportunity of living my dreams warms my heart every day.

Jonathan and his granddaughter at the Pyramid at Kobe in the Yucatan, 2006.

A Merciful Light
Consuelo Luz Aróstegui

One of the world's most inspired interpreters of Sephardic (Judeo/Spanish) music, **Consuelo Luz** *has performed internationally and recorded several albums, including the international release Dezeo, a collection of Sephardic prayers and ballads featured on such prestigious compilations as Buddha Bar and Putumayo. Singer, writer, activist and mother, after hosting and producing a nationally syndicated Spanish radio program for many years, Consuelo has dedicated herself to her writing and exploring her multicultural heritage through music and art.*

MY EYES OPENED TO A DARK PLACE. It smelled of burned mist. I was gasping for air. Where are you I asked myself. My heart was beating fast. I had awakened from a dream.

In the dream I was wandering on a beach. I found a small round entrance into a huge sand dune and walked in, following something. I went deeper. The grains of sand raining down on me. Each grain a world. I saw into one of the grains. It was endless water. In another grain I could see a mountain. There was a church. People were singing an old song that was dying. I kept on. Deeper. The grainworlds covering me. It was getting hard to breathe. The grainworlds entering my mouth. I started running. My legs sank deeper into a cold sand. I could hear my little son calling me *Mamá Mamá donde estás? I chased a goat today. When are you coming to see me?*

Then I remembered. I was 24 years old and living in my bread truck on the northern coast of California. I had parked for the night in the middle of Kruse Rhododendron Forest, somewhere between Fort Ross and Stewart's Point. I sat up in my bed, careful not to knock my head on the upper bunk. Reached under my pillow for the flashlight.

I shone the beam on the kerosene lantern on the floor. Grabbed the matches next to it and lit the lamp. In the flickering glow I saw my green portable Coleman stove on the built-in tapestried bench. A covered pot contained leftovers from my dinner. Brown rice with carrots, onions and corned beef cooked in Tamari sauce. A bag of dried prunes was neatly tied together with a rubber band. My guitar rested against the black padded vinyl driver's seat. This is what freedom looked like.

I stood up. Didn't have to stoop. This 1948 bread truck had been remodeled by its previous owners into a comfortable 60's traveling home. Paisley curtains hung down over the double-decker beds. The Persian carpet soft on my bare feet. I looked up at the zany cartoons painted on the ceiling by some hippie artist high on LSD. Bulging-eyed squat comic book characters running after clouds and rainbows and happy-looking dogs and big-eared cats.

I walked the four steps to the driver's seat. Pulled the lever next to it which opened the double doors of the old truck. Like my school bus in Lima, Peru. Chattering girls. Green uniforms. Brown leather book bags. An innocence that hurt now. The memory of it. I stepped down the two metal steps covered with glued-on rubber mats, and out into the foggy night.

I had not bothered to change out of my clothes when I went to bed. I was still wearing my patched jeans and faded brown T-shirt. A cold breeze sighed. Sad it was, like tired birds looking for home. I wrapped my arms around myself. By the light of a cloudy half moon I walked to a bush, pulled down my pants, crouched and relieved myself, grabbing some leaves off the ground to wipe off the last drops.

I stood, pulled up my tattered jeans and wept. For my little boy across the ocean who was forgetting his mother. For the lost and crazy years. For the dancing fading flower children who had given birth to a vision mad with love. For the assassins with their bludgeons and their money, mad with hate. For the Earth, being devoured by this fearful hatred, for the dying lakes and rivers, for those too blind to care, for the tortured, for the torturers, for myself, seeking my red and golden fate like one of Leonard Cohen's saints.

Was it necessary I asked myself. Yes I answered.

Dearest Mummy and Daddy,

We are paintstrippers my generation and me. Stripping the layers of lies, like coats of paint and dirt grown thick through the centuries. I begin to see something beautiful underneath....the Earth breathing again, and my life surrendered (like Jose Martí, I am part martyr). Please don't dismiss me as mad for all this, but if you do then read Emily Dickinson. "In madness is the divinest sense," she wrote. So it may be that in divine madness is where we will survive. And what is mad? Aren't all the women in our family a bit mad? Maybe the world needs this kind of madness. Love madness. And maybe it's not madness after all....

Thank you for taking care of my precious little boy. I love you both so much.

Your ever loving daughter, caught in the struggle of this century....

The struggle for truth. The truth of our ancient bones. If we were fashioned by kind gods they are now frantic with despair. May a finer world be born out of our greedy careless ashes. Am I seeking nothing to find I asked myself.

I did not answer.

I made coffee as the dawn made its way through the thick rhododendrons. Ate the cold dinner leftovers and heated some more water to wash the dishes which had soaked all night in the large tin pan. I splashed some warm water on my face and on my long curly hair to smooth down the wildness. These ordinary things. To remind me I am still blessed. My son is alive and healthy, waiting for me, albeit half a continent and an ocean away. I wish I could remember how soft his skin is.

I pushed up the heavy fat black hood of my truck and lodged it open with the metal rod I had wired in place under the hood. Checked the oil and the water. I made sure the pencil was well lodged in the carburetor. When I took the engine apart and put it back together back in San Francisco, I had put new rings, replaced two pistons, did a valve job and replaced all of the gaskets and belts. The carburetor seemed fine, but when I got on the road, it kept flooding and then the engine would die. I suspected the air flow adjuster wasn't working properly and tried sticking a pencil in the hole. Since then I'd had no trouble.

I had found the truck parked in a forest in Marin County. Two of the tires were flat and the engine needed work. More work than I had bargained for but I was grateful. The month of being on my back, under the truck, grimy and smelling of motor oil and dank metal, learning to use ratchet drivers and understanding the simple logic of the combustion engine was time well spent. It gave me the confidence to take to the road knowing I would be my own mechanic. If I was planning to drive all the way to the southern tip of South America, I'd better not be at the mercy of macho strangers.

It was March, 1973. The Chilean socialist revolution was struggling. The CIA was at work, sabotaging the economy so the people would rise up and bang their pots, demanding food and jobs. The moderates were abandoning President Allende pushing him into the arms of the extremists who were occupying private farms and homes, creating panic in the middle class. My schoolteacher aunt's tenants were forcefully taking possession of her little house in Santiago. People driven to desperation. The socialist dream unraveling into chaos. My plan to drive to Chile, my mother's native land, to be part of the new vision in the south, was looking grim. I would drive farther south then, to Patagonia, find a sheep farm. When I was settled I would go and fetch my son from my parents in Spain. He belonged with his mother even if she was a crazy Patagonian shepherdess singing songs to cleanse the earth's pores.

I turned the ignition and pumped the gas just so. I knew the carburetor well. The motor turned over on the first try. I let it warm up for five minutes and then set off north to deliver some things from my San Francisco friend Nancy to a women's goat farm in Albion.

The fog started to clear mid-morning but the cloud cover kept things grey and sad. I followed the directions Nancy had given me and found the farm easily. There was a large house with a wooden porch and several outbuildings. It was a lesbian commune. Lots of goats and women. An air of freedom. I delivered the packages and stayed for a lunch of fresh greens and goat cheese. There were three women who seemed to be at the center of the energy, weaving around each other in a kind of tentative dance. This awkward tension disturbed the otherwise bucolic paradise. Nancy had told me it was a ménage a trois.

Consuelo Luz after arriving in New Mexico.

A woman with a feather hanging from one ear mentioned she was going to New Mexico. New Mexico. I imagined a dry, magical land. A desert. A refuge.

Nancy's parents, Casey and John, had offered me what they called their "treehouse" in Whitehorn, much farther north, practically at the border with Oregon. I could stay there indefinitely. It was wet in this north country. Very wet. The treehouse was a multi-sided wooden cabin built on top of a wooden scaffold several feet above the ground nestled in the trees in the middle of a dense dark forest.

I was ecstatic to be in a house. I cooked bok choy and black beans. Oatmeal for breakfast. I played my guitar and sang to the treehouse guardians and the forest spirits and the rain nymphs. I guess the rain nymphs liked my singing cause it kept coming down. Day and night. A steady pouring. A wet gray mist seeped in through the walls and the floors and into my songs. I wrote sad. I wrote dark. Songs of being lost in a damp moss underworld. Songs of drowning.

My clothes would not dry unless I hung them directly in front of the wood stove. I looked for a plastic tarp to put over the outside woodpile. I finally found one underneath the house in a small wooden storage shed. I started bringing in the wet wood to dry inside but it just wouldn't dry fast enough. I was running out of dry wood. Had to keep the fire going by all means, not let the fire go out. Going to sleep was a problem.

I imagined a dry, magical land where the sun would shine a merciful light.

Have you had enough of the wet treehouse, I asked myself.

Yes I answered.

Okay, let's go.

I packed up and hoped the truck would not have trouble in the mud. Grabbed a wrench and turned the latches on the tires which put it in four wheel drive. It made it out of the driveway and onto the road which wound for several miles up and down some hills on its way to the highway. In the dense grey wetness everything looked the same. I couldn't find the highway. Must have taken the wrong turn. Suddenly I was having trouble going round an uphill curve and then the truck stopped. I revved the engine. Nothing. I put it in reverse and it moved back slightly. Put it in first again and this time the front spun around to the right and the whole thing started skidding backwards. I felt a jolt and heard a crunch. Was afraid I was going to go over the side of the road so I floored it. The truck moved forward but I heard another crunchy ripping sound. I stopped, left it in first gear, turned off the motor and pulled the hand brake.

I slipped on my long green plastic rain poncho and went out to survey what had happened and found the bumper had been half torn off by a boulder on the side of the road and the outside right rear tire was flat. It was a half-ton truck with double tires in the back but I didn't want to drive on one tire, dragging a fifty pound bumper without knowing where I was headed.

What are you going to do now I asked myself.

Don't know, find some help I guess, I answered.

I locked the truck door with a padlock and started walking. Water pouring off the edge of my hood onto my nose. Mud dragging my boots into it. The rain cold, relentless, heavy.

I imagined a dry, magical land with a spirit that wanted me.

I came to a grouping of houses. There were several wooden buildings and a few cars. I knocked on the door of the biggest house. A young man opened the door. His eyes huge and blue, his hair long, brown, his smile wide, gentle.

"Praise the Lord, you found us!" he cried out sweetly, "just in time I'm sure."

It sounded like a song. My answer did too.

"Hi, sorry to bother you, my truck is stuck in the mud, my bumper is half ripped off and I'm wondering if you could…"

Without hesitation, he grabbed a rain poncho and an umbrella off a hook by the door and we trudged up the muddy road with the rain coming down, him singing hymns of gladness, the red umbrella dancing brightly in the wet gloom.

It was a Jesus commune I had stumbled on. And a full day of praising, praying and labouring, sloshing through the mountain mud, lay ahead. This beautiful shining youth, about 18 at the most, helped me take off the 50 pound bumper, carry it to their workshop, change my tire and move my truck down to the commune where my bumper was re-attached. The rain kept pouring and he kept praising the Lord. Smiling, singing thanks to Jesus and blessing me. Blessed I was.

At the end of the day I was introduced to their leader. In his early 30's, he looked like one of those Italian statues of gods I had seen in Florence where my parents had taken me when I was a little girl. A mass of brown curls cascaded lion-like around a face that was handsome, intense and serene as an archangel would be. His eyes a blue made of ocean to dive into. He wore a white robe-like long shirt over jeans and leather sandals. In his private sanctum he sat me down in front of him. An archangel cross-examining me. King in his world.

I gathered my will. Both my hands on my solar plexus. I can resist this strange angelic power, I said inside myself. Part of me wanted to crawl up to him and put my head on his lap so he would caress my face with his gentle hand forever. He would recruit me into his joyous band of Jesus freaks if I let him. I was vulnerable. I am a Patagonian shepherdess I repeated to myself. My son needs me. I have to go and get my son I told him. He could not argue with that.

I said goodbye to the shining youth who had helped me and gave him twenty five dollars. He praised the Lord and gave me a Christ blessing for my travels. He surely did.

Back in my truck I looked at my map of the United States. Saw how I could cross the border into Mexico through California or Arizona or through New Mexico to El Paso, Texas, and then to Juarez. Once in Mexico there was a choice of routes to go south, catch the Pan American Highway and keep on going.

New Mexico kept on murmuring to me. A vast murmur it was.

In Southern California I was pulled over by the State Police for going too slow.

"The truck can't go over 55 miles per hour, officer, and that's on a straightaway."

The policeman looked inside the truck at the paisley curtains. No doubt thinking *hippie, drugs.* Then he looked up at the cartoons painted on the ceiling, shook his head and asked,

"Where are you headed in this thing?"

"Patagonia, sir."

I don't think he knew where Patagonia was and didn't want to admit it so he waved me on.

"Well, just stay in the right lane."

"Yes, sir," I replied, glad I was leaving California.

It felt good to drive into Arizona. I got stuck overnight in the Petrified Forest in an April blizzard and had to get a new alternator in Flagstaff. It felt good to leave Arizona and drive into New Mexico.

When I crossed the border into New Mexico something happened. I started picking up hitchhikers. Never done that before. Dropped one off in Gallup and headed on to Albuquerque. A woman at the Albion goat farm had told me that she had traveled around the country on her own and whenever she found herself stranded in a big city she would find the university. They all had women centers now. This was the 70's and women and girls were leaving home by the millions, leaving their husbands, leaving their families, looking for their destinies, out there, alone, needing refuge.

I found the University of New Mexico campus and, sure enough, there was a women's center. There were women cooking in the kitchen, trading stories, phone numbers, rolling out their sleeping bags, young, old, hippie, straight. A young curly-haired brown skinned woman came up to me. Hummingbird she said her name was.

"You need to go to Taos." As if my life depended on it, she said it.

"Taos" I repeated, as if it was a secret prayer known only to a few.

Nancy had given me a name and phone number of a friend of hers who lived in a place called Taos. You should go there she had said, as if she knew something about me that I didn't.

"Go to the Taos Learning Center in Arroyo Hondo," Hummingbird said. "Nick and Adrienne. Good people."

Hummingbird gave me directions.

In the morning I set out north. Passed through Santa Fe. Wondered about it. I'll stop on the way back down I said to myself. All right.

I don't remember why I made that right turn to Nambe but it led me to Truchas and my New Mexico awakening. When I got to the top of the last rise into the mountain village of Truchas, I had to pull over. Something was trembling in me. My heart already knew. It had been begging for this new light for a long time. I parked my truck at what seemed like an abandoned adobe. Later I found out it was the old morada where an ancient Catholic brotherhood met. I got out and walked a few steps, if you can call it walking. More like stumbling and floating at once. I tried to find my breath and what words to say and what thoughts to think. There was nothing to explain this place of awe and silence, majestic and humble in the same embrace. This was the mountain in the grainworld in my dream where the people were singing a dying song. I would help sing it alive again.

The snow-covered peaks filled me with a longing I could not understand.

The simple quiet village made my heart feel safe. The light seemed to come from another dimension, in its soulbreaking glow. Merciful. A sweetness and power to float into forever.

I wept. For my long mad journey. For the harsh grace of it. For the desperate dream of Patagonia that had led me here. For the night soon ahead when I would put my boy to bed, kiss his smooth round cheek and pile him high with blankets against the cold New Mexico winter. Soon this would happen. Soon. I breathed a long gasp, choking with new dreams, and it started to snow. I continued on to Taos on the high road, past the village of Las Trampas where many years later I would give birth to my third child.

Then Taos Mountain greeted me. How much can your heart take I asked myself. Not much more I answered.

Entering Taos I found a phone booth and called Nancy's friend. He gave me directions to his house. John Nichols welcomed me warmly, cooked me scrambled eggs and chile and gave me the political and cultural lowdown on Taos. It was April 10, 1973. He was in the middle of writing *The Milagro Beanfield War.* A funky edgy sweet wild kindness permeated everything around him. Many years later I would work on casting the children and the Senile Brigade for Robert Redford's movie of the novel and both my daughter and I would appear in the film. I slept in my truck in John's driveway that night as my heart continued to break open. The next day I set out for Arroyo Hondo.

Photo by Manuela Asencio

The magic created by Nick and Adrienne Arias Morrow and their Taos Learning Center took me in as if it had been expecting me for a while. In the fire-warmed and dusty pottery barn a young long-haired man held out a hand-rolled smoke to share in welcome. His name was Chuck. And there was

Consuelo with husband-to-be, Jeff, and her children, Lucas and Astrea, Stagecoach Springs, New Mexico 1981.

beautiful Andrea mountain maiden. And wild Pepe riding his horse across the mesa.

I would go east and return with my son before the winter set in. Patagonia would have to wait.

I was home.

Connecting with local villagers in Valdez and Des Montes was like finding lost family. I found open, generous, strong, laughing, spiritual women who taught me to chop wood, make tortillas, pick fruit, preserve apricots, grow vegetables, heal with garlic and survive the harsh winter. María, Olivama, Marlin, Mary, Little Bird, Stella, Crow. I found an old adobe to rent from Eva and Manuel Martinez and their huge loving brood on the breathtaking Rim Road. And I got a PO Box in Arroyo Seco.

Consuelo Luz performing at Peace Day on the Santa Fe Plaza, 2006.

Years later, I would end up moving to Las Trampas and then to Santa Fe, when love, schools and work beckoned. A cozy light-filled house in the West Barrio, then a house designed by Bill Lumpkins on Canyon Road. And then a community getting it together. In Santa Fe is where I gave birth to the rabid activist in me.

Santa Fe and Taos being like two sisters who love each other but need to live apart, you can love them both. One's bigger, busier, with more bustle and carousing and a more sophisticated cutting edge, after all, it is the Capital. The other's wilder, funkier, harder to get to with its breathtaking vastness and edgy sweetness.

But it's the same blood, just depends what your spirit is wanting…

I had imagined a dry, magical land where the sun would shine a merciful light. A refuge.

I found it.

Why I Came to Santa Fe
Ali MacGraw

Ali MacGraw is an Oscar-nominated actress and she made her Broadway debut in 2007. She is the author of a best-selling autobiography and her yoga tape has sold nearly a half a million copies to date. She has also worked in the design field, on houses, textiles, and a restaurant. She spends much of her time in New Mexico working on a wide variety of community causes, and considers herself lucky to be living in such a beautiful and Conscious place.

M Y COMING TO SANTA FE WAS completely unexpected—a fluke, some sort of "cosmic plan" beyond my wildest expectations.

I was brought up in the country north of New York City and went to school in New England. My first real jobs were all in New York (not counting the waitressing, chamber maiding, etc., which put me through school!). I worked in the crazy fashion business of the 1960's and felt that I was a die-hard New Yorker. When fate threw me a totally unexpected surprise in the form of a sudden, overnight career in the film business, I wanted to try that— and stay in "my city." But as it turned out, I soon met the father of my son and only child, and we moved West to live in quintessential (terrifying) film executive lifestyle in Los Angeles. I remember crying as our car pulled away from everything and everyone I knew, to the airport and the whirlwind madness of Hollywood in the 1970's.

Several marriages and lifetimes later I found myself with my son and various dogs and cats in a wonderful rented house on the beach in Malibu—back when it was still a funky surfer and family town, no paparazzi or hedge fun mc-mansions. It was a different lifestyle, but private and comforting. I must have drifted in it a bit, because deep down I knew that after a certain number of years in Los Angeles, I really needed to move on. But where?

One filthy hot, smoggy morning in November of 1993 I awoke to the smell of an enormous brush fire which was raging out of control to the south of my house in the hills above Malibu. Irritated and cranky, I decided to work it out at a yoga class 12 minutes away in Santa Monica. An hour and a half later I came out of that studio to see a huge, tornado-shaped, horizontal column of black smoke settling over the Pacific Ocean, and I knew that the fires had jumped to Malibu. Several hours later (after a drive up the highway which felt like an emergency run out of Beirut), I realized that my rented house was at the very center of a raging, out-of-control firestorm! It would burn to the ground by 2 o'clock, taking everything with it except for, thankfully, my animals; a thoughtful friend had moved them out of harms way.

That year was an interesting time for me, because I stayed on in Los Angeles, looking in vain for a beachside cottage to rent. They were of course all taken, as so many families with children had shared the fire experience and needed a place to restart their lives near the neighborhood schools. I was blessed to have the comfort of a place to stay in Los Angeles, thanks to the generosity and thoughtfulness of my son's father. But I knew it was a temporary solution. Daily I stressed and whined about where I was going to live (with my two dogs and two cats), until one day an old friend from New York said, rather testily, that he was tired of hearing me moan, and why, for Heaven's sake, didn't I just take my animals and a few possessions and go to Santa Fe? After all, hadn't he heard that I had bought a cottage somewhere in the hills north of that town? I was paying a mortgage,

Ali MacGraw seeing her house in Malibu burning down at sunset, 1993.

wasn't I? What was the problem? If I didn't like it, I could decide to relocate, but he was sick of my drama.

In fact, I HAD bought a little getaway up in Tesuque several years before, and I frequently came in for a few days, or even a few weeks, just to escape Los Angeles. I knew virtually no one there at the time, and I cherished the hours walking in silence and the overwhelming beauty of this very foreign landscape. My trips consisted of flying in on (two-for-one!) Southwest Airlines and renting a car for the beautiful, peace deepening drive North. I stopped for food supplies at the stores whose organic produce were a revelation. Then I went to the now-closed Blue Moon Video store, where I rented a feast of old, ethnic, and esoteric films for my quiet evenings at home. Daytimes, I wandered the hills collecting hundreds of rocks of colors never seen in New England or California. They are still arranged in bizarre still-lifes all over my property, where I suppose they might await the puzzled reaction of clue-seeking aliens one day! A hugely "social" day would include time spent at the then fabulous Tesuque Flea Market, where I met amazing new friends whose lives included the kind of romantic travel and ethnic art that so appeal

to me. Those were glorious days for me here in New Mexico—soul-feeding escape from my crazed life in Los Angeles, and a time to begin to discover (or perhaps to remember) who I was, apart from someone else's description of me based on my old, sometime job. Still, I wasn't at all sure I would keep my house, because I frankly cannot bear the confusion of having a second home: I can never find my "other ballet shoe," or remember where my orange

Ali MacGraw on her porch in Tesuque, 1995.

marmalade is, or which book I was reading. Until that little speech from my friend, (about moving to Santa Fe, making it my home), I was planning to sell.

It is funny and amazing how the Universe so frequently turns apparent catastrophe into gift: the fire appeared to be a very personal disaster—to everyone but me. I was healthy enough to realize that I had certainly not been singled out to have this particular experience and very shortly I came to see it as what it was: a kind of cosmic kick in the ass to get me out of a lifestyle which I think would have killed my spirit.

As I settled into my new life in this breathtaking beautiful land, I quickly saw and felt the healing and expansion and connection it offers. I met wonderful people at every turn, and many of them—like me—were reinventing their lives. I found that exciting and inspiring and alive. The stories I had heard my whole life about the rich, multi-cultured energy of Santa Fe were all true, and I have loved living in a place where there is real history. (As a born Easterner, I have missed that terribly.) With my lifelong, romantic idea of New Mexico and the wildly colorful people who have come here, I have had preconceived ideas of a population interest in absolutely everything about which I care deeply. The sheer quantity of cultural opportunity in the form of performing arts and lectures and foreign films as well as the Native American and Hispanic celebrations just boggle the mind; I know of nowhere like Santa Fe in America, and I use every bit of it.

One of the important surprises here has been the commitment on the part of virtually everyone I know to make this community—varied as it is—a better place for all of us to

Ali taking a break during the filming of an environmental documentary in Southern New Mexico, 2002.

be. I have never lived anywhere where I felt so strongly this way life, this respect for the unique mixture of cultures and life styles and opportunities and spiritual paths which make up Santa Fe. There is so much to be done here, and I am quite sure that our concerned, caring population will "get it done," in this difficult, often heart-wrenching world in which we find ourselves at the beginning of this century. I find this to be reassuring and hopeful—a kind of blueprint for the return of civilization.

So my Big Fire was, in fact, a gift. Everyday brings a new, silent, early morning dog walk in this breathtaking landscape, with sunset-pink mountains and the biggest, star-studded sky on earth with which to end it. In between my mind is stimulated as never before, and I feel the certainty of the Power of the Divine Unknown. I am beyond grateful that for the moment, at least, I am firmly planted in this magical, rich, inspiring, friendly, ravishingly beautiful place: I celebrate this blessing every day with my equally grateful animals!

❖ ❖ ❖

Ali at a Pueblo Church, 2004.

Ali with her favorite companions, Amtrak and Cracker, 2003.

We Came to Santa Fe
Mark & Janet MacKenzie

Mark MacKenzie is, by profession, an art conservator and anthropologist. He is the Director of Conservation/Chief Conservator of the Conservation Department within the Department of Cultural Affairs, Museum Resources Division, in Santa Fe, New Mexico. By choice, he is also a photographer, digital artist, database designer, computer programmer, blacksmith, wood turner, appreciator of wine and beer and all-round explorer of the ways things used to be done. Janet MacKenzie has been an anthropologist/archaeologist and artist. She is a student in Museum Studies, writer and gardener. The MacKenzies have two adult children and a three year old grandson.

O H GOD! SHOULD I HAVE ACCEPTED Victor's invitation? I guess I can't back out now, but how am I going to write this thing? That roof has got to get repaired before the monsoons.... This book is a neat project, though. Makes you think. Haven't really thought about this since we got here. We're just so glad to settle in a bit, maybe watch a movie, have a glass of beer, think about working on the property, get to know each other as a couple again.

But it does make you think....The whole thing began so long ago now, it's hard to remember. Some of it I don't even want to remember. The frustration of not being able to make things happen at my previous museum, the lack of professionalism—nobody told me anything necessary—nobody even knew what I did in my job. How they expected me to provide the conservation services they needed without any goals or objectives, I can't understand. You can only stand it so long… Of course, it wasn't all bad. I learned a lot. Taught a lot, too. After 25 years, you pick up a thing or two, especially if you resist the pressure to specialize and prefer to grow instead. When you can't make things happen that need to happen—ethically, professionally, for safety reasons—whatever—eventually, you just have to start looking around. Yeah…well…I never realized what a long road it would be. Looking back I know now I needed a place where the professionalism was high, the work varied and the needs great. I didn't think the search would lead me out of the country. Thank God I didn't have to go to Ottawa. That's a *really* different country!

You know, when I found the Santa Fe position advertised on the Internet, it just sounded right for me. That other position in Virginia might've been alright, but not having been on a university faculty would have meant a big learning curve for me. But being Director of Conservation for the Museum of New Mexico, with its four museums and five monuments, really attracted me. I thought, "Here's a chance to grow again, make a difference, apply a lot of the managerial stuff I've been developing and using without anyone apparently noticing before." And so many of the things I had been doing for so long in the dark were actually wanted and valued by these people! Database design, working with volunteers, getting interns, working with the public, involving parks and monuments—heck, they even needed someone to work on steam engines! And a chance to go to Santa Fe? *Wow!*

It didn't take me long to figure out that the Department of Cultural Affairs never imagined a Canadian would apply! I'm glad they eventually got over the shock and took a chance. God! The hours I spent on the Internet trying to figure out how to get a visa and find out what they would have to do to get me across the border and into the job… I think it impressed them that I came up with the goods PDQ in time for the interview. That guy on the border in Montana was just great—being able to phone him and get him to talk to the people at DCA was wonderful. It was all so confusing. The various official websites dealing with these things were so contradictory. It took a lot of sifting. About the only thing NAFTA ever did for me and mine was to have a ready made set of desirable work visa categories.

Application deadline in October—on the job in Santa Fe by mid-January! Professionals, every one I met, on the Board and off. Scary, but what a treat! I was surprised and pleased when they even had me interviewed by my potential employees! Talk about trial by fire…. When the offer of employment actually came, we accepted almost without thinking. Almost. We Canadians are used to pretty good free health care up there and we wanted to make sure we wouldn't lose on that. There were also all the things that wouldn't or couldn't move with us, like the kids and things collected over a lifetime. At first, I was so excited, I couldn't think of anything else, including what we would have to go through actually to take the job! Out of the blue I would just burst out, "We're going Santa Fe!"

What a schmozzle to make it all come true! We found homes for a huge amount of stuff—10 foot long printers, the air compressor and table saw, a ton of equipment, my stock of furniture hard woods, books, furniture, clothes—boy, the Salvation Army should give us a tax receipt! And the kids got a lot, too. Getting them set up on their own in time to sell the house wasn't easy, I can tell you. With Dan going off to Afghanistan in the New Year, we couldn't load him up with too much stuff. Justina's basement apartment absorbed the dressers and kitchen stuff. I feel a little guilty at how much we dumped on her and little Kieran. But we had to move so fast that there really wasn't much choice. Janet got rid of some of her precious books, and I really chopped my photo, woodworking and shooting stuff down. But having to have Ziggy put down…. I know Black Labs are pretty old at 14 and she was blind and starting to fall a lot, and she would have had a terrible time with the change, but still it was bad. I miss her.

You know, I really, really wanted to drive the trailer down so I would have a cheap and familiar place to live in until we could sell the house. And I was going to do it, too, no matter what Janet said, weather and miles be damned. It was all packed and ready to go when that nasty weather hit—blowing snow

The MacKenzie's when they started their journey to Santa Fe.

and ice all the way down from Saskatchewan to Santa Fe. I just couldn't do it. Who wants to be stuck in Minot for weeks? We sure got a lot of looks when we dragged the trailer through the drifts to a storage lot.

So then I had to fly out to make my 16th of January deadline. Two suitcases and a lap top. Yes, we'd been separated before—me in Belize or Ottawa and Janet in Peru—but it was still hard, partly because we really didn't know when she would be able to come down. Would it be months or more like a year? At first in Santa Fe I was so busy, I hardly had time to think of home, or anything else for that matter. I had to meet my new colleagues, get a handle on the job, get a car, get a place to live, get my Social Security (that's another story!), get a bank account, get my medical and other insurance, find a pub! Keep the family relationships strong at home. It was a lonely time but everyone I met in Santa Fe was so welcoming and supportive that I felt at home almost immediately. I couldn't get enough of the views—still can't.

Meanwhile, back in snowy Saskatoon, Janet was finishing the packing so she could clear the house and continue work we had started some months before. Too bad she would never see her new perennial garden grow in. You just don't know what's coming up around the bend, eh? But, with new hardwood and tiled floors and paint, the house sold for what it was really worth. And we did well, better than we were expecting, which was nice, because housing is expensive down here.

So…. I looked at houses in Santa Fe but we just couldn't afford what's available outside of the "adobe ghettos." We were lucky to find a nice house in the historical Alcalde area and immediately decided that two and a half months apart was enough. I sure was lucky to be able to squeeze in a few days to fly up, load up Janet and the trailer, and say goodbye to the kids and little Kieran. Crossing the border this time was a snap! We drove down at top speed just ahead of a spring blizzard blanketing the northern and middle states and pulled into an RV park in Española four days later. The poor old truck had quite a time hauling us up the Raton Pass in the teeth of an amazing winter gale! Waiting that month for possession of the house was pretty tedious—

especially when the waterline kept freezing in what deluded Canadians fondly think of as the warm New Mexico spring!

Yes, we miss our family and friends—but they'll visit when they can. We'll miss Canada and the prairies—but we can go north to visit. We won't miss the cold, even if it does hail here in June. This is our country now. The languages are stimulating, the food exciting, the heritage and physical environments fascinating, the gardening challenging. My colleagues, at The Department of Cultural Affairs and beyond, are skilled and a pleasure to work with. Santa Fe has so much to offer with its hundreds of galleries and museums, its restaurants, shops, gardens, architecture and cultural life, its history, warm people and physical charm! We've barely scratched the surface and look forward to years of exploration. We've always enjoyed change in our lives and we have a lot to learn and experience in The City Different. Now the tale is told and the rest is the future!

The MacKenzie's at La Villita, 2007.

The Call of the Wild
Douglas Magnus

Magnus was born and raised in the chemical atmosphere of Los Angeles. The chemistry of photography came naturally at an early age. After two years in the US Army, he gravitated to Santa Fe to pursue photography and art, and an eventual career in jewelry work. He has been there ever since.

IRONICALLY, IF I HADN'T FLUNKED ART during my third semester at college, and as a result been immediately drafted into the U.S. Army, I never would have come to Santa Fe, where I have spent most of my life wallowing in the arts.

My California school years had been a mostly dismal experience, save for art and especially photography. Luckily, I became the high school photography teacher's pet, and the opportunities that came my way opened my mind to the excitement of possibility. The camera became my constant companion and passion, an obsession really. After high school came the let down of not being so privileged, but I held on to the dream that photography would take me places and let me accomplish great things.

About then, the word Vietnam was beginning to be heard. Suddenly my good times seemed doomed, with the 'greetings' letter from Uncle Sam. It was May 1966, and I was off to Fort Bliss in El Paso, Texas and Destiny.

It's impossible to explain the magic in life, but that's how I regard my two years in the Army. Magic. A pretty dumb kid given a job in Operation Central, designed to shoot planes out of the sky with guided missiles. No jungle duty for me. I stayed in El Paso the whole time. And wild times they were! Many of the people I'd left behind were hiding scared and dodging the draft, while I was having the time of my life, and never felt freer. I felt totally in control and fearless. Youthful arrogance, testosterone, drugs (I now realize), and luck at not being sent to the war zone.

By the time of my Honorable Release from the military, 60's idealism was spreading like a wildfire. I had become absorbed into El Paso's version of counter-culture, with an amazing assortment of strange and wonderful friends and acquaintances. Among these were artists, musicians, beatniks, feminists, sexual freedom pioneers, drug smugglers, lawyers, runaways, and at least one ex-military guy on acid. Amongst them all was a gorgeous blonde 19 year old Army brat named Lori, who invited me to stay with her at an old mansion on Mesa Street, 'Madness Manor'. Our time together was brief—maybe a week, but one day while out driving in the country and taking photographs (yes, I always carried my camera) she looked at me and said, "You should go to Santa Fe!" I asked why…because "It's beautiful." A few days later another lady friend also advised, that "You should go to Santa Fe." I wondered, what is this mysterious Santa Fe? I determined to go. Besides I was feeling good and in no hurry to return to smoggy L.A. The Southwest had captured my soul and my imagination entirely.

On the day of my departure, Lori hitchhiked off to New Orleans, as I was saying goodbye to others in the house, I heard the longhaired retired ex-Army guy yell out, "Wait for me, I'm comin' with you!" Donald C. Peters, was allegedly 36 years old, and truly outrageous. He looked like a Clint Eastwood spaghetti-western character with a gift for gab and was hilarious. He scared me, but he was someone to travel with. So off we went.

In early May of 1968, the road north from El Paso to Santa Fe was still the old two-lane highway that followed the mostly ancient route along the Rio Grande through small towns and villages. Behind stop and go school buses, we slowly made our way in my '58 Volkswagen, while Don blabbed and the miles went by. The closer we got I remember wondering when is it

Magnus, Rancho de Mora, Santa Fe 1971.

going to get beautiful? Sure the sky is bluer, but so far I couldn't distinguish a great difference from other desert landscape I had seen. Finally, over La Bajada Hill we caught our first sight of Santa Fe nestled at the base of the Sangre de Cristo Mountains. The two-lane highway turned into Cerrillos Road and the anticipation grew. Yucca Drive-In, Chez Rene, pinions, cholla, a few motels. Could this be it? We stopped to eat at VIPs Big Boy (site of the present day McDonalds on St. Francis). The waitress was friendly and we got directions to Canyon Road. We had been told to go directly to Claude's Bar by our El Paso Friends. As we entered Canyon Road "IT" started to hit me. By Garcia Street I was having trouble controlling my photographer's urge, and by Canyon Road and Delgado Street I said, "THIS IS IT!!!" I was already blown away! Claude's Bar was a short way up the street. When we entered, the bar was mostly deserted. We sat down near an old guy with a beer and a dog. We told him that we had just arrived from El Paso. He told us that he had been passing through from L.A. to New York twenty years before and never left.

Santa Fe looked ancient, neglected, forgotten, undeveloped and to me utterly glorious. It seethed with a sense of the gritty and unruly, freedom, danger, and yes "differentness™". I got the notion at the bar, and from people I saw on the streets that the popular idea of a generation gap (the subject of the day in mainstream America) didn't appear to exist here. Eccentric older people seemed to be mingling with eccentric young people. It was all so strange and foreign. I had no knowledge of its history, its people, or even that it was a well-known artists' community! (I wouldn't know know anything about Georgia O-Keefe for years to come) I thought maybe I was the first to discover this place, and I wanted to photograph and document my discovery! Ha!

Don Peters was a charismatic, energetic and gregarious person, a charming outlaw—within our first hours in town, we had made the acquaintance of a number of people. Among them, a young woman named Marcia who lived on Canyon Road at the home of a lecherous artist named Walter Dawely. She invited us to come see her the following day. Don was onto her like stink.

That first night we had the good fortune to stay in an empty apartment on the corner of Canyon and Delgado (now Natahlie). The apartment adjoined was an artsy retail store called the Bo Tree. The owners were acquaintances of the second woman who had urged me to Santa Fe. Turns out, she had ripped them off in a drug deal or something. Yet they still were nice enough to let us stay (on the bare floor).

The following day, we had breakfast at the Plaza Café. Afterwards, we were strolling on the sidewalk amid the amazing buzz of the Plaza. There were people of every description, moving around or just sitting around, doing business or just hanging out in this true center of Santa Fe life. Suddenly, a car honked behind us, we turned to see a city policeman flashing the two-fingered peace sign! There could be no better welcome for us to Santa Fe!

At the liquor store next to Plaza Café, Don bought a gallon jug of wine for about $2.00. And we proceeded back up Canyon Road to locate Marcia. We arrived at the address and went round back. It was an old two-story frame farmhouse-style, unusual for the neighborhood. I parked in the middle of a wide dirt lot. Don got out with the jug and spoke to someone on the back porch. "Excuse me, but we're looking for Marcia," he said, "And we've got wine." From an open second story window, I heard a woman's excited voice, "WINE?!" I looked up to see a sun-kissed nude woman framed in the window yelling, "Well, come on up!" That was our introduction to the notorious 'Sally Anne' (who would figure in many stories to follow in the coming years). Walter Dawely's studio home was a haven for wayward women. Marcia and Don were an instant item.

In a week after this meeting, we three were on our way back to El Paso, along with another character from Claude's, Crazy Dave (Dave wasn't really crazy, just supremely odd). When I first hit Santa Fe I had about $100.00. A week later I still had about $90.00, and Crazy Dave had convinced me that with that money, we could drive to El Paso, take the bus from Juarez to Oaxaca, buy rugs and trinkets, then return to Santa Fe just in time for tourist season! Which we did. The ninety dollars ran out in Oaxaca, and the kindly native people whom Dave knew, gave us weavings on credit, plus cash to return. It was a madcap adventure. Back in Santa Fe we rented a space at the Casa del Sol Stables, owned by Juan Vigil. Later known as Glassworks, the Stables had been recently converted to vendor stalls. We rented one for probably $25.00 per month. I carved the sign in wood, which read 'Zapotec'. Thus began my first business venture in Santa Fe,

I had been out of the Army for over a month and still had not called anyone back home. Family and friends were wondering. I decided to make a quick dash to California. Thankfully, gas was $.24 per gallon and my car got 40 mpg, because I was broke. Back in L.A. I couldn't breath. I visited friends but found the old familiar environment stifling. All I could think of was to hit the road back to Santa Fe. I wanted to get back to Santa Fe to be part of it. IT was the call of the wild. I brought back a movie camera since my still camera had been stolen from my car on my third night in town, which was a tragedy. I loved that camera. But what I really missed was the film and some of the pictures I'd taken in my first days. Fortunately, I do have the very first pictures I took in Santa Fe, and many others that would follow over the years.

Santa Fe fit me like an comfortable old shoe. Inexpensive, too, if material expectations were not high. The Café Beva on Water Street served a whole meal of liver and onions for $.75, fat Santa Fe flour tortillas were $.10 extra. Rents could commonly be anywhere from $25.00 to $75.00 per month for little adobes in great neighborhoods. In 1968 I was offered a house for sale on Camino Don Miguel for $3000.00. Later on, artist Eli Leven bought and remodeled that house. I obviously wasn't smart enough to see the coming changes.

In 1968 and '69 I roamed the north New Mexico villages and Taos, pho-

Photo by Dana Waldon

tographing the life there with the hippy invasion into the old Spanish villages. The Hog Farm and other communes were rich subject material, as well as the hot springs. I documented everything I could during these idealistic times of mixing cultures, outlaws, and social experimentation. A sometimes difficult thing to do, since the camera was a mistrusted material object to many. Local people hated it.

In late 1969, Sage, an alternative political lifestyle newspaper run by publisher Emil Hoffman hired me on as staff photographer. The office was located in a somewhat dilapidated part of Santa Fe on Guadalupe across from the old train depot. I now had a darkroom and felt complete. I went on all manner

Taxco, Mexico 2007.

of photo assignments, from the City Hall meetings, to the Republican Governors BBQ, to strip joints, and everything in between, I was doing what I had set out to do, and was where I wanted to be. There was never much money, but always somehow, just enough. Living in the larger-than-life landscape of New Mexico provided my needs, dreams and desires. It was indeed a love affair.

When Sage magazine finally folded in 1972, times got tougher. To survive I did odd jobs, literally dug ditches, sold firewood and got food stamps. The new Sunday flea market at the Yucca Drive-In, was a much anticipated opportunity to make some cash. Friends would scrounge all week for items to sell. These were the days when everything at the flea market was old, used, unwanted or unknown. Often there were real treasures amongst the junk. It seems to me now that the flea market was a great metaphor for rebirth. For me, it came with news of the next great trend which would change my life. Turquoise and Silver. All things Native American or Indian was a new vogue just beginning to sweep the nation, and Santa Fe sat at or near the epicenter. During the next few years, the frenzied excitement of activity surrounding the turquoise trade was akin to that of the gold rush of 1849. Literally overnight, many of us young neophytes who knew nothing became Indian traders. I teamed up with another starving artist and flea marketing friend, Richard Duchene. Together we pooled what monies we had (my Navajo rug and some money from his wife) into a respectable stash of silver and turquoise obtained from the Hock Shop and sources in Gallup, New Mexico. Our six month run to bust is a story of 'way over our heads'. We bought, sold, and mostly traded ourselves broke again in a wild spree that took us all the way to New York City, where we found older and better jewelry cheaper on Bleeker Street than in Gallup! It had been another rollicking adventure that left me disappointed and broker than ever, but wiser. The turquoise boom continued, whilst I sat sidelined, wondering what to do next.

A film production came to town and I was lucky to find work. "Catch My Soul" was a rock musical, and I decided to try one more stab at photography. I contacted *Rolling Stone Magazine* and offered my services. Editor Ben Fong Torres already had someone covering the story, but told me that if I wanted, I could submit the photos and story freelance. I photographed the scenes as best I could while doing odd jobs for the assistant art director, Tex Reed. Tex was one of the characters from my El Paso days, and he had once threatened to kill me in a jealous rage over a mutual girlfriend. Now, we were working together but his hatred lingered. Finally he fired me in a loud public display at company headquarters at the Inn of the Governors. Tex was greatly disturbed to see me back the next day, re-hired by the special effects director! When it all finally ended I had a lot of photos and a great story. I located a darkroom, bought supplies and went to work. After a week or so I realized the futility of the task. It was more than I could accomplish by myself, and it was all on speculation. I gave up and became somewhat depressed.

Friends and acquaintances were still active in the Indian trade. One day I visited a trader friend at his home and he had a guy sitting at an anvil with a bag of silver dimes, smashing them into buttons. It was then I realized "I CAN DO THIS!!!"

My 25th birthday was approaching and my girlfriend, Terry Hawn, was requesting gift ideas. I asked her to buy me a jeweler's saw and a sheet of copper. Cost $6.00. With this I began my jewelry making career. No background, no instruction, and not even with books. I found some steel, broken tools, and a hammer and began fashioning my first concho in thick copper sheet. It was crude. I showed it to a few people and they loved it! I traded that concho belt for a ratty old Navajo rug at the Thieves Market (now the Guadalupe Café). I was on my way! Cash began to flow with my next series of buttons in brass. My trader friend, Jeff Lewis, still has a few of them. Then came the first silver pieces, more tools and technique. Leo Hakola, of the Trader's Bazaar, took pity on me and taught me how to solder silver in a five minute lesson. My spirits were soaring, and I felt a sense of accomplishment as a silversmith. The silver and turquoise market was raging with unabated enthusiasm and demand. Mine wasn't genuine 'Indian made', but only the better stores cared so long as it looked good.

The 'Go-Go' years of the jewelry trade lasted until about 1977, and by that time I had mastered many techniques including stone cutting and carving, inlay and even some gold work. In Santa Fe, I already had established a good reputation and solid foundation. They were good times. When my love life crashed in 1977, along with a dwindling trading scene, I felt the need for change and accepted an offer to move to Navajo country near Gallup, to run a jewelry production shop, B.G. Mudd & Co., that offered new experiences, education, and a change of scenery. It was another dream of mine, since the old Navajo silversmiths were my heroes.

Always homesick for Santa Fe, my eighteen months near Gallup were another dimension. Santa Fe life was great, but had temporarily stagnated for me. Down there, the people were charged with a spirited vitality. It was the disco era. The diverse and widely scattered residents of the Gallup area included people imported from everywhere to work for Indian services. Nurses, doctors, teachers, traders, cowboys and Indians, native and newcomers—all ready to party. All the Navajo women had Farrah Fawcett hairdos and dancing was the rage. It was a truly surreal scene.

My work with the Indians enabled me to develop my design skills and learn production methods. The experience altered my level of thinking that would allow for me to someday produce greater volumes of high quality jewelry in my own business, rather than just one piece at a time. That opportunity would come towards the end of 1978 when the company slowed production to a yearend trickle and could not afford to pay me. I had to take jewelry instead of a final paycheck.

It was my thought at that time that I had had enough of making anything that resembled Indian jewelry. I am not Native American and no longer wanted to ever be asked if my jewelry was 'Indian made'. I knew that I wanted to produce items for volume sales using my new skills and build a product that would sell nationwide, even worldwide! Friends in the leather business indicated that great hardware for leather was hard to get. Also, great silver belt buckles were impossible to get. BINGO! The WESTERN genre buckle business sounded perfect for my next venture. Of course, I would design my way, my own contemporary style. Also there was no competition at the time.

Back in Santa Fe, a cool little pad came up for rent just as I was

Photo by Dana Waldon

At Turquoise Hill, 2006.

arriving and a friend Jim Manning was vacating. Located in the woods of Arroyo Hondo, it had served as home to at least one other jewelry maker. I referred to it as the Zen Bunkhouse. While I was setting up there, jewelry maker Valerie Fairchild invited me to work in her well-equipped studio in Tesuque. It was there that I worked and cast my first production buckles during a torrid love affair. The buckles were an instant success. The affair was not. I sold everything I produced, and was told by one veteran belt maker in Tucson that "these are the finest buckles I have ever had." I felt good about that. Some months later a large photo of that buckle appeared in a *Playboy* fashion article. I felt I was on my way, again.

Santa Fe has really been good to me. My business has continued and prospered. I own my own production studio and have produced many thousands of silver, gold, gemstone belt buckles, and also significant quantities of jewelry. I have always kept photography, film and video in my back pocket. Continuing to document the life around me with the goal that this will some day be a part of the historical record of the area. I even began a serious hobby of oil painting and the study of art. I've created hundreds of paintings and even sold many. Art has influenced my jewelry design and expanded those horizons.

I now work and live in my own compound near the center of town with the love of my life, Dana Waldon (photographer extraordinaire in her own right!), her son Dylan, dog Scout, and Lettuce the cat. And life is complete.

Oh yes, the turquoise gemstone mines. Since the middle 1980s, I have been privileged to own some of the oldest gemstone mines in North America. The turquoise mines on the Cerrillos District, located 17 miles south of Santa Fe, provided the gems most valued by the ancient Mixtec, Aztec, and Anazazi peoples. In the 1880s–90s, gem grade turquoise was mined from there for the Tiffany Co. Now it is my honor to use this rare material in my finest jewelry.

And I continue…

So, yes, I came to Santa Fe, and when I leave I will have left something of myself here.

Punk Monk Enters State of Enchantment
Willem Malten

Willem Malten, *well known as founder/owner of Cloud Cliff Cafe/Art Space, was instrumental in setting up the Northern New Mexico Organic Wheat Project. Also an activist and a filmmaker, Willem filmed and directed three highly acclaimed films: Staff of Life, Cry at the End of the 20th Century and Shipibo-Konibo..*

I T'S BEEN SO MUCH TIME—memory is starting to fade…or is it? Has it been lifetimes?

Moving in those days—was mainly a mental affair. Now, of course that would be different considering all the property and things that Santa Fe has gifted me with over the years. But at that time—the fall of 1983—there was not yet a noose of responsibilities and dead weight around my neck like that—I was free. Coming from the Zen Center in California I had just a couple of bags carrying all my belongings when I arrived in Albuquerque. In them were an odd mixture of Buddhist books, robes, an old brown leather vest (a little too small), some shirts from the Goodwill at Tassajara (always good stuff because of the quality of the guests that visited that Zen Resort in the Carmel Mountains), a hat, and curiously, a pair of black leather pants that I must have carried around from an even earlier previous life—coming of age in Amsterdam. Remnant of urban angst.

I wasn't hauling that much stuff, and after four years of sitting Zazen I was relatively free from preconceived notions as to where I was going. Frankly I had no idea other than some vague expectations that came from children's adventure books that dealt with Hopi children, Yazze and Kiwani, and the Wild West. Carl May and stuff.

Some months previously things had hit the fan in Tassajara Zen Mountain Center between Richard Baker Roshi and Paul Hawkins, and many others who played some role in the affair were affected. It has been written about elsewhere and it is not that important any longer to repeat the story here, other than to say that the whole tragedy had been a totally humbling experience for me personally.

In that situation I had to realize what Trungpa calls "Cutting through Spiritual Materialism." In the process of the Zen Center falling apart around me I realized that I had practiced Buddhism kind of as a carrier. Regardless of any of the deep yogic states of mind I may have been able to access sitting, day after day, on top of a black zafu—breathing in, breathing out, hour after hour, the thing about it was that I had a certain pride in them. And in having no hair, self-righteously having no property to worry about and meanwhile being a monk—it was like an addiction. All of these fantasies came tumbling down like a rain of bricks, as I lay hours on my futon staring at the wood ceiling of a cabin—way away from anywhere, while a palace coup was unfolding elsewhere on the grounds of the monastery.

Coinciding with Baker's loss of status as the Roshi, head monk and CEO of the Zen Center, somehow I had personally run into a wall. And I think that many monks and lay people alike felt like that, around that time. A sadness and desperation had taken hold of the sangha—much like we feel now about the war in Iraq.

The tensions were kind of brewing at a dangerous level in meeting after meeting within the closed monastery. It seemed that things could go wrong, very vague echoes of Jones town had started to resonate. I felt most concerned about Baker Roshi himself—whether justified or not—I thought that suicide was a real possibility and that would be the last thing that I wanted to see happen—the master committing hara-kari—imagine another stain on one's soul! So I sought him out in nightly meetings during his time, and my time, of need.

Why? In my case this was simple: Richard Baker and his Zen Center had provided a refuge for me, this intentional commune had welcomed me and re-formed me from an Amsterdam Punk with suicidal romantic notions, into a disciplined yogic monk, with a will and commitment to live. It taught me how to bake bread. I have always felt grateful to him for that.

William Malten on his arrival in
Santa Fe as the "Punk Monk", 1983.

Anyhow it was during this time that Baker brought up the possibility of going to Santa Fe and live in the Chorten on Cerro Gordo Road—a Tibetan stupa and Zen meditation room, next to what is now Upaya. The idea to live in a desert some 6,000 feet high sounded exotic. After all I was born some 12 feet below sea level.

Meanwhile during meditation I tried to visualize what I was going to do in Santa Fe. Finally, after years of Anthropology study in Amsterdam, and then years of meditation in California I felt ready for the challenge of stepping into the "real world" with no other protection than intent and energy. Practicing yes, but as an anonymous person in society. Yet it was totally unclear how or what things would manifest. This was a source of some anxiety and when that samsara was finally exhausted in meditation, suddenly an image came up in my mind. A Gate, and over that entrance way it said "Cloud Cliff." This was the seed.

Ungan (Cloud Cliff) asks his master: "What are all the hands and eyes of Avalokiteshvara all about?"

Tozan answers: "It is like groping for a pillow in the dark."

Ungan: "Oh....I understand now...."

Tozan:.... "How do you understand it....?"

Ungan: "All over the body there are eyes and there are hands."

Tozan: "You are almost right...."

Ungan: "What would you say, master?"

Tozan: "Throughout the body there are eyes and there are hands?"

I no longer wore my robe to the Zendo and I announced that I would leave the monastery after working as a baker during the summer guest season.

One day in early August I slipped out of the monastery and met Baker at the San Francisco Airport. This was going to be a re-connaissance trip into new territory.

After landing in ABQ, still morning, Richard Baker drove the rental car over the I-25 to Santa Fe. At that time—perhaps more so than now thanks to the recent years of more rain, the fragile hills along the I-25 looked like one step away from stone and sand desert. Really barren, punctuated by small piñons—like a giant kitty litter box.

Baker was thinking aloud about the possible health hazards that are associated with living in El Norte. He said to be careful with extra ultraviolet (now of course intensified by a thinning Ozone layer also) over a place like New Mexico, he wondered about food and water quality, And then, looking at the Jemez Mountains he said, "And in those mountains is Los Alamos, birthplace of the bomb that might carry some health risks as well."

Like so many of us moving to New Mexico at that time, I had no idea that living in a adobe new age Santa Fe meant being neighbors of the laboratories that produced the deadly weapons that befell on the people of Hiroshima and Nagasaki, and claimed so many indigenous peoples and others all over the world. A very shocking awakening. Still sitting in the car I made a vow to resist, expose and speak out against the nuclear mission like I do now. It has been one of the few vows I have been able to keep in my life, and it has drawn me closer to native people, to the earth, and to the life of Jesus.

The nuclear weapons mission is really the epitome of injustice, perpetual inequality, torture, destruction, terror and fear and death all rolled into one little ball of plutonium and controlled by very few members of the human race. Places like Los Alamos call forth tiny elites, effectively dictatorships. Think about it: genocidal weapons hollow out the very possibility of true democracy.

Thus the sacrifice that we make to keep hosting this genocidal machine on our soil goes much deeper than environmental or health abuse—it eats away at our souls. We become unable to take care of each other, unable to commit to a different future, slavishly believing that the federal money that comes with the labs is the only way to economically survive in New Mexico. Dead inside. Let's wake up to the lie of New Mexico, throw those lying clowns out of office, unmask the hideous nature of Bechtel and Lockheed Martin, Invest locally, become carbon neutral, become nuclear free and gain some self respect in the process. It started here—let's stop it here. Land of Enchantment can no longer mean "State of Delusion."

What Enchantment means is to endow everything with song and make it sacred.

William Malten as the dedicated and responsible filmmaker, entrepreneur and socially responsible smiling guru of the Cloud Cliff Restaurant & Art Space, 2007.

We Came to Santa Fe
Tom Margittai & Richard Tang

Tom Margittai is a Holocaust survivor, a noted restaurateur with an international reputation, a bon vivant as well as a noted story teller whose partner, Richard Tang is a consummate artist in terms of both sculpture and jewelry with an international clientele.

IN THE SPRING OF 1988 I turned 60 and my thoughts wandered to another spring afternoon a long time ago.

It was Sunday March 19, 1944, a pleasant early spring day in my home city of Budapest. Strolling on Elizabeth Ring Road I saw an endless column of German tanks with heads of German soldiers sticking out. My 15th birthday was less than a month away but I knew instantly that my life had changed forever.

I ran all the way home but my parents already knew from the radio that the Germans occupied Hungary. The weeks that followed brought law after law curtailing the freedom and every right known to man of the Jews in Hungary. Rumors of mass deportations from the countryside were rampant, and plans how to escape that fate were made by my parents.

My father bought false birth certificates and identity papers for himself, my mother and me. We were going to separate and live in different parts of Hungary under assumed names. I was to go to a large estate of friends where I was going to be known as a recently orphaned youth from Budapest. Being an only child, never separated from my home or parents, I refused to cooperate and my parents had to cancel their plans as well as a consequence.

During those troubled and nerve wrecking weeks following the occupation I was recruited to work as a courier at the headquarters of the Jewish Community Council where the Gestapo and the SS made daily appearances with demands and edicts. I possessed inside knowledge, most of it horrifying, of what was going on. One of the things I learned was that there was a secret "rescue committee" headed by a Zionist journalist called Rezso Kasztner who was negotiating with Adolph Eichman, head of the Gestapo, to ship a large transport of Jews to Palestine via a neutral country such as Spain or Portugal. I offered this solution to my father who managed against great odds and a pledge of foreign funds to become part of this transport.

The Kasztner train, as it became later known, which left Budapest on June 30 with high hopes and 1,842 people contained many prominent Hungarian Jewish families, intellectuals, writers, journalists, religious leaders, industrialists, etc. It was like all other deportation trains, empty freight cars with 30 to 40 people crammed into each car but with the difference that doors were not sealed. The train made frequent stops in the countryside for calls of nature and to take water.

The journey to Bergen Belsen, where Eichman decided to put us "on ice" lasted 10 days. The stay, with all the horrors of a German concentration camp, lasted almost five months. Kasztner's negotiations resulted in our arrival of the group almost intact on December 3, 1944 in Switzerland which made sure that in August 1945, end of the hostilities concluded, we left our temporary asylum there and were transported by the British (as promised by the allies) to Palestine. There is a vast library of literature of this group's history written over the years as well as the assassination of Rezso Kasztner, as an alleged traitor, in Israel in 1955. A brand new comprehensive book on the subject by Anna Porter in Toronto is awaiting publication this summer.

My first three years in Palestine were spent in learning the language, a trade (diamond cleaving), and being called to arms in 1947 to fight the first Israeli-Arab war.

In 1950 I came to my adopted city. I had been living and working in New York City, with a couple of interruptions, in the hospitality trade for 38 years culminating in the ownership of the Four Seasons Restaurant in the Seagram Building. Which brings me back to my musings in 1988.

The restaurant business is a very intense and time consuming profession. You get to work in the morning like everybody else but do not break for lunch. Lunch is your busiest two hours. You do your accumulated chores in the afternoon and in the evening you get busy again with your customers, supervise your kitchens and your staff, and it is late night by the time you get to bed. In addition New York winters started getting to me and I thought a second home in a better climate where I could spend a couple of months during the winters and regenerate my system would be a good solution. I decided on California, San Diego in particular, and La Jolla as a preference, and scoured the area for a suitable abode.

As providence would have it two things occurred.

In 1986 my best friend, Marvin Sloves, Chairman of an advertising agency bought a house in Santa Fe and insisted over the next year or so that I come visit and see it. In the summer of 1988 on my way to yet another trip to La Jolla, I stopped for three days in Santa Fe.

It was love at first sight, from the incredible cloud formations to the green desert, it was a place I wanted to be. After three days, when I left for La Jolla,

Richard Tang and Tom Margittai at the great doors of their house in Santa Fe.

I made an offer on a house I saw on the north side and by the time I checked in at La Valencia, my offer was accepted, and I started coming for short periods of time to Santa Fe.

The second occurrence, shortly thereafter, was my meeting my future partner, Richard Tang, in New York. Richard, after visiting Santa Fe, expressed the desire to live here. He moved here in 1993. I kept spending more time here, commuting to my business as best I could.

In 1995 the President of Seagram, Edgar Bronfman Jr., made an offer to buy the restaurant I could not refuse, and *voila,* here I am.

I might add to say!

Richard Tang is on outstanding artist well known for his classic jewelry and his ceramic sculptures, Chinese calligraphy and paintings. His Chinese heritage brings a sensitivity to his work that is both forcefully unique and delicate. His jewelry studio is on the top floor of our guesthouse and his ceramics are done in an all window framed floor addition. My own working space is a small study next to the master bedroom where I maintain contacts and friendships I have made all over the world of art, literature, finance, hotel, and the fine dining worlds. There are many proverbs in many languages that address the pleasure of having found peace and accomplishment after long and hazardous journeys. Each of those proverbs are applicable to our lives.

Tom Margittai
on his arrival in
Santa Fe in 1985.

How I Came to Santa Fe
Nedra Matteucci

Nedra Matteucci, a native New Mexican who treasures the people and cultural traditions of the state, has focused on celebrating the arts of the region through her ownership of three premier fine art and antiquity galleries in Santa Fe. An avid art collector, Nedra gives generously of her time and energies to institutions including the Georgia O'Keeffe Museum, the Museum of New Mexico, the Santa Fe Opera and numerous local public education programs in the arts, including ArtSmart. She has caringly supported the efforts of the Santa Fe Animal Shelter and numerous other local charity organizations such as, Aid and Comfort while serving as a director of First State Bancorporation and as a member and former President of the New Mexico Amigos.

I'M FORTUNATE TO HAVE CALLED New Mexico "home" all of my life. Growing up in Southern New Mexico in the quiet, close knit town of Dexter, I've enjoyed solid, life long friendships and my family has never been far. Being a fourth generation New Mexican, I love being able to travel the state for business, finding so many friends and familiar faces. I even get to do business with my high school roommates from my years in El Paso at Loretto Academy.

From the agricultural and ranching traditions that kept life simple and in rhythm with the seasons, life also had clarity and kept business straightforward, something I took with me as I made my way north to Albuquerque. I was struck by the new energy of a big city and the vibrant campus at the University of New Mexico. But amid this dynamic, the remarkable history of New Mexico was brought into focus, and for me, the instrument through which it was revealed, was unquestionably, the amazing arts tradition in New Mexico.

The University is where I met my husband, Richard. It also became clear to me that I was not only New Mexican, but somehow, I must be Italian, too!

Richard had his own sense of design and love for art that, yes, I think runs in his Italian veins. Between the two of us, finding a work of art to bring home was beyond par with a new piece of furniture. We loved it. Latin American prints, paintings by early Albuquerque artists and some of the younger painters making their mark on the local art scene found space on our walls.

By then I began to make what would become one of hundreds, maybe thousands of treks further north, to Santa Fe. Richard sold his Anheuser-Bush distributorship and I had to get serious about work; for me that meant becoming a student of the art business beyond collecting. In 1983, I took a part-time job at Fenn Galleries in Santa Fe. I don't think I took that drive back to Albuquerque whole-heartedly ever again.

I was fascinated by the layers of the gallery business and poured over auction catalogues, tucked away in the gallery's wonderful art library where part of Forrest's collection of Indian artifacts surrounded me. I met collectors from around the world and found the sales challenge to be exciting. I took chances on historical paintings as I eventually began selling those early purchases made in Albuquerque—the proverbial "trunk show period," meaning the trunk of my car! I traveled the state buying and selling art but realized that not only did I need roots, but my young business needed a place where it could be nurtured and grow, as well. There was no question that Santa Fe was where I wanted to be.

Nedra Matteucci, 1981.

I humbly opened my first gallery *Nedra Matteucci Fine Art* at the bottom of historic Canyon Road, near where the very first artists to settle in Santa Fe built their adobe homes and studios in the early 1900's, igniting the art community that continues to flourish today. It seemed that beyond every corner there was a piece of Santa Fe's rich artistic history that resonated within me, prompting me to build my first home in the foothills, just below the landmark Cross of the Martyrs.

In 1988, with a stable of talented artists and a growing historical collection of my own that now included Spanish and Native American antiques, Richard and I purchased the *Fenn Galleries*. I felt that the beautiful gardens of the gallery could celebrate the growing monumental sculpture market and so I opted to make them more accessible. I brought in several key, contemporary artists to complement the gallery's solid and respected offerings of historic American and Southwestern paintings and *Nedra Matteucci Galleries* has grown yearly since our inception. The clients, dear friends and experiences I've had through the gallery have shaped my life, affording me the opportunity to participate in Santa Fe's civic and charitable community for two decades, one of my great rewards.

I had always considered *Morning Star* the paragon of Native American galleries and it stood in a beautiful historic adobe on Canyon Road,

Nedra Matteucci, 2002.

next to our present home in Santa Fe. We were able to purchase the gallery in 2002 and it added an entirely new dimension to my existing galleries. I personally became more involved in collecting Native American artifacts and especially love the form and design of historic pueblo pottery. But if anything, my collection is eclectic—almost beyond description. I can find the artistic beauty in the most mundane of tools, even having a collection of over 100 antique Guatemalan slingshots.

But my first and greatest love in art remains the historic paintings of New Mexico, and this reflects where I live and work—my beloved Santa Fe. As I prepare to celebrate my 25th year here, I can think of no other place as wondrous and beautiful to call home.

❖ ❖ ❖

Nedra Matteucci today.

I Came to Santa Fe
Maryann McGraw

Maryann McGraw *manages the State Wetlands Program for the New Mexico Environment Department. She is on the Board of the Association of State Wetland Managers and is also a member of the Environmental Protection Agency's National Wetlands Monitoring Workgroup. Presently she is working on a book about New Mexico wetlands. Maryann paints en plein air in pastel, concentrating on New Mexico's scenic vistas and how time and seasonal changes affect those places. She serves on the board of the Pastel Society of New Mexico as Treasurer. Maryann has been a volunteer driver for Kitchen Angels of Santa Fe for the past 10 years.*

Prelude

It took about a year
To get used to the idea
Leaving Tucson.
But the opportunity presented itself
To him and to us,
Once in a lifetime.

Leaving this sacred place
Where my children were born,
And also my friends
 Javalina,
  Desert tortoise,
   Gila monster.

continued

Keeping watch over hummingbird's eggs
While their mother performed her solitary duty
Catching tiny bugs
Where coyotes stretch their legs
Sleeping like favorite dogs.

Leaving clear skies
Where telescope eyes
On mountaintops
View paths across the universe
While capturing a moment
Of stars and galaxies.

Leaving behind Indian feet
Running unharmed by cactus spines
Elf owl dances in
The circus of desert nights and
The fragrance of cereus flowers.

No more checking for
Edward Abbey at Allsups
Running in front of big wheels
Rescuing ancient cacti
Spilling Eegees
Quietly laughing in excitement
Of a mid-night poor-will dance.

Simple to understand how
Lives are formed by the land
We live in.

And then came the time to go
To this new place in New Mexico.

FOR THE RECORD

I have lived my entire adult life in the southwest, and I have cherished all of the places that I have lived. My story may be a little different from the rest because I am one of those beings that commutes daily to Santa Fe from outside the city, and the city has had a profound influence on my New Mexico life. My husband John, my two sons Tom and Daniel and I moved to New Mexico in 1993. John is a Professor of Astronomy at the University of New Mexico and his daily life is entwined with the campus in Albuquerque. We live part way between Albuquerque and Santa Fe in Placitas. Because I spend about 75% of my waking hours in Santa Fe, my dear friend Victor di Suvero thought I belonged in this book.

HOW I GOT TO SANTA FE

I always fall in love with the places where I live. However, when John announced that he received a job offer full of opportunity in New Mexico, I was not altogether happy with the thought of leaving Tucson. I had grown very fond of Tucson and the Sonoran Desert landscape in which we lived and I was fully engaged in the community, schools and the environment. How could anything be better?

Wetlands restoration activities at the Leonard Cartin Wetland Preserve, located just south of Santa Fe with Maryann (left) participating.

I reluctantly spent time fixing our house up for sale, while cherishing the minutes and watching our remaining year unfold in Tucson, trying to remember each nuance of the desert and hoping my children would remember this unique part of their lives. We made trips to the Albuquerque area and central New Mexico. It was OK, but where were the saguaros and palo verde trees?

So when it was time to relocate, I packed up a trailer full of enormous cacti, succulents and other bits of my life from the desert and decided to take the desert with me. We hooked the trailer to our car, separate from the moving van with our regular belongings. We moved to a wonderful home in the high mountains on the north side of the Sandias and I spread our cherished desert flora around the outside of our new home. After all, it was still quite warm — in August.

It was nice, but what was I going to do here? I spent my earliest days in New Mexico exploring, longing for that feeling that I belong here. The piñon-juniper savannah of the foothills of the Sandias is quite serene, quite unlike the cacophony on a Sonoran Desert morning. I was taken by the magnificent views of the sky from our mountain home, vistas that stretched for miles in any direction. That first month, I would regularly look to the sky for connection to something. One day, while carefully inspecting my cactus garden, I heard a faint beeping sound. Where was it coming from? It disappeared and then I heard it again. Was there a car show somewhere in the valley below? Was it children or chickens? Then I heard it again, but this time lots of beeps and honks at the same time. This required some further investigation. Wherever I went it sounded the same.

Then I looked up to my new friend, the New Mexico sky. Straining to see I saw a faint V-shape wobbling against the clear blue. As I looked more and more, I saw many of these V-shapes slowly heading in a southerly direction. And then, one especially large V-shape had a white dot on the tail end of one of the V's arms. The faint honking and beeping appeared to be coming from these V-shapes. I ran in to the house to get my binoculars. Flocks of sandhill cranes were flying right over my house in formation catching a ride and lift on the mountain thermals. The little white dot was a lone whooping crane trailing at the end of a flock — relegated to the rear as an outsider. My heart sang with joy at the site of the magnificent birds on their journey to somewhere, at the time I did not know.

The Sandhill Cranes that brought me to Santa Fe.

This was the sign I was looking for. From that day forward, I called New Mexico my home.

Little did I know at the time that those cranes were on their way to their winter wetland home just south of Socorro. Later that year I started working in Santa Fe as an environmental specialist for the State of New Mexico and as time went on New Mexico's precious water resources and wetlands became the focus of my efforts. Even my commute to Santa Fe allows me to study the landscape as it changes with the changing weather and seasons. In Santa Fe, I have made many close friends and allies with the same passion for wetlands and the environment and have been exposed to other disciplines that further my intimacy with the landscape such as plein air painting.

My heart still sings about New Mexico, and until water runs uphill it always will.

I
once
walked
in the woods when
rain fell
Rivulets of water
ran where I walked
Water fell
from the branches
blowing where the wind
rushed
And the water
wept from seeps
and winks
And leaves and debris
keep
the water winding
down the deep
where waters sleep.

Maryann standing next to the New Mexico Environment Department Wetlands booth at H₂O 2005 Water Festival at the Center for Contemporary Arts in Santa Fe.

We Came to Santa Fe
James McMath & Sabine Steinhardt

James McMath and Sabine Steinhardt are co-owners of the Emerald Earth Shop - a retail business which specializes in natural health and eco-friendly products. Emerald Earth is also the "First EM Retail Shop in America." EM stands of Effective Microorganisms, a certified organic product which naturally detoxifies and restores the health of the micro-ecosystems—whether it be for the soil, water, plant, animal or human levels. Their motto is "Nature Does it Best!"

James McMath

MY STORY IS A BIT DIFFERENT than Sabine's. My roots are here in Santa Fe. Although I wasn't born in New Mexico, my father and grandfather were. My great-grandfather, James, moved to Raton in the early 1870's to open a creamery. Keep in mind, this was still a part of the Wild West, when New Mexico was a large territory—long before joining the Union.

After my great-grandfather died, my grandmother was eager to take all of the kids back to Indiana. But that didn't stop my grandfather, also James, from taking his new bride to northern New Mexico. Here, he became the caretaker of the large ranch estate called "Vermejo Ranch." This was the famous Chandler Ranch (the Chandler's also owned the *Los Angeles Times).* Chandler would take his Hollywood friends, people like Clark Gable, Greta Garbo, Will Rogers, Spencer Tracy, Katherine Hepburn, and the like, to his wilderness ranch for fishing and hunting expeditions. My grandfather served as their host and tour guide—and thus became close friends with many of the celebrities.

Eventually, my grandfather was made managing editor for several New Mexico newspapers owned by Chandler. From this important position, he became a champion for progressive and environmental causes. Once New Mexico became a state in 1912, he went on to become a state legislator. My father, who was born in Wagon Mound, can remember Grandpa presiding at the opening ceremonies of the newly-constructed Federal Courthouse Building in Santa Fe.

I can remember coming to visit my grandparents in northern New Mexico when I was only five years old. While touring the Indian Market at the Santa Fe Plaza, I can remember holding my grandfather's hand and earnestly looking up and proclaiming, *"You know, Grandpa, some day I'm going to live here in Santa Fe."* At first, my grandfather looked down at me with amazement, and then a proud smile slowly grew on his face.

In many ways, I am a great deal like my grandfather, James McMath. He used to say, *"You know, G.O.D. stands for the Great Out Doors! And that's the place where I worship!"* As far back as I can remember, people used to refer to me as the "nature freak." I went camping as often as I could. And I loved taking friends along to experience the *great-out-doors!* Although I grew up in northern California, I always knew that some day I'd end up in Santa Fe. After being a successful city administrator for many years in Portland, Oregon, I up and decided it was time to move home to Santa Fe about 20 years ago—just about the same time that Sabine decided to move here.

Jim McMath in 1989 when he moved to Santa Fe for good.

It's no wonder that Sabine and I have a "natural living shop" here in Santa Fe. We love hearing the numerous stories from our customers about the many health benefits obtained from the natural microbial products we sell. For us, its time to take it to the next step and begin demonstrating how to live sustainably with integrated water, energy, and green building designs.

What better place than Santa Fe to discover new and innovative ways of living. Our high desert climate is a strong motivator for responsible water conservation and recycling systems. Our bright sunny skies inspire inventive solutions for clean and renewable energy systems. And the ancient, earthen architecture of the area beautifully demonstrates how to naturally optimize our solar designs. What better place than Santa Fe to truly start building "ecovillages"!

Sabine Steinhardt

MOST OF ALL, I CAN REMEMBER how much I wanted to leave the bleak, gray, and crowded land of Germany, where I was born. Shortly after my 30th birthday, I was ready to take the leap. I sold everything that I had, bought a backpack and a sub-zero sleeping bag, and secured a plane ticket for Vancouver, Canada. Finally, I was on my way to America — ready to simply get away and find some peace and quiet.

It was the end of January, and I decided to take a housesitting position for a couple seeking to escape the deep winter snows of Canada for the warm sunny skies of Mexico. I traveled by bus about 600 miles inland through British Columbia. I had never seen such wide-open country, uninterrupted by villages and people. My housesitting job was to last until May.

Here, I hoped to find the peace and solitude that I sought. I began my venture by reading a number of books that I found in their library. This is how I learned more English — far more than what I had learned in school. I would

Sabine on her arrival in Santa Fe in 1992.

look up the words that I didn't know from my tiny travel dictionary. Each night I would cuddle up and read next to the warm glowing fire where it was very safe and cozy inside—with deep snow and strange, unusual animal noises outside.

I enjoyed being by myself in the middle of nowhere. It was a new experience not seeing any night lights from the neighbors—as the closest village was a half hour walk away. Each morning, I would go through my set of rituals. I would wake up to a cold house, rush outside and carry in the wood. Then I'd quickly build a blazing fire in the woodstove. Next, I'd rush in the bathroom and take a hot steaming shower. Then I'd briskly stroll into the kitchen and brew a warm cup of coffee. The quiet and solitude was great for awhile. But by May, I was ready to return to civilization—as the snow was still knee-deep outside.

Now I was ready to see the beautiful Pacific coastline that I had heard so much about. I had booked a round trip bus tour for Baja when I first arrived—but alas, that tour was no longer available by May. They did, however, offer a 10-day round trip excursion to the desert southwest. So off I went on the "Green Turtle Bus Tour," which departed from San Francisco for the destinations of Canyon de Chelly, Shiprock, and the Grand Canyon. I was in awe of the desert with its bright sunny skies and grand open spaces. On the trip, I befriended a fellow German from Berlin named Karin, who also wanted to explore the open spaces of America. So, in returning to San Francisco, we decided to join forces and explore together.

At first, we considered buying a used car. But then we discovered a flyer offering "drive away cars." For the price of gas, our job was to deliver new cars to specified locations around the country. Sounded perfect. So we picked up our first car, which was to be delivered to Los Angeles. Finally, I had my chance to see the beautiful Pacific coastline, as we slowly drove down the very curvy and scenic Highway 1. Then we were offered a delivery from LA to Portland and, of course, another opportunity to drive along the beautiful coastal routes. Once in Portland, we picked up a brand new silver Mercedes Benz that a doctor wanted to give to his son in Atlanta as a present. Another opportunity to see the grand expanses of America, so off we went in style—sun roof, air conditioning, padded leather seats…the works!

We wanted to see the southwest again, so we headed straight for New Mexico. By the time we arrived in Taos, we were dead-tired and were ready for a real bed. We stayed at the Plum Tree Hostel in Pilar. Then we immediately took advantage of the hot tub, went swimming in the Rio Grande, and had our first New Mexican food at the Mainstreet Bakery in Taos. Once fully rested, we decided to head south for Santa Fe. Coming up the final hilltop, we had our first panoramic view of Santa Fe—spanning before us like an island on the ocean's edge. It was magical! Our first destination, of course, was the city plaza that we'd heard so much about. Now this was my kind of town! Charming, peaceful, narrow winding roads, and beautiful earthen architecture.

I decided to look up an old friend from Germany, Michael, who used to date my sister. A friendly mailman at the Main Post Office offered to help me locate Michael. The postman had just started his route and let me follow behind—where he led me up to the Santa Fe Ski Basin. This is where Michael worked and lived. After a few directions from employees, I was shown where he lived.

James and Sabine still smiling after all these years—2006.

James and Sabine in front of their store The Emerald Earth Shop in Santa Fe 2007.

Michael was totally surprised when I showed up at his doorstep! After his shock slowly wore off, Michael suggested that we go to the Ore House for dinner. This is where I had my first chips and salsa and a margarita! We were sitting on the balcony overlooking the Plaza and I was feeling right at home! I loved the feel of Santa Fe. Much like my memories of Greece—a desert town having an ocean feel with its bright blue skies. Very charming. Lots of history. Karin and I decided to stay an extra day and explore more of its festive galleries, enchanting museums, and colorful foods! It was difficult leaving the following day, but I promised to come back—and I did, as soon as we delivered our car in Atlanta!

That was over 20 years ago. I've since grown to love everything about Santa Fe. Its colorful seasons. Its bright, sunny skies. Its ancient traditions. Its year-round festivities. I love hiking my favorite trails. Visiting my favorite restaurants. Exploring the Farmer's Market. Celebrating opening night at the opera with our delectable tailgate parties. Swapping stories of renewed health and revitalization at our Emerald Earth Natural Living Shop. And seeing the passion in Jim's eyes, as he envisions a world living in peace and balance.

With every seed that is sown in my garden, I feel more and more rooted in this special place called Santa Fe. I now realize that Santa Fe was calling me from far away, across the seas, to a place quite the opposite from where I grew up—to a place that I now love calling "home"!

A Confluence of Events
Donald & Barbara Meyer

Donald Meyer, *noted lawyer and outstanding public servant has been recognized and honored by the City of Santa Fe and the State of New Mexico for his successful and dedicated community service and is fortunate to be married to* **Barbara,** *jewelry artist and community activist. They live their lives in Santa Fe when not traveling to visit children and maintain their many contacts on the East and West coasts.*

DONALD: **AFTER A 36 YEAR SUCCESSFUL,** yet stressful, legal practice, specializing in civil litigation, in New Orleans, during which time I underwent a triple bypass at the age of 44, was married and divorced, had two wonderful children, and was the day to day operating partner of a theatrical and entertainment company which presented touring Broadway shows and other events at the major cultural venue in the city as well as the Superdome. Being heavily engaged in chairing arts and cultural non-profit boards, I was advised by my cardiologist to "slow down." Being an A+ personality, I found this difficult to accept, but realizing the potential consequences of not doing so, I retired from the practice of law and moved to Santa Fe in 1990, having first been here for a few days in 1956 and having spent extensive periods of time here in the 1980s as a tourist.

BARBARA: I had lived in Miami, Florida for more than 36 years where I raised a son and daughter as a single mother and started, ran, merchandised and marketed a very successful retail store. I had computerized monogramming machinery and most things in the store were embroidered. The store also took in outside work for Bloomindales, some prominent men's stores, and did logo work for race car drivers and other events going on in the city. This kept me busy 15 hours a day, six days a week. I still played competitive tennis, went on 50-mile bike rides, sailed on the weekends, fished, and took as many art courses as I could fit into my available time. In the back of my mind I knew I needed to continue enhancing my skills as a sculptor and ceramicist. This was a goal I had continued working on for 35 years.

I was involved in community non-profit organizations, but my proudest achievement was being an active participant in a start up group of women who began an experiment called "1000 Plus." Our only goal was to raise money for cancer research by having each woman raise at least $1,000 per person per year for cancer. It became a successful movement in Miami with each member trying to "out-raise" each other.

In 1992 after my children were married and Hurricane Andrew had destroyed my home, I made a decision that I wanted to pursue my art full time in some location other than south Florida. I had previously visited Santa Fe and knew from my first visit, that I HAD to live here. The sky, the light, the mountains, and the spiritual calling of the land formed my future direction. The second half of my life was going to be for me to live to my fullest. I rented a furnished house over the telephone, sight unseen, with a one-year lease in 1992. I thought I would give it a one-year trial.

BARBARA AND DONALD: In October 1990, I was hired as Executive Director of the Western States Art Federation (WESTAF) and shortly thereafter Barbara moved permanently to Santa Fe. My Director of Development at WESTAF met Barbara at a party the week she came to Santa Fe. My director told me I should meet Barbara since we were both Southerners, both tennis players, both involved in the arts, both community involved, and both of us were of the same religion. At a social gathering, Barbara and I finally met each other, but at the time I was living with a very young woman, and was not looking for another relationship. Barbara said as far as she was concerned, I was as good as married and she did not want to get into a relationship that would take time away from her art. We saw each other at numerous art openings and social occasions during the next few years, but nothing more significant than that.

In mid-1995, WESTAF moved its offices from Santa Fe to Denver, Colorado. I was not interested in moving, so I stayed in Santa Fe. At approximately the same time, the woman I was living with decided to move to California.

Shortly thereafter, I called Barbara and said, "I may be five years too late, but what are you doing for dinner tonight?" Hearing I was "single" again, she accepted the invitation and the rest is history. After a period of time, we eloped with the blessings of our four grown children and were married in the cave on top of the mountain above Rancho de San Juan on August 23, 1997. Barbara wore a large brimmed white hat, which I had bought for the occasion at the Saratoga Race Track in Upstate New York while I was there on a business trip. We both wore blue jeans and she had a blue satin garter that her kids sent for the wedding, on the outside leg of her jeans. We drank fine champagne as the sun set and toasted a glorious new beginning for two middle-aged lovers.

Our life together has been full. Maintaining our commitments to community work in non-profits, sitting on the Board of Directors of SITE Santa Fe with Barbara being on its Foundation Council, staying involved for 13 years on the Santa Fe Railyard Community Corporation Board of Directors and its

Barbara Meyer then.

Donald Meyer then.

Barbara and Donald Meyer today.

current Vice President, being involved as a member of the College of Santa Fe Board of Advisors, the United States Post Office Board of Advisors, and also sitting on the Citizen Board of Advisors to Blue Cross and Blue Shield of New Mexico. I have been the Chairman and on the Board of Directors of the Santa Fe Arts Commission and in 2003 was a recipient of the Santa Fe Mayor's Arts Award.

We built a studio for Barbara on the grounds of our home and now she is a full time artist specializing in sculptural, one-of-a-kind, hand fabricated gold and silver jewelry. She markets her own work and shows in galleries across the United States. She has produced jewelry shows in Santa Fe with jewelers from across the country participating.

We love Santa Fe and continue to be involved in the community and hope that we have given back to our adopted city as much, if not more, than it has given and continues to give us.

Santa Fe, By Way of Russia
Bruce Moss

Retired publishing company executive, world traveler, successful novelist and Dante aficionado. **Bruce Moss** *calls Santa Fe home when not traveling to Italy where various parts of his many lives still thrive and inform his appreciation of Santa Fe.*

IN THE SUMMER OF 1993 I flew from New York, where I lived and worked, to spend a couple of weeks with my son, who was a Junior at the University of Colorado in Boulder. We rented a car and drove down Route 285 to Santa Fe, where we stayed with an old friend, Louisiana Longwell, who had a ranch at that time in Pojoaque at the base of the *barrancas*. I was staggered by what seemed infinite space on both sides of Route 285—so impressive after closed-in Manhattan with its glimpses of sky between overhead ramparts. In retrospect I know the landscape reminded me of San Antonio, where I had spent eight months at Fort Sam Houston as a medic in the '60's, where for the first time I saw what sky was.

On the drive back up to Boulder I decided that sooner or later this would be where I would live, if I could find a way. In New York I had a lucrative job, a newly bought six-room apartment in a great old building, and was in the middle of a fiery relationship after my divorce five years earlier. Yet I had a vision—I am not prone to visions—that the Southwest was where I would be able to grow, spread my putative folded wings, as if my life so far had been a pupa stage or chrysalis, and it was time to break out. But could I? I had just begun writing a dark, comic novel on the New York advertising world after a year of evenings in the Columbia Writing Program, and I couldn't see how I could fit the American Southwest into my future.

By a year later, much had changed. The downward slide of my company's fortunes—and my job of 20 years—turned into a plunge when the company was sold as if for scrap...by 1994 advertising was no longer being bought and sold as it had been for decades. With my pay package cut in half, I could no longer afford the mortgage for my apartment, and as if on cue the cooling relationship I had been trying to keep alive hit the wall toward which it had been heading for months. It was time to opt for a severance package, rent out my apartment (with the co-op's permission, no sure thing), and hope for a turn in the real estate market, considering the extravagant money I'd sunk into its improvements two years earlier.

By this time I was exhausted. The East Coast was beginning to remind me of all things dead: my job, my divorce, my relationship, my apartment. If I was going to survive I was going to have to go West, I told myself. But my ex-wife's brother—my ex-brother-in-law—had another idea.

Three years earlier, Walter had settled in Moscow after spending a year in Santa Fe near his sister Janet—my ex-sister-in law—who had moved to Santa Fe in the '70's. Walter had been with Phillips in the oil business for some years, both in Alaska and doing seismographic exploration work in the Gulf. A world traveler, one day in 1991, Walter ran into a Russian in a bar in Bangkok who told him that with Yeltsin opening things up in the defunct Soviet Union, there were all *kinds* of opportunities there. Specifically, in the oil industry. He explained to Walter that the Western oil majors wanted to get in on developing Russian mineral resources—and the Russians needed them, at least for the time being—but without an organized personnel infra-structure of scientists and technicians to present to the West there existed no way for the Yeltsin government to make it happen. Walter took the next flight from Bangkok to New York, bought a couple of used PC computers, flew to Moscow, hired an interpreter, and within a couple of weeks was seated before a half dozen of Yeltsin's ministers, explaining how he was uniquely qualified to set up a data base of Russian scientists and technicians from whom West-ern oil companies could draw employees (the Russians naturally insisted that the oil majors employ only Russians). Walter would build the data base in a form that the Western companies—not only oil companies—could use in the future, providing a basis for all future international business dealings. Wal-ter walked away with a two year exclusive contract for his fledgling company, whose name he had conjured on the flight to Moscow: *Eurospan.*

Walter wanted me to come to Moscow to go in with him on a project. He had an idea for a hardware distribution center in Kaliningrad, the old Prussian Baltic city of Koenigsberg (home of Immanuel Kant), which in Soviet days had been the super secret and closely-guarded warm-water headquarters of the Soviet Baltic Fleet. In the postwar years this once sophisticated city, with its highly complex 100-year-old system of hydraulically engineered canals had been allowed to fall into complete ruin. In fact, raw sewage ran through the streets in places. Ever the optimistic entrepreneur, Walter called this the ideal ground-floor opportunity. All we had to do was round up U.S. investors. The Germans were already moving in with their mighty Deutschmarks.

But it soon became clear that every known (and unknown) Kaliningrad official, from the mayor on down, would not move a constantly redefined and fluctuating inch if their palms weren't first crossed with impressive quantities of silver…best deposited in foreign bank accounts.

Bruce Moss boating in Italy on Lake Como on his way to Venice, 1992.

Back in Moscow, Walter tried to interest me in joining Eurospan anyway. I was flattered, but could not for the life of me figure out where I, an ex-advertising man whose interest was in writing novels—including one I was now in the middle of—would fit into his company, assuming I wanted to. Could I live in the Arbat, Moscow's quickly reviving Bohemian district, and write novels by moonlight?

Walter decided to introduce me to some of the "ex-pats"—especially female ex-pats—to whet my interest and show me that Moscow rocks. He took me to lunch at the trendy Restaurant Santa Fe to show me that I could have the Southwest in Moscow if I so desired. With its meticulously-copied adobe-esque walls covered with Navajo rugs, its vigas and its saltillo tile floors, and its menu straight out of Maria's or Tomasita's, it was a kind of Disney World mirage. He invited five attractive young female ex-pats of his acquaintance—one beauty from South Africa caught my eye—to join us. The ladies soon began complaining that the *male* ex-pats dated only Russian women, leaving them stranded, at which point I asked why they, then, didn't date Russian men. Silence. "We don't *do* Russian men," one said; they all agreed that Russian men were prone to drunkenness and violence, and tended to bathe rarely… obviously poor romantic prospects. I later got into a conversation with the Santa Fe's manager, their fifth in two years. He was an American, and I asked him about the surprising manager turnover rate. "They were all shot," he said. He explained that everyone from mob bosses to street hoodlums wanted a piece of the restaurant profits, selling protection. The tricky part was telling the real muscle from the street bums, the real from the fake. If you paid everybody you'd be bankrupt. Yet if you made a mistake and brushed off a mob envoy—the real McCoy—it was generally fatal, life in Russia—and bullets—being cheap. I asked him in a friendly way why he thought he would be more successful than his predecessors. "You've got to have the instinct—the intuition. I've got it, and I can read these guys," he said. "I can tell the difference between run-of-the-mill con artists off the street—the ones you ignore—and the genuine article—the enforcers you pay. It's a survival skill." He seemed quite sure of himself, and I wished him luck.

A few days later, late for my return flight, I was sprinting around barriers and butting ahead of clumps of patient passengers to reach a remote gate in Moscow's airport. Sweating, finally settled in my seat, I reflected that Russia had its attractions, but I wasn't sure it offered the serenity that a casita in the high desert would provide for my novel-writing.

Two weeks later, with my apartment safely rented for two years with the building co-op's permission, my furniture stowed and stored, my new Subaru Legacy packed and loaded, I headed west. A few days later, arriving under cover of night, I checked in at the Western Scenes Motel. Aged 53, I was exhausted and cautiously pleased that things had turned out as they had. The next day I drove into town. It was early October, and beyond the city, on the peaks of the Sangre de Cristo Mountains, was early snow. The sight seemed a kind of imprimatur, approving my arrival in Santa Fe.

Bruce Moss when sailing as First Mate on the "Santiago" a 36-foot Grand Banks fishing trawler in the Inland Passage off British Columbia before coming to Santa Fe, 2004.

How I Came to Santa Fe
Lily Aliza Nathan

Lily Aliza Nathan is about to complete her studies at the College of Santa Fe and expects to obtain her Bachelor of Arts degree in 2008. An accomplished artist with initial recognition of her painting in two group shows and a pending solo exhibit, her writing skills have been flourishing and her promise as both writer and painter bodes well for her future.

E VER SINCE I BECAME AWARE OF THE WORLD as a child I recognized the beauty and the wonder of my existence. I have sung, praising the awareness and integrity of being alive, praising the grace of transcendence, the gift of simple wellness. I have gone from child to woman and within that growth I have used my voice to try to express the wonders that lead to wisdom. To lift a pen and make words roll out on paper, to discover in tones of music and lyric play, to move a paint brush over canvas making portraits of human beings that have mysteriously touched my life and resemble myself hauntingly, as if each portrait I paint, each poem I write, is autobiographical and a manifestation of my being. Yes, such creative activity has rescued me, has enabled me to express the angst and grace of a very particular existence.

Horses have galloped through me, leaving hoof prints on my life. My father and I rode through the Redwood forests of Woodside, California when I was a very vivacious child growing up and it was there that I began to feel wisps of poetry sweep through me and an urge and ache in my breast to paint the colors of the moist forest, as thick and dank as they were. The classic Paso horse of Peru nuzzled a place for itself in my chest and I grew up on horseback. My childhood was innocent; I had no inkling of what depth and fighting was yet to come.

At 12 years of age, my family moved to Santa Ynez, California with 22 Peruvian Paso horses and my sister and I braced our hearts for the strange gifts that would come with this migration. I was a child coming into womanhood; I was a young girl, quite delicate, who would fall and fall hard. Brace yourself, child, for the passage into adulthood will be rough, rough like a cow horse stomping in the mountains, I thought.

Sexuality found me very young and I fell in love at 14. I was lost. I wandered recklessly and there was some part of me that was grasping onto any strain of stability that might hold me together. Damit, I won't love like this. Dearest God, I fought, let me survive this. And I found a path that would never be unfaithful to me; I found pigment and ink, I found oil paints and charcoal. I found guitar and voice. I would sing to my love and sing about the fight within myself to stay grounded. It felt as if my mind was lifting, lifting and I would cling to anything that might pull me back down to the earth. I moved into a new identity, one of a young woman who needed desperately to express the furies and the other emotions within. It was through my voice that I was able to release this painful love, this coming of illness, indeed, this very life I have lived that has been carefully documented by my making pictures of the images within.

I spent two years in high school and I remember walking through the halls repeating in my mind, I am a self-made woman, a self-made woman. This was the beginning of the voices, the voices that began as a whisper and that would soon consume me. In the beginning it made for very intriguing art, and in

Lily as a young girl riding her pony.

the end it led to hospitalization and it forced me to have great faith in an outcome I could not imagine. At 16, after completing my sophomore year in high school, I became lost. I spent the summer walking the hills of Santa Ynez, painting, making words and music, and all at once, I could not hold myself as a whole person. I joined my mother and sister at the Siddha Yoga Ashram in Southfallsburg, New York and with the grace that comes out of meditation and the strength of the Saints, I began a voyage to wellness that had an unimaginable breadth.

At 16 I was hospitalized and diagnosed with schizophrenia. The flowers bloomed within and while in Ward 2 South of the facility, I cried in the day room relieved that I had reached rock bottom. With some shadow of faith, I agreed to try a new medication that might quiet my mind. After a month, after fainting in the shower, after tears and fear, I was let out of the hospital and I stepped onto the streets of Westwood in Los Angeles, holding my mother's hand.

I was on the outside. I was in the process of returning to this life, leaving the underworld with all its stink and wretchedness. I was hospitalized once more the following year and after two months, I again stepped onto the streets of Los Angeles, only this time I had come into a new strength. This strength had not ripened, but I had faith that it would, and believed that this new power would take me further than I had ever thought I would go. The nurses and patients at the hospital would remember me as the young woman who organized poetry readings in the wards, taped dozens of portraits drawn and painted of people she had met in the hospital on her wall, and who, indeed, inspired others to have the faith that wellness would come only through devotion.

In the time that I spent hidden away at my parents' ranch in Santa Ynez, between hospitalizations, my mother organized a family vacation to visit New Mexico. I brushed my hair one morning in a tiny cottage in Taos and I marveled at how fast it was growing after I had cut it short the year before. With the growth of hair came a clean and new countenance. I was becoming a woman, and through the fog, the nightmares and the intensity of disease, I was blooming with grace. The light of New Mexico pushed me into a state of utter awe and I didn't want to leave, I didn't want to go back to my life in California. After visiting Taos and Santa Fe, I returned to Santa Ynez completely transformed, as if I had been told a secret, one that would ensure grace and stability for the rest of my life.

At 18 I stepped out of my little cave on the ranch and took a painting class with several elderly women. I was shockingly quiet. My images expressed a great pain that was misunderstood but appreciated. Slowly, I came out of the cocoon that had covered me and kept my eyes closed. After painting with the old ladies for a semester, I began taking junior college classes of all sorts, having been granted a high school diploma by taking the proficiency exam. I worked slowly toward a degree, with the anticipation of someday attending a university, achieving what would ultimately become a Bachelor's degree in Creative Writing.

I moved to Santa Barbara on my own. My sister returned home from New York where she had earned a Bachelor's degree from Sarah Lawrence. My father and mother held my hand and kissed me and loved me and encouraged me as I took this step away from home. My sister and I moved into a little cottage on Chapala Street, near the down town area and I enrolled and attended Santa Barbara City College. I had actually gone out into the world! I was free.

I went running. I went playing. I went, sometimes aching and ever lustful, down the streets of Santa Barbara, three steps forward, one step back, amazing grace. I reunited with my high school love who came home from Italy for just an instant, and I became lover, friend and someone who could actually be depended on. I created paintings, wrote songs, became part of a group that worked on and established art exhibitions and watched the whole world spin around me. I found myself realizing this is what it is to be a real person, to not hide out in the Santa Ynez Valley, to really live and to really be seen by the world and become part of it.

I held my visions of New Mexico in my breast and I began to travel in my mind away from Southern California. I began to ache for new land. I began to want unfamiliar winds to blow through my hair. I reached the end of my stay at City College and since I could not pass college level algebra, I knew I would not be eligible to continue on at a UC school. My love for New Mexico swelled in my heart and in June of 2005, my mother and I boarded an airplane and flew into Albuquerque. We had a mother and daughter adventure and came to Santa Fe. I felt my heart swell. I was home. I had come home to the comfort of home. Oh mother, take me into your body and rock me, I am yours.

The College of Santa Fe had no math requirement and a fantastic Creative Writing Department. I applied and waited on edge for several days for

Lily in Santa Fe, 2007.

news. I waited and was accepted by the College of Santa Fe's Creative Writing program. Growth continues to ripen a woman beyond imagination, and beyond clairvoyance. Set me free into the South West. Watch me love. Watch me learn, I said to myself.

I am now a Senior at the College of Santa Fe. This is my third year of study here. I have painted, I have played songs with my guitar on my lap, touching my womb, I have written a memoir of my young and deeply felt life and I have come into a greater womanhood that is ultimately supported by faith and intimate devotion to wellness. I have come close to marriage but I have backed away from it knowing that I must be my own lover before I can be the lover of anyone else.

Santa Fe takes her inhabitants into her breast and rocks and rocks. She forces her lovers to look her straight in the eye, all of those demons and terrors that would lie dormant in any other land. I have been torn and tattered here, and yet I have come into a beauty and a faith in myself that transcends schizophrenia and that is ultimately expressed in the art pieces that I create. I have become unafraid because I know that in Santa Fe's breast, whatever pain I feel, I will be redeemed with this amazing grace that has become mine and that I am pleased to share with all those who see my work.

I Came to Santa Fe

Yolanda Nava

Yolanda Nava is an Emmy Award-winning broadcast journalist, author, and motivational speaker. Her best-selling book It's All in the Frijoles *(Fireside/Simon & Schuster) was the recipient of the Latino Literary Hall of Fame's 2001 Best Self-help Book Award. That same year she was also selected as one of "5 Key Latino Leaders" in California by the State Department of Education for a statewide campaign to encourage people to enter the teaching profession. She was featured in the writer's section of the Remarkable Women series exhibit "Latinas: Spirit of California" at the California Museum of History in 2005–2006. Ms. Nava is also featured in the book* A to Z Latino Writers & Journalists *published in 2007.*

A SERIES OF SYNCHRONOUS EVENTS guided my journey to Santa Fe. It began with a fascination with Mabel Dodge Lujan as a graduate student at U.C.L.A. Another 15 years passed before I made my first visit. My dear friend René Enriquez (Sgt. Ray Calletano on *Hill Street Blues*) had invited me to participate as a "celebrity" guest at a gala fundraiser in Santa Fe to benefit the National Hispanic Endowment for the Arts. René and I had become friends after I interviewed him for the nationally syndicated television magazine *Latin Tempo.* He also invited 20 or so of his Hollywood friends, including Gene Hackman, Diane Ladd, Michael Warren, Steven Bochco, among others.

It was a grand introduction to the City Different. Toney Anaya was governor. Bill Richardson had recently been elected to his first term in Congress. We were invited to a reception at the Governor's Mansion. We stayed at the Inn at Loretto which captivated me with its luminaria-lit adobe walls and quintessential Santa Fe charm. I walked the streets around the Plaza, discovered Canyon Road and the original Fenn Gallery. We visited the Sanctuario de Chimayo, La Fonda Hotel and the Tesuque Flea Market.

It was an enchanting time for a wonderful cause. By the time we departed, I was hooked and vowed to return again soon.

I became a regular visitor, exploring Galisteo and the Light Institute, Bandelier National Monument, and Georgia O'Keeffe's home in Abiquiu. I slept in Mable Dodge Luhan's famous bed. The bed with the carved pineapples on each post that was so heavy it had to be constructed on the spot. I hung out with my sorority sister, photographer Linda Carfagno, and made new friends.

It was to Santa Fe that I escaped after the death of my mother in 1989. I spent a month mired in grief on the exquisite grounds of La Barbaria Ranch, thanks to the generosity of a friend of a friend. I took long hikes into the surrounding national forest and had massages in Madrid with John, the masseur whose technique not only soothed, but opened up glimpses into past lives that brought tears of release and healing.

And it was to Santa Fe that I brought my children, Joaquin and Danielle, for summer vacations by car following my divorce from their father.

Grief was transformed into inspiration. In 2001 I was back for Spanish Market and book-signings for my award-winning book *It's All in the Frijoles* — the book inspired by Mom's death-bed wisdom.

Yolanda Nava and co-anchor Jay Scott with Walter Cronkite at CBS/TV in New York, 1978.

Frijoles had created an extraordinary consulting opportunity in Boston where I had just landed—a fish out of Los Angeles waters.

A year later an unexpected marriage to a wonderful man I never dated would finally bring me to Santa Fe from Boston. While attending a two-week spiritual retreat in Albuquerque just weeks after our marriage, Finn and I were talking by telephone. I was speaking about the mountains, the sky, and the magical clouds. Finn tells the story of how he noticed a new, joyous quality in my being, an *élan vital*—he hadn't experienced before....

—"You'd like to live there wouldn't you?

—"Yes, in Santa Fe."

—Let's do it. I'm in transition and your clients will fly you in from wherever you choose."

I was incredulous. Was it actually possible to realize my decades old fantasy?

The next day he flew out to Albuquerque and we began a daily trek to Santa Fe in search of a place to live. We quickly leased a guest apartment near Museum Hill and moved cross country in July. We rescheduled a formal wedding at Lamy Chapel for September.

Yolanda and Finn leaving Lamy Chapel, September, 2002.

Yolanda and Finn at wedding reception at Bishop's Lodge, September, 2002.

Yolanda Nava in Santa Fe, 2007.

In December we purchased my "dream" home, a rambling pueblo style historic hacienda built during the Spanish/Mexican period known as the Rocking Horse Ranch.

And so our new life together began. My husband Finn founded his fourth school—the first three were in his native South Africa. Innésence School lovingly serves local children K–8 while bridging spirituality and education. I traded a broadcast and consulting career for the Department of Cultural Affairs where I have directed marketing for museums and then State Monuments. Finn and I have never been so productive, elated, frustrated, or challenged.

And so the pull to this unique and special place has brought us thus far. Many come to Santa Fe to escape the maddening crowd, the *anomie* of the big city. Some to start a new life, explore a spiritual discipline, or to find themselves. My own journey of discovery continues. But I believe we are here to confront life on new terms and to learn to tackle our own as well as the issues of our difficult times in a fresh way. Because New Mexico is a microcosm of all the issues that confound our global community, I believe we are here to find likeminded persons with comparable goals coupled with the skills, talent and courage that can help transform this community and the world. This is the challenge that answers the question why we have made Santa Fe our home.

Catching Up With Miriam
Neil & Sonia Nelson

*After thirty year in Health Care, **Neil** is retired, writing, and is looking forward to increased opportunities for travel. As founding director of Antaranga Yoga and the Vedic Chant Center in Santa Fe, **Sonia** teaches Vedic Chant and mentors teachers and gives workshops locally and nationally.*

O UR DAUGHTER, MIRIAM, brought us back to New Mexico where Sonia and I had met some 30 years before. It was 1998 and Miriam had just begun her freshman year at the College of Santa Fe. We had come out from New Hope, PA to visit over Thanksgiving break and see her settled. After an initial tour of the campus and dorms we drove back to Cerrillos Road by way of St. Michael's, heading for the Inn where we were staying, but a no-turn lane forced us to cross Cerrillos onto Osage. At the first stop sign we turned left onto Hopi Road intending to work our way back to Cerrillos. Almost immediately Sonia spotted the "For Sale by Owner" sign in front of a low fenced front yard on the right. The sign had a small box with fliers. "Pull over, I just want to get an idea of prices," my wife commanded, as only wives can. The dimensions on the flyer belied the seemingly tiny, unobtrusive stucco in front of which we were parked. In fact the only thing at all remarkable, visually, was a mature Katalpa tree in the yard, the biggest I'd ever seen, perhaps the only one I'd ever seen. My partner had her cell out in a flash and was punching numbers before I could protest. "Let's just get a peek," she said. It was Thanksgiving weekend and by the following Monday we had placed an offer on this three bedroom with oak wood floors and vigas throughout, and replete with outdoor spa and Casista. It was in walking distance to the dorms at the College.

Sonia and I met in 1967 when we were, each of us, living separate lives north of Albuquerque in the then rustic Village of Placitas. I was an undergraduate in the English Department at UNM. Sonia had recently dropped out of grad school in UNM's Art Department and would soon become one of Albuquerque's first Head Start teachers, and the priest, Father Baca, at the Duranes Church where her classes were held, would marry us in the Rectory of the San Filipe Church in Old Town. But just three years earlier, inspired by the restless energy of Jack Kerouac's epic prose/poem *On The Road*, and recently having completed a tour in the U.S. Navy, I had thought myself to be "just passing through" New Mexico when a chance encounter in Albuquerque with another Bay-Stater, the poet Robert Creeley, altered the trajectory of my intention.

IN AN INSTANT
for Robert Creeley

I was moving
alone &

so without shame,
& it was

belly up to the bar
when we met &

I sd, "Give me a
beeha," & you

turned, sd, "Boston?"
"Nope, Newton," I

sd. "No shit,
sit," you sd;

&, like they say,
things change, —

"in an instant"
cd have been

what the poet sd.

That brief happenstance, in what was then a University area landmark, the Triangle Bar & Restaurant, resulted in this high school dropout's enrolling at UNM. Sonia on-the-other-hand, also from the East Coast, had chosen UNM Graduate School after finishing her BFA at Philadelphia's Temple University, Tyler School of Fine Arts; in part, she reminds me, because a friend had just graduated UNM and was living in Albuquerque. I would go on to complete an undergraduate degree and, thanks to its editor, the late poet Gene Frumkin, I placed two poems in the final celebratory issue of the *New Mexico Quarterly*. I've discovered since that our friend the long time St. John's tutor and scholar, Charles Bell, who was then unknown to me, was one of the more prominent writers and poets represented in that final issue of the *Quarterly*. (Incidentally, it went on to be translated and reprinted in its entirety in Spanish by, I believe, an Argentine University Press, as an example of North American creative writing of the time.) Shortly thereafter and following a failed attempt to purchase land in Chacon, New Mexico, Sonia and I made the first of what was to prove to be many subsequent moves. We left Chacon for Berkeley, California in 1972, and 1975 would find us on our way to Madras, India. My own pursuit of Yoga studies would lead me back in the States in 1979, into the field of Physical Therapy. However our interest in Yoga became for Sonia her life's vocation.

Over the years she would return to Madras regularly to continue studies with our teacher, T.K.V. Desikachar, son of the legendary T. Krishnamacharya, and a prominent yoga authority himself. Our mutual interest in Yoga and in the writings of the philosopher/"non-guru," J. Krishnamurti took us to Ojai, California where Sonia helped start Krishnamurti's U.S. school, the "Oak Grove School." She taught there for 14 years while I worked in the Physical Therapy department of the local hospital. Our daughter, Miriam, would know no other school until the ninth grade when, having accepted the challenge of developing and directing a startup Physical Therapist Assistant program at Alleghany College of Maryland in 1994, I moved us to Cumberland. However, the ninth grade class at Cumberland had a larger enrollment then the entire Oak Grove's K thru 12, and while Miriam finished out the year there she then transferred to Solebury Boarding School in Pennsylvania. Two years later, following the national accreditation of my program, I resigned and we began "catching up with Miriam." We moved to Pennsylvania for her "at home" senior year during which time she would be recruited by and receive a scholarship from the College of Santa Fe. Miriam graduated with honors from Solesbury and, familiar with New Mexico from various family trips over the years and her parents reminiscing about the "sixties" there, she was gone to begin college life in Santa Fe.

Catching up with Miriam

How is it far if you can think of it?
— Ezra Pound

Just outside
the back gate

still breaks green
that scrawny scrub

oak bifurcate —
& was it

taller then than I
who am not tall

daughter nor tended it?
yet will

not with yr tiny goldfish clay
nor with this mine arcane art

in antique words preserve
as ancient amber would

but by Gold's tiny votive kindle glow
our one-root-memory two trees grow.

After our Santa Fe Thanksgiving visit, and following Sonia's annual trip to Madras, we moved permanently back to New Mexico, and into our new house in Santa Fe. But Miriam had moved on, transferring to UNM before we arrived. We settled, however, into The City Different with minimal difficulty and only a little disappointment. I quickly found employment with a local home health agency, and not long after with the hospital's Rehabilitation Department, retiring at the close of 2006. Sonia, already teaching workshops nationally, opened her Vedic Chant Center on Second Street here in Santa Fe and was soon seeing both local students and those who come from around the country to study with her privately. Teachers of yoga, they come for further training and/or for instruction the art of Vedic Chanting. In 2007 Sonia was one of the prominent American women Yoga teachers featured in the book *YOGINI*.

YOGINI

The song is not in the sound but in the silence

J. Krishnamurti

yr name is
SONIA

& yr every
waking sleeping

breath's a
song

not the sound
but the silent

sacred chant
the sacred

.....!!

As for Miriam, who drew her parents back to New Mexico and here to Santa Fe, we've still not caught up with her. After receiving her BFA at UNM, she went to England completing a first MA at the University of London. She now lives in Bloomington, Indiana, where she's just completed a second post graduate degree in Library Sciences/Visual Resources from the University of Indiana. But I think we have stopped trying to catch up with her. And, as I write, that three bedroom house with oak wood floors, vigas throughout, hot tub and Casista is on the market and we are preparing to move to Albuquerque's North Valley, not far from Old Town where we were married. Sonia will continue her teaching at the Vedic Chant Center, only now she will do more teaching in Albuquerque as well, and I will continue to meet each week in Santa Fe with our Charles Bell inspired Dante group. And, just as Paradise was for Dante, Santa Fe for us will always be *a state of mind*.

Neil, Sonia, and baby Miriam.

Miriam's Reprise

Kittens come in kindles
& Rabbits likewise breed
So why can't a tiny gold
Fish kindle family trees?

Neil and Sonia with "stand-in" friend, Theresa
("we've given up trying to catch-up").

Miriam today.

Why and How We Came to Santa Fe
Catherine Oppenheimer

Catherine Oppenheimer is a former dancer with New York City Ballet and Twyla Tharp Dance Company. Her professional career included performing and choreographing for the stage, television, and feature films. Catherine spent four years as an instructor with Jacques d'Amboise's National Dance Institute in New York City, and in 1994, with the help and guidance Mr. d'Amboise, founded National Dance Institute of New Mexico (NDI NM). Today, NDI-NM directly teaches more than 6,700 children and public school teachers throughout the state.

I WAS INTRODUCED TO SANTA FE by Jacques d'Amboise, principal dancer extraordinaire with the New York City Ballet (NYCB), and founder of National Dance Institute (NDI). Jacques used his MacArthur Fellowship award to purchase a second home in Santa Fe and in 1990 began an annual, one month NDI workshop in the Santa Fe Public Schools. In 1992, I was lucky enough to join the team and spent the month of September working at Salazar Elementary School.

I drove down from Colorado and followed directions to some place called Tesuque. I arrived very late at night and slowly made my way to this house that had been donated to the NDI staff for the duration of our program. As a born and bred New Yorker, I was stunned by the dirt roads and homes and was relieved when I finally found the house. In the morning, I realized I would be spending a month in Eliot Porter's home, surrounded by his art work and apple trees nestled in the Tesuque Valley. Paradise! I was hooked.

In 1994, I decided to leave New York. I too had been a dancer in the New York City Ballet and with Twyla Tharp, but I was 30 and knew my professional dancing days were over. I was faced with a common dancer's dilemma—I had no money, and I had left Columbia University after just two years when I was invited by Balanchine to join NYCB. So, I had no money and no degree.

I decided to move to Santa Fe because it enchanted me. I was one of those people who came and felt that inexplicable draw to the land and its people. I figured I didn't need any money to enjoy an outdoor life in New Mexico and I could cheaply finish my undergraduate degree in an affordable fashion. In September 1994, I packed up my tiny, five-flight-walk-up apartment in Greenwich Village, whose only window opened out over a 24-hour falafel restaurant, and drove West.

When I first arrived, I slept on an acquaintance's couch, enrolled in school and began what is accurately described as the "Santa Fe Shuffle." I taught Pilates; I taught at the College of Santa Fe; I taught in the public schools; I taught at the Aspen Santa Fe Ballet School: and I traveled and worked as an independent choreographer. As life happens, months after I moved, with Jacques's and other's help, I also formally started NDI-New Mexico as a non-profit organization. Much to my surprise, in no time at all I was

so busy teaching NDI, learning how to operate a non-profit business, writing grants, and overseeing a growing program, that I stopped all of my other activities to concentrate on NDI-NM. It wasn't much of a financial living, but I felt enormously challenged and on a mission.

NDI-NM uses dance and music to inspire and motivate children to strive for excellence. We use the arts to teach an important life lesson;

Catherine with the child is from 1997 in Albuquerque at Eubank Elementary.

that joyful learning, tenacity and hard work can lead to success in life. NDI-NM targets the schools and communities that have the least financial resources to give the program to children who wouldn't otherwise have access. For many children in New Mexico, NDI-NM is their first introduction to learning through the arts or through physical activity. For many it is a revelation and it changes their lives. The demand for the program has been overwhelming!

In 2003, NDI-NM built a permanent facility, The Dance Barns, and started an endowment. Now in addition to our character building work in the public schools we are also able to offer children access to pre-professional after school classes in dance, theater, and vocal music. In just four years, our students have won scholarships to dance and musical theater schools all over the country including my alma mater, the School of American Ballet. The innate potential of all human beings, especially children, to learn, achieve, and transform themselves continues to inspire me.

In 1994, I ran NDI-NM out of my shack in Tesuque and taught 100 children in one public school. Today, NDI-NM is a complex and multi-dimensional organization that teaches over 6,000 children and public school teachers each year in communities all over New Mexico. The meteoric growth and constant challenges of running NDI-NM have taught and shaped me both as a human being and as a professional. I am grateful for having found this work.

I recently watched a performance of 500 children that

Catherine and Jacques D'Amboise the founder of NDI in New York.

I had nothing to do with preparing and then attended a community dinner organized by scores of parents that I also had nothing to do with. There were people of all ages and backgrounds dancing together, smiling and celebrating, and it occurred to me that the organization is here for the long run. That astonishes me and is very gratifying.

Santa Fe has been good to me! I am very happily married to the most wonderful person and have two fabulous children. A few years ago we remodeled our kitchen and went looking for a piece of art. We found a large Eliot Porter photograph that we loved and were told it was of one of his apple trees behind his house in Tesuque. Needless to say, it hangs in our kitchen and reminds me of that first glorious introduction to this special place.

Teaching Excellence® Teacher Training Workshop 2006.

Socorro Residency Performance 2007.

JACONA *(A Dark Fairy Tale)*
Nathaniel Owings

*Today **Nathaniel Owings** lives in Santa Fe and runs Owings-Dewey Fine Art Gallery. The gallery is still in the same location after 22 years.*

HOW DOES ANYONE COME TO BE in one place or another at any given time when one is young? It must be some combination of accident, luck, fate and destiny that brings us to a place near the beginning of all we do and become.

The very young coyote had found her place high on a willow shrouded bank overlooking the Little Tesuque, not by accident, but with the help of her pack whose tracks were all around her in the soft earth. I found her there last week, her tail curled around her and her head resting lightly in death on her gently folded paw. As if asleep, she was in that final moment, perfect in her death. For some reason, there by the river, I thought of my mother Emily who first came here to Santa Fe as a beautiful young girl from Chicago.

My grandfather, Joseph Otis, brought her on his private railroad car and each morning, that first summer in 1924, she would ride her horse along the Acequia Madre and down to the Plaza. Emily told me of how she found Santa Fe full of wonder. A place so different from her family's Monroe Street Brownstone in Chicago, that she felt she had stepped off of the Santa Fe Chief and into another world. For years at a time Emily would leave Santa Fe, but she always came back. Then finally, with the help of her friends at age 92, she died in Santa Fe in her wonderful little home on East Houghton Street.

It was Emily who brought me here to New Mexico and to Santa Fe and Jacona and Black Mesa and the Rio Grande. My arrival was, as Emily told me one day when she pointed out the room with the balcony on the second floor of the La Fonda Hotel where I was conceived, not an accident, but quite intentional on her part. It was April of 1945 and it was a chaotic time for my parents. My father Nathaniel Owings, and my uncle Louis Skidmore, were the chief architects and builders for the Manhattan Project, in Oak Ridge, Tennessee. My father was gone much of the time in very secret ways. This left Emily alone with my three sisters and various nannies, trying to renovate a group of very old adobe buildings in Jacona, New Mexico, north of Santa Fe, so that the buildings could actually be lived in. And of course now she was pregnant with me.

That summer in New Mexico was very hot, but in July the monsoons came with the beginning of the dances in the Pueblos of the North Rio Grande Valley. Emily went to those dances many times that summer, with me inside of her. I often think that must be why the sound of a drum in a Pueblo is the one sound that makes me feel like I am home.

Emily also went with my father to Chaco Canyon that summer. She said she went there just to be with the Anasazi. It was a hard trip in those days, taking the better part of two days and then having to camp-out. They slept on the edge of the main Kiva in Pueblo Bonito and built a fire under the huge rock on the edge of the ancient road that goes perfectly straight out of Chaco to the east. The rock has now fallen, but the road remains. Just before she died, Emily told me that on their last night there in Chaco, she walked with me among the ruins and believed that she could see every star in the universe.

In the fall of 1945, Emily and my father and sisters returned to Chicago and on December 24, 1945 I was born at Passavant Hospital.

Nat with his father Nathaniel Owings at the Leaning Well Ranch in Jacona — 1947.

There in the hospital, Emily told me that she whispered to me that she couldn't wait to get me back to New Mexico.

The following spring my entire family, together with two full-time nannies and me in a basket, embarked by train from Chicago for our newly renovated ranch in Jacona. My father had named it the "Leaning Wall Ranch", because none of the old adobe buildings had straight walls. Once in Jacona, my parents lived in the large main house. The children, all four of us, were housed one hundred yards away in a special separate dormitory style wing with a full staff to care for us.

As children, we really never wanted for anything except perhaps parental supervision and love. The ranch in Jacona was a wonderful place. We had a pool where I learned to swim when my sisters threw me in the deep end to see if I would sink. I also had a personal fulltime nanny named Francis. She had been brought to Chicago from Jacona when I was born and then returned when the family came back that first spring. She was well meaning, but often cruel and I decided that if I could live through her care, the rest had to be easier.

The structure of life for me at the ranch really never changed during my first six years there. However, perhaps for reasons of self-preservation, I have no really solid memories of life there until perhaps age three. By that time the family was living in New Mexico fulltime. It had been established that if our parents were in town, and assuming that we had been good (an undefined state of grace at best), we were allowed to see and visit them on Friday afternoons. I have no idea why Friday was chosen as the day. But then again why not, it was as good as any other day and there was a chance my father would be in for the weekend from his many travels to his secret far-away places.

When my memories begin, I was spending most of my time with my sisters

Nat in his mother Emily's arms at the ranch in Jacona — 1948.

and of course my ever-present nannies. The pool and horses were a big part of my life and I really can't remember a time when I wasn't either on a horse or going to the barn to be with the horses. It was a safe place to go and unlike my parents, I could visit the horses whenever I wanted to. It was sometime around age six that I began to slip away on my horse for long rides, often with one of my sisters, to the Pueblos, the Rio Grande and sometimes up Black Mesa. But my greatest joy came when I rode alone in the sand hills we called the Barranca.

The Barranca is a series of large high sand hills long back that rises to the north and east from the Pojoaque wash. It is Pojoaque Indian land with many Indian burial sites, but in those days there were no fences to keep us out. There I would ride through the gullies and piñon and juniper and imagine that I was an Indian scout, the best tracker in the world. I would ride with my 22 rifle and hide and walk the hills leading my horse and fight off outlaws and rescue maidens in distress and always get back to the barn before dark. It was there on my horse in the arroyos of the Barranca, overlooking the Rio Grande and Black Mesa, that I got away from the chaos back at the ranch and from my ever-present nanny.

So much happened in those many days and years after my mother Emily brought me to New Mexico inside of her and then brought me back in a basket. I grew up a bit in those early years and I like to think that I grew a bit wiser as well. When it came time to leave for school, and perhaps for good, I knew I wanted to return. I really just had no idea of how I would get back. As it turned out, it was the death of my father that eventually brought me back to Santa Fe for good.

I left New Mexico at age twelve for boarding school. I was, at that stage of my life somewhat feral, not good at group activities and I did not take direction well. The year before I left New Mexico, I managed to shoot myself in the upper right leg with a 22 rifle while trying to protect the women and children trapped in the Alamo. In truth, it was a deep drainage ditch that I was in, but the Alamo idea worked better as a story. I also found that once at boarding school I was, being a good shot with a rifle, a natural for the rifle team. And at least I now had some supervision, if not parental supervision. From here at age 12, it would be close to 30 years before I would return full-time to my beloved New Mexico to finally stay. When I did return, I now realize, it was indeed like coming back to the beginning and seeing it for the very first time.

During my there and back again much happened, much seemed to change but really, very little changed inside of me. I went through high school and then to college and I married Cindy Hagan. I was drafted in 1969 and served in the Army as a medic and then went back to graduate school. In 1976 I was granted a PhD in Communicative Disorders from the University of Wisconsin in Madison, and my beautiful daughter Maya was born. Then I did the unexpected. I ignored the big schools and went to Montana to work with developmentally delayed children in a rural setting, to teach at Montana State University in Bozeman, Montana, and to fly fish in some of the most pristine water in the world.

New Mexico continued to beckon. By now I was re-married to the lovely and talented Page Randolph Allen. Emily introduced us at a party at her home in Santa Fe and one year later we were married. Page is an artist and was happy in her studio in Montana, but she loved New Mexico as well. The problem was how to make a living in Santa Fe. Then in 1984 my father became terminally ill with pulmonary cancer and that spring I went to Santa Fe to be with him in Jacona.

That might have been the end of it, but while I tended to my father at the hospital, I also hung out at the Dewey Gallery on the Plaza. It was owned by my friends Ray and Judy Dewey. One day I brought in a Zuni fetish owned by my sister. Ray bought it and gave me a $20. commission. That was it. I had found a way to make a living. Really it was just coming home to what I had always wanted to do. As a child my mother would drop me off on Canyon Road at Eleanor Bedell's store called "The Shop". There I would sit for hours in fascination, watching Eleanor talk with people and sell art. I realize now that I knew then what I wanted to do. It just took Ray and his $20. bill to awaken the sleeping thought and to arrive back where I started.

Nat and his dog Walter—2001.

RIGHT: Nat fishing again, Boulder River, Montana 2006.

BELOW: Nat salmon fishing in Alaska 2003.

All of this of course, took time. While my father was sick, Ray and Judy let me work and sell things for fun in his gallery. It appears I was a natural when one day a man from Nome, Alaska came to the gallery and I sold him an ice maker. Thanks to Page and Emily, and Ray and Judy, I had found my way back to New Mexico.

In March of 1985, with Ray's help and Page's tireless support and encouragement, Emily's hand-made lace curtains on the three windows, and Susie Herter's hug, I opened Owings-Dewey Fine Art on the Plaza in Santa Fe. We did it truly on a wing and a prayer with no money and no inventory. We only had the idea to do something beautiful. I am happy to say that so far it has worked. The spirit of Emily lives on in Santa Fe.

A Young Man's Driveabout
Richard Polese

Richard Polese has been active in publishing and community concerns in Santa Fe since 1963. Ocean Tree Books is his private press, focused on peacemaking, travel, and general nonfiction titles (The Book of Kindness; Peace Pilgrim: Her Life and Works; Chaco Astronomy). *He authored* Discovering Dixie *and recently co-wrote* Passions in Print: Private Press Artistry in New Mexico *with Pamela Smith. Previously he has written for* The Santa Fe New Mexican, Santa Fe Reporter, *and was for five years editor of* El Palacio, *the Museum of New Mexico's magazine. He has served in a variety of church and civic positions and is today Executive Director of the New Mexico Book Association. Richard was elected to the Santa Fe Public School Board in February 2007. He has three children and lives on Cerro Gordo Road, where he perpetually restores both his adobe home and an accumulation of Hudson motor cars.*

HIGHWAY 66 BECKONED, enticing me east out of the California clutter and out across the expanding openness of the American Desert. Summer of '62! Unexplored territory! Saddled up in my 1951 Rambler coupe, this 19-year old adventurer headed alone into unfamiliar land—the Mojave Desert, Colorado River, and beyond. As the character Sally explained in the recent animated film *Cars,* "Today we take the interstate to *make* good time; in those days we drove the highway to *have* a good time".

After two years in journalism school at San Jose State, near my birthplace in the San Francisco Bay Area, I took a "personal sabbatical," working in a Chevron station as a gas jockey while taking night classes. But I had larger plans. I'd always been intrigued by desertscapes and the possibilities beyond, sketching desert scenes of Nevada while daydreaming through Algebra 1 in high school. So, I saved a few dollars, bought that Rambler (its fold-down seats made into a convenient bed, skirting the need for a leaky tent or the expense of motels along the way). When the time came to go, I left a note on my folks kitchen table (shame on me!), letting let them know I was heading out on what I later called my "Great American Driveabout" and would be in touch when I reached Crawfordsville, Indiana, where I'd find safe haven with family friends.

Vacation motor trips and camping out were my family's summer recreation. As young kids, my sisters and I went hiking, fishing or gold panning in the Northern California mountains with our folks every year. But the Southwest and points east were for me *terra incognita.* I had to find what was out there for myself.

The Rambler and I paused for a couple of days at the Grand Canyon's south rim, made friends with other travelers, then we were back on Route 66. I reversed the trek of Dust Bowl migrants of the 1930s, motoring on through Flagstaff, Winslow, Holbrook, and into New Mexico at nightfall. A few miles out of Gallup, the Rambler's engine began making a steady ominous clacking sound. As I pressed on through the New Mexico night, the racket got louder and louder. I worried that a connecting rod would let go in the middle of the night, ending my adventure for good. How sweet it was when, sometime long after midnight, I topped Nine-Mile Hill and saw the glorious lights of Albuquerque spread out before me! After a sound sleep in an old Route 66 motor court, I pulled into the local Rambler dealer to learn the verdict about the now cacophonous noise up front.

"Yup," said the old-timer Nash mechanic. "It's most likely a rod." He saw my downcast look, then asked, "How much money you got, son, and where are you headed?" I told him I was on a very lean budget and was thinking that maybe I'd head up to Denver before pointing east across the Great Plains.

"Well, I've known these Ramblers to have a certain peculiarity. Sometimes a piece of piston ring breaks off and will bang around in the cylin-

A younger Richard Polese, at the door of Jack Rittenhouses's Stagecoach Press in 1963.

der head. Sounds just like that. Then that chip may just pass out the exhaust valve by itself and no more noise. It's worth a try, considering your situation."

Encouraged by his suggestion, I made a left turn at Albuquerque, and headed north toward Santa Fe. Halfway up La Bajada Hill, the hammering racket just went away. The old wrench-slinger had been right! Much relieved, I pulled into the most interesting town I'd ever seen. Santa Fe was virtually unknown to much of the world in those days. Before that moment it had been for me just a dot on the map.

But look! Real adobe houses! Spanish spoken on the streets as much as English. Winding dirt streets, and what romantic mysteries might lay behind those earthen walls? Relaxed, enchanted and filled with new confidence, I decided to splurge and stay at gracious old La Fonda (which appears much as it does today). There in peaceful slumber I spent my first night in Santa Fe, at $16 for the night.

Next day I poked around Canyon Road (artists actually lived in their studios then), Candelario's Curio Shop, St. Francis Cathedral, and appreciated how genuinely itself this place was. Tolerant, relaxed, steeped in history, and completely inviting.

But the road beckoned again, and soon I was on my way north, then east, to Indiana—were I picked up forwarded mail—including a Dear John from a ballet dancer I'd met a few months earlier in Los Altos, California. My last incentive to return to California suddenly gone, I set my sights on checking out colleges as I made my way south and east, through Kentucky, the Appalachians, to Washington D.C., New York, and Boston. In New York, I received word that a small liberal arts college in Indiana had accepted my application for the fall. Hanover College is a beautiful campus on a bluff above the

Lindsey Clark and her grandfather Richard Polese, skipping rocks in the fountain at the Inn at Loretto.

Ohio River. I stuck it out there through two harsh Indiana winters, graduating in 1964.

But during those Indiana ice storms, I found myself daydreaming in class again, drawing sketches of Santa Fe landscapes on the margins of notebooks. During Christmas break, I wrote to the *New Mexican,* asking if any *Santafesinos* had the time to write me about their town. The letter appeared in newspaper on New Years Eve, 1962, and three young people responded. One note was from Gayle Carnes Stromei of Calle Torreon, daughter of a cowboy family, who became a lifelong friend. So, with these connections and increasing dreams of the Southwest, I immediately headed west to Santa Fe at the end of the Spring semester.

An exchange student from Germany rode shotgun with me as I headed back to New Mexico. Our very first stop in town was at The Three Cites of Spain, a semi-bohemian coffee house (now Geronimo's), which I'd discovered earlier was one of Santa Fe's best people crossroads. I informed our waiter, Bob Garrison, that I was looking for summer work in Santa Fe — perhaps with a printer, so that I might learn the arts of journalism and publishing from the ground up.

"You won't believe this," Bob replied. "Not ten minutes ago this man came in and said he was looking for an young apprentice at the Stagecoach Press, and gave me his card."

Jack D. Rittenhouse, long a passionate student of everything Southwestern, printed his own books and historic reissues at a tiny shop on Tesuque Street, across from White Swan Laundry. I quickly found myself learning to set metal type by hand, running Colt's Armory and Vandercook hand presses, and operating a now quaintly antique Linotype machine.

My apprenticeship with Jack was half-time, so to help pay my rent at Annie Burris's Boarding House on Don Gaspar Avenue, I picked up work

Polese transplants a neighbor's spare day lilies at his "contributing historic" hours on Cerro Gordo Road.

interviewing opera stars for the *New Mexican* and helping the Santa Fe Public Library haul hundreds of books into new quarters (now the Fray Angelico Chavez History Library of the Museum of New Mexico). During that sweet Santa Fe summer, I found time to explore the landscape beyond town, enjoy a mutual flirtation with a lovely Spanish girl, got to know several local characters, danced on the Plaza at my first Fiesta, and made firm plans to return to this delightful, welcoming, unique, genuine, deeply historic, and remarkably inexpensive town.

And return I did, the following year, after completing studies at Hanover and San Jose State, bringing with me my new bride, Maggie. I resumed my printer's apprentice job at the Stagecoach Press, where Jack Rittenhouse helped me publish my first book, a reissue of *The Original New Mexico Cookery,* in 1965. Maggie and I next worked for Rudy Rodriguez at the *Santa Fe News* (later the *Santa Fe Reporter),* then I inherited from Rittenhouse the book editor's job at the Museum of New Mexico. Those were indeed halcyon days, where we made friends with many of the City Different's very colorful variety of individualists, including Tommy Macione, Charlie DuTant, Alice Bullock, Will Harrison, Gus Baumann, Jene and Jetta Lyon, Peggy Pond Church, E. Boyd, Betty Kuhn, and Jack Schaefer, as well as a handful of local politicians, monks and pocket change entrepreneurs.

When Rudy Rodriguez found us an old, three-room adobe on Cerro Gordo Road, our roots became set, deep and permanent. Originally built by Miguel Lamy (an orphaned Indian raised by the famous Archbishop Lamy) the house was offered with a couple of charming amenities—a WPA outhouse and a legend of hidden treasure. This house became my long-term teacher in the native crafts of adobe construction, fireplace building, brick floor laying, emergency flat roof repair, as well as plumbing and wiring. Our house set us back something in the very low four figures when we acquired it from Lamy's daughter, Patricia Lamy de Lucero, in 1967.

The doors to Santa Fe and all it offered seemed open to us then—quirky opportunities and easy delights—for a young couple freshly in love with life in the City Different!

The Real Story & a World of Difference
Earl & Deborah Potter

*During his 37 years in Santa Fe, **Earl Potter** has been a father, soccer coach, first Attorney/Director of Legal Aid, County Attorney and author of the first Santa Fe County Land Development Code, founder and President for 20 years of his own law firm (last known as Potter & Mills), with his wife **Deborah**, a managing Partner in Hotel Santa Fe, and founder of Five & Dime General Stores (locations in Santa Fe, Branson, MO, and San Antonio, TX). He was Chairman for both the New Mexico Democratic Party and the New Mexico Delegation to the 1996 National Convention.*

Earl Potter

WHEN ASKED HOW I CAME TO SANTA FE, I used to say, "I was sent to New Mexico as a VISTA volunteer in 1968, won a stiff competition for the job of first director of Santa Fe Legal Aid, and never left." Thanks to my wife Deborah, I've learned that is not the real story.

I *was* sent to Albuquerque in that year to work at the Legal Aid Society. I *did* begin my career there as an attorney with an incredible group of new New Mexicans—Michael Broude (now a distinguished law professor and counsel to the Legislature), Chuck DuMars (also a professor and Super water lawyer), Michael Messina (entrepreneur/Lawyer husband of Patricia Madrid), Peter Mallory (such an effective lobbyist you probably don't know who he is), Paul Bardacke (former Attorney General, Governor's candidate, and Governor Richardson's lawyer), and Supreme Court Justice Richard Bosson. Under the enthusiastically anti-establishment leadership of ex-Detroit criminal lawyer septuagenarian Bill Fitzpatrick, we fought fearlessly for the rights of our clients

Two years later, I did see an ad in a legal publication for a job as the first director of a new legal aid program in Santa Fe. We were often in court and the legislature there, and I had fallen hopelessly in love with the town. I submitted my application the next day.

Then came the interview with the full Board. We crammed into the small house on Baca Street that had been chosen for the office. A few days later I learned I had the job.

Bill Lumpkins, the distinguished architect, was a member of the Board. Often when we were together at social occasions in later years, he would tell those present that after meeting me, the group had caucused and decided to remove the requirement of fluency in the Spanish language because I had made such an outstanding impression. I would smile self-consciously, and sneak a peak at Deborah beaming!

A few months before Bill died, Deborah stopped at his lunch table at the Pink. "Bill-it's so wonderful the way you tell the story of how Earl came to Santa Fe," she said. "Do you want to know the real story?" he said, with the patented Lumpkins twinkle in his eye, "Earl was the only one that came in sober."

Deborah Potter

I HAD BEEN TO SANTA FE ONCE, way before they coined it "The City Different." It was back in the late 50s when La Fonda was considered elegant, and their restaurant had metal umbrellas to protect diners from the sun. People wore large-brimmed cowboy hats then, and snap-pocket western shirts. I remembered riding a horse across a forest stream and trudging up a mountain in the middle of town at night, along a path lighted by candles in brown paper bags. The city had a lot of dust and no car wash.

Deborah with actor Richard Egan and her father, TV executive William Dozier at a La Fonda dinner, approx. 1962.

So when a childhood friend told me the most desirable old boyfriend in my entire life had moved to that high and dusty place, I was a little confused. What was a gorgeous Yale graduate who had always loved water sports doing in a place like that? However, I was certain that no highly educated young man would ever be curious about the esteemless underachiever I was becoming.

A few years later, I was told he had two little boys and was divorcing his wife, but I changed the subject. I had seen my own family's divorces and didn't want to hear about another. Those memories repulsed me, but I wasn't self-aware enough to realize it then. Another year passed, and I was told he had married someone else. I wondered why my friend kept providing these bulletins.

Almost half a decade later, I had built some self-esteem through hard work and good use of my talents. I was about to turn 30, and was afraid to dream I could ever have a relationship with a man I respected. Then several fond and vivid memories of that old boyfriend surfaced in my mind, all in one week. I started to write a check in a hardware store and said to the clerk, "Today is August 14th. I used to have a friend whose birthday is August 14th."

I phoned Santa Fe information and got his home address. Then I wrote a simple note that ended with, "I wonder whatever happened to you." I sealed the envelope, addressed it, and kept it in my purse for almost a month. I was

afraid to mail it. Afraid he would think I was an idiot. There's a reason why this is happening, I said to myself. You have to break through your fears about being good enough. You have to put that letter in the mail, just to push yourself through this. He'll probably never answer it anyway. So I closed my eyes,

Deborah and Earl drive to
New Mexico after their wedding.

Deborah and Earl in Santa Fe, 2006.

deposited the note into an anonymous corner mailbox, and listened to the clunk of the heavy metal flap.

That boyfriend and I plan to celebrate our 30th wedding anniversary next year. From the beginning, we knew we would have a lifetime together. Steadfast hope helped us through those first ten years of adjustments and acceptance, then the boys' college graduations, our changes of careers, building our island vacation home, and menopause (his and mine). But whenever my husband tells people about that note, his story gets longer and more emphatic.

Last night, at dinner in one of our city's many world-renowned restaurants, he told it again. "I drove to the end of our driveway to get the mail. I reached into the mailbox and pulled out a light blue envelope. As soon as I saw it, I recognized her handwriting. It was from the most beautiful girl I had ever known, and I knew I was still in love with her. Before I even opened the letter, I sat there in my car for half an hour, with the engine running, stunned. I made a determination right there and then: I was going fly to California, I was going to find her, and I was going to convince her to become my wife. Then I would bring her to Santa Fe to spend the rest of her life with me."

❖ ❖ ❖

I Came to Santa Fe
Nancy Red Star

Nancy Red Star *descends from Redman/Parker Cherokee bloodlines and John Burroughs—the first American Naturalist writer, on her mother's side and is of Sefarditas descendant on her father's side. Red Star is a citizen of the Sovereign Abenaki Nation in Missisquoi, Vermont.She is the author of the* Star Ancestors Trilogy *(Inner Traditions/Bear & Co., 2000-03-08, Wilheim Heyne Verlag, Germany),* Life With A Cosmos Clearance *(Light Technology Publishing, Inc.,) and* UFOs *—No Threat, Official Eyewitness Testimony (Willow Spirit Press LLC 2005). Now residing in Taos, New Mexico, Red Star became the Executive Producer, writer and host of her upcoming feature documentary entitled "Star Ancestors…Guardians of the High Frontier"—narrated by Dean Stockwell and slated for theatrical release and worldwide TV distribution in the winter of 2008.*

I CAME TO SANTA FE, NEW MEXICO via Roma, Italia. It was another world…another war—called Vietnam. This was a good time to leave America and that I had done, right out of high school.

First stop back in America was Taos, New Mexico where I languished at the mysterious Mabel Dodge Luhan estate. Dennis Hopper, who was editing his "The Last Movie" shot in Peru now owned the home. My boyfriend, Corsican and French actor Pierre Clementi was going to meet me there…but ended up in prison in Rome. He was a political actor and it was political times for my generation.

I moved into the DH Lawrence house and found the winds of change upon me. The magical colors, the sounds, the reverence of New Mexico began to enrapture my spirit. I knew I was home. The winter played songs of wilderness dancing in my head.

I had slept in the mountains, followed the trails of the Snake River and the Grand Tetons but the Sangre de Cristo Mountains whispered calls that captured my pathway. The Medicine Mountain held the sweet breath of my life casting a reflection. A transformation was occurring at the footsteps of my walk.

I loved to talk with *Tell Us Good Morning* from Taos Pueblo. He would pass by often and we would walk the rugged terrain. The sky had become my ocean passing over me cool and blue…waves I surrendered to. The trees bowing to the wind encouraged me to quicken my pace as the beads on my moccasins caught the sunlight.

I lamented about my love interest, Pierre Clementi. As Brendan Gill, a writer for the *New Yorker* magazine, once said to me in an interview I did with him for *The Paris Review*… "Oh, to be lonely, lonesome and alone."

I knew that I would have to go back to Rome to try to see Pierre in prison. I was lovesick and not able to truly focus on my life—I was mired in a restless kind of bondage. So, I left for Europe again.

Once more, the city of Rome wrapped me in ancient splendor. I visited Pierre's lawyer but I would not be able to go to the prison. I was lost in sadness and the streets offered no solace. How could I stay here? My dreamtime memories swept me back to the Medicine Mountain.

Santa Fe embraced me as a Mother holds a child. The dirt roads leading into the Plaza held my walk with the exhilaration of a foreign country. The old structures of the past spoke their history with grace. My faith in America had been restored in the relics of a cultural history standing proud.

I would find a home here and nest. I did not have to run anywhere. I could stay and become who I am. Even with the loss of love, the sunlight cured my morbid tendency for sentiment. As an

Nancy Red Star with her "Auntie Susie"
at the horno in Taos Pueblo.

artist I could recreate my life and charge a new direction. I could draw upon the colors of my palette to restore my spirit.

I loved the faces of the people…all the people. Like me they were dark and exotic. A warmth came through their eyes as we met. In those days, some 30 years ago, Santa Fe was a neighborhood…there were no strangers. The people were the town. I wandcred up and down the streets to find the areas where I could sit like I did in the cafes of Europe.

I began to study Flamenco with Maria Benetiz and Vincente Romero. The music and movements were passionate and alluring. I loved the colors and sensuality of my wardrobe. The stride, the mood, the strength of the Spanish gate all challenged me to be a better dancer. As good students, a group of us would follow our teachers to all their recitals. I could walk to the dance studio off Canyon Road and it all was truly blissful for me. There could be no better place to live, I was sure.

As time passed, I began to work with "Youth at Risk" through the State of New Mexico and Eight Northern Pueblos. I was welcome into many villages and got to know many families very intimately. I helped to set up the first live-in residential program and I had an extensive client base. Many times we would be invited to pueblo dances that were not open to the public especially during the winter season. My heart was totally committed to this wonderful program which was the first of its kind for New Mexico. That brought me to work within the prison system with the "Scared Straight" program. It was astonishing to me that so many people who traveled to New Mexico had no idea of the deep sorrow that lay beneath the outer façade of a fashion driven tourist trade.

Nancy Red Star at
Chaco Canyon, 2003.

There were many elders and youth that had lives that were very difficult to survive. In fact, many of the youth that even passed through our program did not survive in later years. I still remember their faces and those that did make it I see today and even visit with.

I served an elder on one of the pueblos for six years and her picture is with this story for you to see. She was the last one living on her pueblo at night. She kept her Daddy's promise to never leave or use the wires (electricity). She heated her house with wood and lived with no running water and gathered her drinking from the river that ran through the pueblo. She never watched TV (the shadow) or used a telephone.

Auntie Susie told me that she was born in 1904 and remembered when President Roosevelt gave the Apache their land. She taught me about wild crafting medicine; everything I know today is because of my Auntie Susie.

It is exactly a year since she passed on—I write this piece in her loving memory. Before she passed she gave me her Indian name…in English it is "Green Leaves."

As she used to say, "Those days seem like a dream."

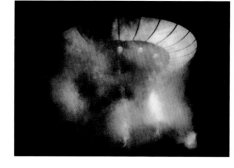

UFO Photographs
© Top Secret VIP Navy
Transport Commander
Graham E. Bethune @
Cosmic Intelligence Awareness

"Inspired by the work I have done, I have been researching existing data in our various aboriginal cultures of the contacts we humans have had with extra terrestrial beings and life forces. My current books deal with this generally unacknowledged but very provocative area of intergalactic communication. Based in the Santa Fe area this work has sent me all over the world and will bring me to Australia in the near future."

Nancy Red Star

I Came to Santa Fe

Mary Redmond

Mary Redmond has lived in Europe, Chile, New York City and California before settling in Santa Fe. She worked in sales at Tiffany and Co., I Magnin and Coldwell Banker. She is manly interested in the protection of all animals as well as the environment.

W HEN I CAME TO SANTA FE ELEVEN YEARS AGO, I had pretty much decided that this was to be my final move. I had come here before on a few short visits, and I definitely liked what I had the opportunity to see and enjoy—the climate for one, with its change of seasons, the clear blue skies, and the atmosphere which reminded me strangely of other places—a small village in Guatemala or maybe in Mexico.

When I decided to retire, my mind went directly to Santa Fe as a good place to go to. I came here on a Thanksgiving weekend, found a house in an older Hispanic barrio in the north east part of town, bought it, and moved in six months later. From that moment, I never looked back.

My father had been in the U.S. diplomatic service, and we, my parents, my sister and brother, my nanny, their nanny, etc., lived in Europe for the first 14 years of my life—in France, Germany, Spain, England, and Switzerland (alas, never in Italy!). On top of that, we must have moved households at least 10 times by my last count. So naturally, I was thrilled to finally board the Queen Mary and head on to what I thought would really be home—New York City! Then the humdrum life began, four years of boarding school and then college. But after two years of that, I went down to Santiago, Chile, and stayed for a year while my father was stationed there. It turned out to be one of the best years of my life—carefree, fun filled and a source of wonderful memories. I came back to New York, and as all my friends and contemporaries were getting married, I followed suite. I got married, moved to the San Francisco Bay area and we proceeded to raise four children. We lived happily for 30 years, moving to a larger house as our family expanded. Then we divorced, and I went to work for the first time in my life, as a sales person at first and then in real estate. I actually made some money in that difficult and competitive area.

I occasionally think of my roots. Where are they planted? Then I realize that I don't really have any, not real roots anyway. The curious thing is that my father born and raised in Omaha, Nebraska, left in 1914 to join the Navy in WWI, never set foot there again. However, in the codicil to his will, he specifically requested that at the time of his death, he be sent back from Spain (where he lived) to Omaha to be buried next to his father, his mother

Mary Redmond on a ride with Gordon Miller, Pecos, 2006.

Mary at her grandson, Jesse Wilson's wedding to Seleta Reynolds with part of the bridal party, 2006.

and his brother. My mother who was born and partly raised in New York, is buried there next to her mother, her father and her sister. Curious how strong an individual's roots can be. As for me, the jury is still out.

In the meantime, however, I am having a wonderful time with the best of everything at my disposal. I can ski in the winter, golf and fish in the summer. There are concerts of all kinds during the year and opera in the summer, and my favorite, a small theatre that puts on excellent plays. And I have been lucky in finding many new, wonderful friends of all kinds and stripes that really make my life compete.

I don't think that I'll be leaving any time soon and Santa Fe's brilliance has never tarnished.

Why We Ended Up in Santa Fe
Tom & Nan Rees

Doctor Tom Rees, world renowned plastic surgeon whose practice though based in New York has taken him around the world as a primary advisor as well as practitioner in a variety of governmental and NGO situations, is the only survivor of the original threesome that organized the African Medical Research and Educational Foundation (AMREF), otherwise known as "The Flying Doctors of Eastern Africa" whose outreach and accomplishments have saved thousands of lives and serve a multitude of needy people not only in Kenya but in other parts of Africa as well. Nan Rees, his wife and familial manager had a brilliant career in New York where her sense of style and management capabilities were well recognized. Having married Tom, Nan embraced her husband's humanitarian approach to life and has been his partner in the work of the Foundation as well as managing the various personal contacts created around the world because of the work they have done and are doing together. Tom also plays a mean sax when he takes the time for it.

W HEN WE BEGAN TO SERIOUSLY CONSIDER how and why we settled our post career lives by moving and living in Santa Fe, NM— the answer emerged and became obvious. Our many years in New York were pointing in this direction from the start. We developed close ties to Western America ever since Tom moved from his native Utah to New York to begin his career in surgery. Many very happy vacations were spent over a period of 45 years in places like Sun Valley, Aspen, Vail, Snowbird, Sundance and Alta pursuing our skiing addiction. In addition to skiing in the winter, we visited Montana, Idaho, Wyoming, and Utah packing into the mountains on horse-back, fly fishing and boating on Lake Powell. We stayed at "dude ranches" in Arizona and Montana. In short, and in retrospect, we scouted off to the West at least once (and usually more frequently) each and every year to

Tom and Nan Rees at camp in Kenya.

recharge our batteries, precariously run down by the pace of New York City. All this was natural for Tom who grew up in the western mode in Utah where his family lived in Salt Lake City and where he worked summers on the family ranch in central Utah, but was all new for Nan who grew up and received her schooling in New York and New Jersey.

Without really being aware of it, on these many trips, we were unconsciously evaluating Western towns and cities as to their potential as a retirement location for us. As the years went by, many attractive early possibilities were abandoned because of inevitable change resulting from growth. Scottsdale for example, was a very small village when we first went there, with only one paved street. We watched with dismay as the retirement population exploded and this charming town became a city with all of the attendant problems of a city. Likewise, Palm Springs, once a charming desert destination, evolved into a mega golf culture with little else to offer except a superb climate for eight months of the year and an uninhabitable summer. Not much culture going on there. Ski destinations were scratched due to our aging bones and joints, and other indignities of advancing age.

We cannot remember who first suggested that we take a look at Santa Fe, but Nan did an initial reconnaissance on trip with Cheray Duchin Hodges to visit the museums and explore the area in general. Nan was hooked, so that in the winter of 1992 while Tom was recovering from orthopedic surgery, we decided to rent a house in Santa Fe and get a true feel of the place. We thought it particularly prudent to see what Santa Fe was like in the winter, supposedly its least attractive season before taking any serious steps in moving there.

We loved the ambience of Santa Fe and New Mexico in general. It so reminded us of East Africa where we had spent considerable time during our yearly trips working with the Flying Doctors of East Africa. Looking out over the landscape surrounding Santa Fe, it was easy to imagine oneself in Kenya. Santa Fe shared many positive characteristics with Africa; pure air, crystal clear starscapes, an almost magical feeling about the place that is difficult if not impossible to describe, but experienced by many, including Native Americans who considered it a sacred place. Santa Fe is probably the largest art center in the World as well as home to a World Class Opera House, a symphony and chamber music.

During that winter visit of three months we met an astounding number of very interesting people who were friendly, gregarious and willing to share their ideas and dreams even with newcomers like us—we were so acquainted to the somewhat reserved and guarded attitudes of many Easterners. The Santa Feans represent a cross section of every imaginable profession and occupation: writers, artists, professors,

Tom and Nan Rees at home in Santa Fe.

entertainers, actors, directors, producers, ambassadors, horse lovers, and so on. We were fascinated meeting new people who did not immediately try to impress us with how important they were (or had been), but seemed genuinely interested in us. It was this human factor and the mild, but four season climate, that finally persuaded us to build a house and change our permanent address to Santa Fe from New York City and the Hamptons. We have never looked back, and find ourselves more in love with Santa Fe each year.

Having said all of this, we hope not too many people who might read these words decide to move here because we really want to stymie growth and keep this secret all to ourselves and our many friends.

Flying Doctors: (back row) East Africa Nurses and Paramedics;
(front from left) Dr. Tom Rees, Dr. Bettina Vadera, Nan Rees, and Nicky Blundell-Brown.

I Came to Santa Fe
Godfrey Reggio

Born 1940, New Orleans; moved to Santa Fe in 1959; member of Christian Brothers Roman Catholic order for 14 years (Brother Godfrey); teacher (St. Michael's); street gang organizer (YCTA); social activist (La Gente); lecturer; filmmaker (Koyaanisqatsi, Powaqqatsi, Naqoyqatsi, Anima Mundi, Evidence); member of IRE collective for 35 years.

SHOWTIME

1959

2007

Summer of '62! Photo @ Lisa Law

What you see is what you hear
Language, but no words
Faces on a sundial
of the one that came here now

Scheming Our Way to Santa Fe
Bob & Mimi Rhodes

Mimi and *Bob Rhodes* came to Santa Fe in 1974 fresh out of Mexico, with Bob's PhD in hand and Mimi still working on her MFA in art from the University of Guanajuato. Bob got a job on the staff of the Board of Education Finance. They found a house on Canyon Road and Mimi, their kids, and Bob set out to make the most of Santa Fe. Ole!

WE LIKE TO THINK OUR LIVES are planned, that where we are is where we're meant to be, but we know this is not so. Life happens to us; if it's good we take the credit; if it's bad we find someone to blame. Mimi and I have had a good life and we mostly have ourselves to blame. I like to think we schemed our way to Santa Fe.

We came to Santa Fe 30 years ago and it was a good thing we did. We came here out of Mexico where we had gone to look for ourselves in San Miguel de Allende. I working on translations of three contemporary Mexican poets (Efrain Huerta, Alejandra Aura and Margarita Michelena) for my dissertation while Mimi worked on an MFA at the Instituto Allende. I was able to do a bilingual reading with Aura of his poems at the Instituto. Mimi had classes with Pinto and Samuellson in the Bellas Artes art program. I taught publishing and was in a class with Tony Hillerman. I took a class in poetry writing with Patricia Goedicke. (She liked my stuff!) One of our great experiences in San Miguel was taking part in a play by Garcia Lorca. The Keoghs who were Canadian puppeteers produced the play and I played the part of the father. We raised money to renovate the Peralta Theater and later took the play to Guanajuato. I tell you this to display the wide range of our risk taking activities.

What of our kids I hear someone ask. Did you not take five kids with you and put them into parochial schools and the older one into the Academia and how did they adjust to Mexican society? The answer is that we did take them and they tell us it was good for them. The real test is what they have become. Karin, the oldest, is at the University of Pennsylvania where she is an Assistant Professor of Medicine and Director of the Division of Health Care Policy Research in the Department of Emergency Medicine. Julie, the next oldest, is running her own business, Kleenslate Concepts, which sells a device she invented to erase white boards and other products still under development. She recently went to China to oversee production of her materials. Laura, the middle child, is the family lawyer and works for a firm in Portland, Oregon. Aaron, the only boy, was a student, actor and teacher at the Second City in Chicago. He does some of all of that here in Santa Fe. He recently has been teaching improv and working on his art. Kim, the last of the lot, has a BA from the University of Vermont. She has managed a dialysis center and is currently working as a critical care nurse in Santa Fe and Las Vegas.

Meanwhile, back we came to Santa Fe where with my new PhD in American Studies I was able to get various jobs in State Government which was good because we had used all our savings. My first job was with the Board of Educational Finance

Bob and Mimi in 1989.

where I dealt with creation of new programs on a state-wide basis. My office was in the Capital building close to the Senate chambers. There I became friends with Ernie Mills and as Director of the Commission of Public Broadcasting I was able to help him in the development and startup of his "Report from Santa Fe," which taught me a lot about matters having to do with state government. It was at this time I noticed that New Mexico was not taking part in the national State Student Incentive Grant program and was able to get the various agencies and colleges to join in what has become a multi-million dollar grant program for students in public and private colleges throughout the state.

In another area of state government I was able to persuade agencies to support the participation in the National Historical Trust's Main Street program. As a result, several cities in New Mexico now have ongoing Main Street renovations. Santa Fe needed no encouragement for such a development.

One last example of my loyal service is the time that I served as Director of the Natural History Museum where I did planning, hiring and fund raising for our Museum of Natural History. By now you are asking yourself is there nothing this man would not do to avoid getting into one line of work and sticking to it? Later I will tell you what my real work was and how it relates to our lives in Santa Fe.

But what of Mimi I hear you asking. Was she idling away her days in Santa Fe. No, she was painting and showing her work. She had a show at St. Johns and works at the New Mexico State Fair, the Fine Arts Museum as well as galleries about town. In addition, she taught in the Amnesty Program at the Community College as well as teaching English as a Second Language. She also worked as a literacy volunteer. She now has her own studio and would be pleased to show you what she is currently doing. She has recently hung the walls of the First National Bank with many paintings and drawings.

What has all this to do with Santa Fe? It has everything to do with why we came and why we stay. In Mexico we warmed up for our full frontal assault on the educational, cultural, and political institutions of Santa Fe. Santa Fe continues to provide the creative context for our lives. Santa Fe like San Miguel has a special beauty all its own. Here our juices continue to flow. Everyday we walk about and find more reasons for being. We live on a hillside close to the National Cemetery with a million-dollar view of the Sangre de Cristos.

But wait there is more! I will now confess why I really came to Santa Fe. I needed money to support my habit. I am a habitual poet. All this time while I seemed to be earning a living I was stealing time to write. Yes, I went to UNM pretending to get a master's degree so I could do a book of poems for my thesis and yes, I returned to do a PhD in American Studies so I could do another book of poems in the form of a dissertation. I confess that I have used the system to support Mimi and myself and when you come to see Mimi's studio I will show you so many poems that you will weep at my audacity.

But wait one last time! I have a last confession to explain why I hide here in plain sight ever closer to the cemetery. I have joined and continue to belong to the Live Poets' Society. Mimi knows this and is to blame for my recent book of poems (Smoking the Bees) for which she did the cover. For that group I produced a live performance last year at the College of Santa Fe and this year I was the editor of *Volume III, Scenes of the Live Poets' Society.* I'll show you my books if you come by and we will lift a glass to what is left of our lives and its subterfuges. In the meantime a poem, ready for my next book:

Layered with old scars
The ghost of my missing hand
Reaches for a pen.

Your ever scheming friends,
Bob and Mimi Rhodes

Bob and Mimi today.

Inherit the Sand
A play in one act
by Claudia Jessup & Jonathan Richards

*T**HE SCENE IS A SANTA FE BAR**. For want of a better word we will call it La Fonda. An uncommonly handsome couple of uncertain age are sipping margaritas at a table. They are CLAUDIA JESSUP, an author and practitioner of healing arts; and JONATHAN RICHARDS, a man with a shifty résumé spread around the arts.*

JONATHAN: How the hell did we wind up here in Santa Fe, anyway?

CLAUDIA: I've told you the story a hundred times, darling.

JONATHAN: Tell me again. I'm bored.

CLAUDIA: In Charlottesville, Virginia, where I grew up, I was good friends at boarding school with a girl from Santa Fe. I thought New Mexico, back then in the early '60s, sounded like the most exotic place in this country, if not the world. Liza always wore turquoise jewelry and Concho belts (her mother owned a jewelry store on Palace Avenue), and for class gatherings she made guacamole, which *no one* in the East had ever tasted back then. When we were seventeen, she got engaged and invited me to be a bridesmaid. I was so excited, because I was finally going to get to visit a place that was actually called The City Different in a state called The Land of Enchantment.

But, alas, Liza had second thoughts and broke off her engagement.

JONATHAN: That was inconsiderate.

CLAUDIA: I was so disappointed. Then I went to college, and moved to New York City.

JONATHAN: Where you met me.

CLAUDIA: Where I met you, darling. Then my friend Genie and I started Supergirls.

JONATHAN: A very glamorous business where you did all sorts of exciting things, and went on the *Tonight Show,* and....

CLAUDIA: Don't get off the subject. Who's telling this story?

JONATHAN: *(contrite)* You are.

He signals to the waitress for another round of margaritas.

CLAUDIA: Okay, so we sold the business in the spring of 1973. I'd started writing, and my first book had just come out.

JONATHAN: And I'd just signed to write a novel, *Cherokee Bill,* about a real-life outlaw in the Oklahoma Territory....

CLAUDIA: I decided that maybe we should get away for the summer, for both of us to write. You said, "Where should we go?" I blurted out—without even having to think—"Santa Fe!" So I called Liza, who was now married to someone else and still living here, and asked if she could look for a place for us to rent for the summer. In due time, she called back, reporting that she couldn't find *anything* for less than four or five hundred dollars a month, because of the Opera. Then she said, "But if you'd be interested in house-sitting, my mother has friends who are looking for someone to commit to four months."

JONATHAN: Housesitting! That's the ticket. No rent! Of course in those days, you didn't get paid for it either. Our timing was a little off.

CLAUDIA: We had planned for two months, but what the hell; we weren't on any schedule.

JONATHAN: We spent that summer in Santa Fe, writing. The kitchen had the first microwave we'd ever seen, and we discovered marshmallows would swell up insanely if you nuked them. We gathered mushrooms at the ski basin, and

Liza's mother looked them over and threw out the ones that would kill us, which was about two thirds of them, and we were still terrified to eat the rest.

CLAUDIA: It was a great summer. We made friends. We went to the dances at the Pueblos, and Indian Market, and Zozobra. There was the fragrance of fresh piñon after it rained. And on cool mornings in September there was the aroma of burning piñon in the air. And those incredible sunsets! We both fell in love with Santa Fe, which was a lot different back then.

JONATHAN: A friend wanted me to do a cartoon with a sign on the highway: "Entering Santa Fe. Pavement ends." Remember buying seafood from a freezer truck that came once a week to Pen Road Shopping Center? There was one Chinese restaurant that served Chop Suey and Parker House rolls. Nothing was open after eight in the evening.

CLAUDIA: Which may explain why I got pregnant.

JONATHAN: Well, it was that or the Opera.

Claudia sings "Donde lieta uscì al tuo grido d'amore." from Act III of La Bohème.

JONATHAN: It was another ten years before we moved here.

CLAUDIA: But we kept coming back every year for a few weeks to visit all of our new friends. We always had a wonderful time . . . but it was a bit of a Yin-Yang experience, going between New York and Santa Fe.

JONATHAN: Our friends started leaving brochures for time-shares on the night table of their guest room.

CLAUDIA: Remember the fight we had in that restaurant on 105th Street? After we came back from Thanksgiving in Santa Fe?

JONATHAN: Fight?

CLAUDIA: I threw a fork at you.

JONATHAN: Oh, *that* fight.

CLAUDIA: I *was* pretty upset. And then I realized why I was so unstrung.

JONATHAN and **CLAUDIA** (*in unison*): *Because we were living in New York and not Santa Fe!*

JONATHAN: It had snowed, and there were gray moats of melting slush at every curb.

CLAUDIA: And there was all the school stuff and ballet and piano classes to schlep the girls to. It seemed as if it was always pouring rain, and you could never get a cab. The subway at rush hour with two little girls did not thrill me at all.

JONATHAN: Dog poop. Trash blowing everywhere. Weeks without seeing the sun.

CLAUDIA: So we decided to give Santa Fe a year, a sabbatical of sorts, just to get away.

JONATHAN: Who were we kidding? We bought a house. You came out alone for a week to house-hunt.

CLAUDIA: The house was to be an investment. And it was only five days. "If I find a place, we'll move. If I don't, we stay put." That was the deal.

The Richards on arrival in 1983.

JONATHAN: Every night you'd call me. "I've found the perfect place! I'm just going to look at one more tomorrow."

CLAUDIA: I know, I know. But each one was better than the last. And then I found the house on Apodaca Hill, and that was it.

JONATHAN: "We'll try it for a year." That was 1983. We weren't even unpacked till '85.

CLAUDIA: And here we still are. Alex was four and India was nine when we moved. They grew up here and loved it. When Alex's fiancé was here last year, he told her,

Jonathan and Claudia today.

"Now I know where you got your sunny personality." Of course, both girls are back living in New York now....

JONATHAN: How ya gonna keep 'em down on the farm? A lot's happened over all those years, hasn't it?

CLAUDIA: Well, there's Whole Foods, for one thing. And a lot more wonderful restaurants now.

JONATHAN: They've paved the streets. Movies, music, culture...it's the Paris of the Desert.

CLAUDIA: Santa Fe's so much bigger, for both better and worse. I do worry about whether there's enough water to sustain all the new growth.

JONATHAN: Well, should I go look at houses in Costa Rica? Just for a week?

CLAUDIA: Maybe. But where would we get our green chile fix?

The waitress brings more margaritas, and a bowl of green chile.

CURTAIN

We Came to Santa Fe
Orlando & Rebecca Romero

Rebecca (Becky) Romero is a former journalist and retired state employee. **Orlando** *is the retired director of the History Library at the Palace of the Governors. He is an NEA fellowship recipient in Creative Writing and was named Eminent Scholar for New Mexico. He has published numerous essays, columns, articles and is the author of two books.*

I T WASN'T EASY GETTING HERE. We not only had to prove our worth; we had to have our own tools, animals, seeds, and farming implements like shovels, hoes, picks and saws. Some of us were peninsulares from Spain, some of us were Mexicanos Espanoles, born of Espanoles in Mexico, some of us were meztizos, Espanoles mixed with Indians, and some of us were mulatos, Indians and Espanoles mixed with Africans. We had one desire, starting a new life. Like all emigrants and in all our mixtures, it was this mix that was to bring diversity to not only Santa Fe but all of New Mexico.

The journey was difficult after leaving Zacatecas, Mexico. It was the year 1598 but by April of that same year we celebrated the first recorded Thanksgiving in what is now the United States of America, and on the banks of the Rio Grande there was much feasting. The men killed game and caught fish and eels from the sparkling clean waters of the Rio Grande. Men, women and children feasted, prayed and gave thanks that we had made it this far. But after much rejoicing by this mixed bag of wealthy, middle-class and peons, we realized that we still had passes to cross, barren plains to wander, and to find a place to settle.

After settling nearby San Juan Pueblo, renamed San Gabriel de los Caballos, and known to the Native people today as, we celebrated by putting on a grand play of Moros y Cristianos both to impress the Natives and to assure ourselves that we had arrived.

But those years were tough. It has been considered by some as a minor ice age. The rivers froze solid. Firewood was scarce and by 1605–1607 we started, like all immigrants looking for a better place. Despite the terrible harshness, desertions, and internal turmoil, the gold was not in the ground but in the settlers themselves.

One of our colonists, Martinez de Montoya, started a small finca in Santa Fe. Santa Fe was ideal. It was cold in winter but cool in summer and for a small colony the stream was more than adequate. Game abounded, there were trout in the streams and, most important, tall pines for vigas and home construction. Before we knew it, we were all living in Santa Fe, creating a Plaza that was large and went as far as the Parroquia. We constructed las casas de gobierno, the Place of the Governors. Our governor Peralta officially called it La Villa de La Santa Fe in 1610.

When Becky and I moved to Santa Fe in 1968, some 375 years later, it wasn't as hard as it had been for our ancestors. In fact, the town had a population of about 35,000. I was an undergraduate at the College of Santa Fe while Becky had completed a tour of Peru as a journalism student. Life in Santa Fe in those days was wonderful as it had been in the late 50's when I was growing up.

In reality, I had been born in Santa Fe in 1945. Becky had been born in Alamosa, Colorado, but of New Mexican ancestry that went back to the colonial period.

Santa Fe in those days was intimate, graceful, polite and full of artists and writers. It was so afford-

Orlando and Becky bringing their contribution to a "bring your own" party in Santa Fe, 1968.

able that our apartment with a corner fireplace and vigas was a mere $45 a month. We walked downtown to the high school tennis courts to play tennis. We walked to the moves at the El Paseo, the Lensic and Spanish films at the Alley where Tia Sophia's is now. On special evenings we would walk up Canyon Road to Three Cities of Spain, have dinner, drinks and stay for a play. And if we really wanted to be rowdy and dance we would walk up to El Farol, dance and meet bohemians from all over the world.

But in those days you could count the galleries on your hand. In fact, a cursory glance at the 1951 City Directory shows only one gallery listed and that was on Burro Alley. But by 1991, it had jumped to some 171 art galleries, many of them replacing the clothing stores that filled the Plaza earlier. Downtown was full of wonderful stores, like Goodman's, Levine's Bell's, El Pavon, etc., all great places for a good sport coat, a pair of work boots or a sturdy bra. People gathered from all the villages as far away as Vadito, Penasco, Cordova, all speaking the dialect of Cervantes with the older Hispanic men tipping their hats as ladies walked by. Santa Fe was polite in those days.

And restaurants abounded just as today. On San Francisco Street, Becky and I had Chinese at the Canton, Greek food, close to my heart could be found in various locations and for the real New Mexican you had so many choices it was hard to choose, but my favorite was "El Parian," where the old Bull Ring used to be.

Life in Santa Fe in the 60's, even with the hippies' arrival, was dignified but without pretensions of the nouveau riche. It didn't matter if you drove a Porsche or a Ford, parties were not catered, and your status did not depend on the square footage of your house or how many boards you belonged to, and no new arrival searched for the ideal

Becky and Orlando at home, 2007.

Becky and Orlando in the Plaza Mayor, Sebastian, Spain 1998.

casita in a gated community. Santa Fe was civilized in those days.

And graceful. Santa Fe in the 60's and earlier was this elegant Spanish woman whose gestures, nuances and flirtations were old world, dignified, graceful, polite and full of the romance and mystery that accompanies a malaguena. Santa Fe remains Spanish, but in those days Santa Fe was as close as you could be to a foreign city without leaving the U.S.

Its plazas, courtyards, its genteel people and their relaxed manners, customs and celebrations made you think you were in Spain, Italy, or Greece. With a huge proportion of Santa Fe's population being Hispanic, many of them retained their culture and customs, whether it was a viuda with a tapalo dressed all in black or a group of nuns walking under the portal of the Palace of the Governors on their way to St. Vincent's or Loretto Academy, nothing in our time can bring back those treasured visual portraits. It was truly old world at its best and Becky and I savored every moment of it.

But a city may keep its facade but it is its residents that give life to this ancient place. If the children of the founders and creators of this beautiful gem can't afford to live here because high prices have turned it into the new Provence or Tuscany for the rich, then much of its passion, romance, diversity and historical integrity will disappear into the sameness that plagues most of the United States.

Yet, despite the sense of loss we feel, this elegant lady is hard to leave, actually it's impossible. When your first love was as beautiful as she, the love only continues to grow.

An Immigrants' Tale

John & Robin Rubel

*How **John** and **Robin**, then of a "certain age," left their comfortable home nearly a quarter of a century ago for the matchless vistas of New Mexico, where, having attained notably more age and markedly less certainty, they reflect upon their Immigrants' Progress with considerable satisfaction.*

I T ALL STARTED WITH THE *WALL STREET JOURNAL* in the Spring of 1983. It was a beautiful day in Santa Monica, California. From my office window I could glimpse the blue of the sea stretching to the lighter blue of the sky at the distant horizon beyond the lazy palm trees gracing the near skyline only a couple of blocks away.

Still, not everything was perfect. Homeless wanderers, having gone as far as they could go on dry land, were bunched amid the scattered detritus of sleeping bags and worn blankets and discarded plastic objects of unknowable provenance among the majestic palms along the Palisades overlooking the infinite ocean. An ominous brown haze was oozing toward shore from its nighttime abode a few miles out to sea to the south. It would soon cover much of the Los Angeles basin and obscure the scenic rim of mountains that help trap the daily and mounting invasion of gases from millions of separately innocent and collectively noxious exhaust pipes. By day's end, perpetual sunlight would create even more smog out of these gases, compounds of nitrogen, carbon and oxygen that burn the eyes, irritate lungs and corrode the leather stops of church organs for miles among millions.

But I digress. *The Journal.* It featured a special interest story about St. John's College in Santa Fe, New Mexico. It was about the *Great Books of the*

Western World, the Socratic Method, seminars. I was a few years past 60, retired after decades of various and oftimes unrelated undertakings. During most of WWII I worked on electronic countermeasures in the Research Laboratories of the General Electric Company. The war ended, we (my childhood sweetheart and then wife, Dorothy, and our year-old baby) fled Schenectady and settled back in Los Angeles. Thirteen years later, now heading a large electronic development laboratory at the Hughes Aircraft Company, having seen Sputnik 1 in the skies over LA, I found myself in the Pentagon. Now, again the beneficiary of a couple of happy accidents, (I had read about the Pentagon opportunity in *Time* magazine), I was Assistant Director of Defense Research and Engineering for Strategic Weapons. A couple of years later I was Deputy Director and Assistant Secretary of Defense for Research and Engineering. A couple of years after that I was a vice-president of Litton Industries in Beverly Hills. A dozen years later I was working on novel schemes for distributing movies, and a widower. In the Spring of 1983, married to Robin for two years, (now for 26), I was…reading the *Wall Street Journal.*

From an early age I had imagined myself going back to school when I no longer had to. Maybe St. John's would be the place. Maybe this would be the time. So I wrote to St. John's, and lo and behold: they told me about the Graduate Institute, there was a summer session, it began in late June. Why not?

That's how Robin and I began in Santa Fe. We rented a house at the far upper end of little Pacheco Canyon in Tesuque. It had just been built by Murray Gell-Mann, the Caltech physicist and Nobel laureate well known for quarks and the Eight Fold Way describing certain elementary particles. I went to school, read books and wrote papers. Robin met people and looked around.

One day she announced that she had found a wonderful piece of property. Five acres, not far away. What did we need property for? Never mind, come and look.

It was at the end of a ridge, the edge of a steep arroyo, in Vista Redonda, the uppermost development east of the Village of Tesuque. By Los Angeles standards, it was "cheap." For no particular reason, or at least none we were ever able to articulate, we bought it. We remembered that Charles F. (Chuck) Johnson, whose masterful "Rock House" in Carefree, Arizona had made the front cover of *Architectural Digest* in February (1983), lived in Santa Fe. We met him. If we decided to build, he would come to Los Angeles, stay with us a few days, get to know us and our thinking, and proceed to design a house for us.

A huge stack of mail awaited us back home. We gradually sifted through it. I was president of the Brentwood Park Property Owners' Association, and received a monthly report showing burglaries or any other crimes known to have taken place in our neighborhood. We had waged an increasingly successful campaign of awareness, patrols, reports and the like that had reduced crime far below what it had been in earlier years.

But now, in early September 1963, the August report told of a murder that had been perpetrated just a block outside the boundaries of our official neighborhood designation. A psychiatric inmate from the nearby Wadsworth Hospital, (a V.A. facility), had come looking for the young woman who volunteered as an aide there. Disappointed and angered at finding only her father at home, he had killed the unfortunate victim and left his lifeless body in the swimming pool.

The next day, taking our usual walk along the Palisades bordering the vast Pacific, we spoke briefly about this sobering news. Without ever discussing the pros and cons of selling out in LA and moving to Santa Fe, we put our house on the market and invited Chuck Johnson to visit us. Together, we composed a comprehensive document, entitled "Functional and Design Requirements and Desirements," in advance of his arrival. It was some 26 pages long. He edited and amplified it. When he left, it was 34 pages long. A few months

later, in February, 1984, we moved into a rental house in Santa Fe. Two years after that we moved into our Tesuque house. Nineteen years later, having outgrown our dream house, we sold it, bought in Las Campanas,

Robin and John circa 1998, at a daughter's wedding.

where we live more modestly but more easily in increasingly golden but existentially challenging years.

Moving to Santa Fe turned out well for both of us. For one thing, married only three years (Robin divorced, I a widower), we started anew in a place where everyone we met was new to both of us. Much sooner than we could have imagined, we discovered a circle of good friends who, like us, needed new friends, too. I completed the Graduate Institute program at St. John's in 1990. At 70, I may have been the oldest graduate that year, but it didn't matter. Indeed, I learned a lot from undergraduates in classes peopled by students who could have been my grandchildren. Robin was active for many years in community affairs, including the Buckaroo Ball, FOCA and the Repertory Theatre. Among other activities, I worked with now Speaker of the House Ben Lujan from 1992 through 2000, when we were finally successful in passing the legislation needed to reform New Mexico's residential property taxation laws. The kind of tax escalation that was threatening to drive people from their homes, often ancestral homes, has been largely if not entirely eliminated.

But most important to us, we not only are happy here, but uplifted by the physical and cultural ambience that surrounds us. Like many who pass from middle age to the next stages of life, we have both been repaired in one way or another in the past few years. Those repairs—open heart surgery, spinal surgery, cataract replacement surgery among others—and the modern pharmacopoeia that controls once-injurious or even fatal bio-physical changes associated with aging, endows us with fully functional, energetic and alert lives for which we try to be duly grateful.

Charm, it turns out, is a heavy burden. Bali, 1995.

Of course, the "world" falls far short of what most of us would prefer to be hearing and seeing and reading about. It *is* a bit dismaying that the polar ice caps appear to melting, the seas appear to be increasingly polluted and slowly rising, all sorts of animal and plant life is gravely endangered, nobody seems to understand how the world's money system works, or even imagines how it can keep on working without first collapsing, America's health care system is not very healthy and is increasingly costly—on and on, a long litany, far more vivid to our retired population than to those preoccupied with small children or immolated in work or distracted by the follies of the most recent celebrities.

But here, in this land of the Lotus Eaters, bright sunlight, calm winds, refreshing vistas and Rio Grande Valley breezes that sweep most of the smog away to other places leaves us time and space and multiple opportunities for a level of civil life never known or rapidly eroding in many a town or city across the world.

So I no longer read the *Wall Street Journal* regularly. Perhaps I have a repressed fear of reading an article that might entice us to consider changing to another venue as we did 23 years ago. But no, not really, that is not it. The fact is—no offense, please—we can't stand the editorial policies of the venerable *Journal.* The Neanderthals, after all, did NOT have it better than we do.

Besides, nothing could budge us now. Santa Fe is home for us for the rest of our lives!

Portrait of the author.

The Road to Santa Fe

Gershon Siegel

*In June, 1981 **Gershon Siegel** arrived in Santa Fe to begin a simpler, more contemplative life following his crazy hectic decade in the Bay Area. Now, after 26 years in this land of enchantment he is thinking that some form of regular meditation might prove salubrious for his peace of mind.*

LONG-TERM PLANNING has never been my forte. Flying by the seat of my pants is more my style and I understand how those more methodical with their choices might accuse me of allowing my life to be ruled by a loony, pie-in-the-sky, and possibly even risky attitude. However, one must consider those faraway times of my youth that helped shape my character.

As the 1960's counterculture was born and was glamorized in mass media, the psyche of society's ship made a radical left tack. This sudden turn tossed many of my peers overboard into a swirling sea of confusing ideas, churning cultural choices and self-defeating backwater lifestyles. Some of those pitched into that uncharted ocean were never heard from again.

The stronger swimmers among us gathered whatever pearls they could in those roiling waters and after a time managed to jump back onto main-stream-society's deck. The most determined "seafarers" plotted a different course altogether, building their own boats, leaky and not so leaky and offered to the still drowning a place to catch their breath.

Then there were people like me, who, not yet ready to jump overboard without a backup plan but still curious, clutched little homemade "lifelines" such as steady jobs or professions to keep from going too far adrift. Such tethers gave a certain freedom from the mother ship while at the same time, kept us skimming along the surface without getting in over our heads. Sometimes we'd be intrigued enough by one exotic passing vessel or another to climb aboard for a while, but our lifelines would soon reach an end and we'd be snapped back behind the wake of our parents' giant ocean liner. Occasionally the line would break and then our families might send in a "deprogrammer" to rescue us from this or that cult or group.

So if there is theme to my story, "experimentation" must be one of them and "media influence" the another. For it is an actual Hollywood movie, a national glossy magazine and a local weekly alternative newspaper that propel this plot.

Throughout most of the 70's I had been a hair cutter in the Bay Area and had always felt self-conscious about it. Catering to people's vanity had never felt like my "real" destiny. Fortunately, fate took a hand. After seeing the Warren Beatty movie "Shampoo," I noticed that staring back at me from my bathroom mirror were the same vacant eyes of Beatty's character, George a Beverly Hills hairdresser. I was shaken and knew the time had come to "get serious" and begin my "real life." The very next day I went to a pawn shop and purchased a used typewriter in order to chase my, as yet, unpursued dream of being a "writer." Any kind of writer.

Later that same day I picked up a copy of the free alternative newsweekly *Berkeley Barb,* still out on the street but long past its venerable incarnation as a leading voice of the 1960's counterculture. On that issue's cover was a headline screaming "What Do Men Talk About When Women Are Away?" and the article was a thinly disguised feminist man-hating screed then quite popular.

The author's slurs upon the masculine gender rubbed my chaps a bit too hard, and she had challenged any man to write in to counter her list of snide innuendoes against my perhaps clueless yet still-noble gender. I rose to the challenge and sat down with the second-hand IBM Selectric, taking up the gauntlet for men everywhere. Determined that my "letter to the editor," even snider than the article inciting it, be published in next week's *Barb,* I walked into the weekly's office to hand-deliver it.

And there, in the converted warehouse offices of the *Berkeley Barb,* is where I first laid eyes on the tall, blonde and beautiful Barbara Ann, who would, much to my surprise, consent to marry me not too many months afterward. An attraction sparked by our opposite colorings, her's Nordic-light, mine Semitic-dark, was all the more piqued upon discovering that we shared a love of unicorns, a bit of astrological knowledge, an interest in the Tarot and a general sense of magical thinking. What more did I need to know? At the age of 29, my destiny was revealed at last. Like purchasing the typewriter, deciding to marry Barbara was all a part of getting serious about pursuing my real destiny.

Part of that seriousness was a coinciding Saturn-return interest in anything related to survival. Loads of books about catastrophic "earth changes" were becoming popular, the most compelling containing maps illustrating the soon-to-be reconfigured North American continent. Those of us paying attention knew the big California earthquake was on its way and those who survived would be those who were prepared. Barbara's friend Jeff, who was selling some of those gloom-and-doom books, told us of a man named Richard who had "inside" knowledge regarding these changes. Jeff had a shoe business on College Avenue. He was solid. He was a Capricorn, like me. If Jeff said this Richard knew something, then he was worth checking out.

Richard turned out to be quite extraordinary in his very ordinariness. A bald-headed, cigarette-smoking, pressed-slacks kind of white guy, he was straighter looking and acting than anyone I had been acquainted with in about a decade. Middle-aged, he alleged to be the former chief investigator for "Operation Blue Book," the U.S. Air Force's famous collection of anecdotal stories gathered in the 1950's from hundreds of eye witnesses claiming to have seen UFOs. Looking, talking and acting like he *could* have been the Air Force's chief UFO investigator, who was I to question that he hadn't? His total absence of charisma only added to his believability.

In three months or less, a group of about 50 or 60 of us were meeting weekly in Jeff's Birkenstock/metaphysical bookstore to hear Richard talk about Solar Cross, an intergalactic confederation of extraterrestrials who were organizing Earthlings to establish "base camps" across the continent that would serve as "light centers" after the "earth changes." From there, we chosen humans would "hold the light," thus helping to calm the chaos. Once that phase was over, the "space brothers" would "air lift" us in giant ships to safe harbor inside secret installations under Mount Shasta. Before we knew it, Barbara and I had purchased 500 pounds of food sealed in nitrogen-gassed buckets. Once alerted through the Solar Cross phone tree, we were to pack up our vehicles with our survival gear and head north toward Santa Rosa to wooded land donated by one of our members.

Before that fated time, however, Solar Cross did a kind of weekend practice exit from the Bay Area, and our group drove to the future "light center." The special enticement of direct contact with the "brothers" was promised. What was not mentioned before the trek north was that the direct contact would be channeled through Richard. Thus did we hear a message of love and light from Kadar Mon-Ka of the *Saturn Tribunal*. However, certain implied warnings were also woven in the subtext. Always having been suspicious of authority figures, Kadar's message via Richard smacked to me of manipulation. At that point Barbara and I decided to sell our buckets of survival food and seek our fortune elsewhere.

Not long afterward, Barbara and I checked out Sunrise Farms, another California UFO survivalist group that seemed more "credible." Sunrise had already been established for many years, founded by a fellow who had once been Paramahansa Yogananda's right-hand man. Yogananda fan that I was, any group associated with the Indian saint could have no better spiritual pedigree. A new door to an authentic UFO survivalist community was opening just as we were leaving the more fly-by-night UFO group.

At the end of the 1970's Sunrise Farms claimed to be the largest wholesale organic grower west of the Mississippi. They had thousands of acres of coastal farmland on which they raised their produce and goats. In common they owned an impressive number of thriving enterprises: several retail health food stores; a large roadside restaurant; a coffee shop/bakery. However, their most exotic possession was a three-masted schooner waiting for the escape planned just before the Pacific inundated the coast.

Our arrival at Sunrise was inauspicious, to say the least. As we learned on the second day of our visit, a week earlier the commune's charismatic leader had gone into the desert on "retreat" after declaring himself the "Second Coming" of Christ. A severe shake-up/wake-up had occurred within the community. Half of its 200 members left en masse, putting the stay-behind loyalists in a bind. Was their readiness to welcome Barbara and me into the community because the "skeleton crew" left needed help?

I was offered a job working in the avocado orchard grafting Hass tops onto Fuerte rootstock, or maybe it was the other way around. For Barbara, it was suggested that they could use her skills with the goat herd that grazed up in the canyon. Since my concern was "getting out of Dodge" for good, I was ready to do whatever, and Sunrise Farms seemed like a pretty neat place to do it. There was a purity required of all collective members. Vegetarian meals were shared and everyone meditated together each morning. They believed in sex only for procreation.

Barbara didn't feel comfortable with the requirements of Sunrise Farms. She was ready neither to become a goat herder nor celibate. That I was ready to interrupt making love to my lovely bride just months after we married in order to fit in with the regulations of a very far-out commune demonstrated my desperation to change my life.

Despite my enthusiasm for moving to Sunrise Farms, Barbara suggested instead that we move to The Claymont School for Continuous Education outside of Charles Town, West Virginia. There I would attend a seven-month course, as she had done several years before, based on the consciousness teachings of G. I. Gurdjieff, the Greek-Armenian mystic and one of the unsung "founding fathers" of what was then known as the "human potential movement." At the time, however, I had no real knowledge of him, and the idea

Barbara Doern and Gershon Siegel's wedding announcement picture from the summer of 1980 as it appeared in the Berkeley Barb, *a publication where they were both employed. Although no longer married, Barbara and Gershon still love each other and work together on the publication,* Sun Monthly.

of attending a "mystery school" seemed too short-term. The course would be over and then where'd we be? We'd have to decide all over again what to do with our lives. I wanted finality. My resolve to join the Sunrise commune strengthened. Barbara refused. We argued. A month later we had a giant "lifestyle liquidation" sale, keeping not much more than my '75 Honda, in which we loaded our few remaining belongings and headed east to West Virginia. Not before, however, I had saved my dignity by having Barbara pledge that after Claymont our next destination would be my decision and mine alone.

The 600-acre Claymont property had once been the estate of George Washington's great-great-grand-nephew and boasted a colonial-era mansion in various states of disrepair. A number of buildings required maintenance, and these jobs fell to the course students as part of their "practical" work. In addition to this upkeep was added kitchen duty, gardening, stall mucking and mastering the "sacred gymnastics," as Mr. Gurdjieff liked to call the consciousness raising "movements."

Our days were filled from morning to night "working on ourselves." To break the intense pace, about every two weeks all students were given an "exeat," allowing them to leave Claymont proper for 12 hours. This usually meant driving into tiny Charles Town for real coffee and food from the greasy-spoon diner. After satiating those basic desires, I might end my media "fast" with a quick gulp of the magazine racks in the 7-Eleven. How could I know that my destiny lay in those racks?

Claymont traditionally ended its course with a seven-day silent mediation retreat lead by Bhante, a 90-year-old Cambodian Buddhist monk. In preparation for the arduous week we students were given one last exeat to blow off some steam. As usual Barbara and I headed for the diner, followed up with a trip to the 7-Eleven where I could scan the headlines. And there in the magazine rack was the May 1981 issue of *Esquire* magazine. Pictured on its cover was a smiling, handsome, well-groomed man sitting at the wheel of a top-down convertible Jeep with an endless Southwest landscape behind him. The headline read: "Yes, there is ONE last place to go!" In that instant I knew with utter certainty that whatever place was named in that cover feature was where Barbara and I were going to start our new life. The trick was to skip over the contents of the article and hunt for the name and the name only, like a thunderbolt from Olympus.

The table of contents open, I scanned for the story. No city's name peeked from the teaser line under the article's title. Turning to the beginning of the piece and restraining my eyes from reading any of it, I ran my finger down the lines of type, looking for the give-away proper-noun capital letters of our new home. And there in the third paragraph was the city's name, "Santa Fe, New Mexico."

Determined not to spoil the moment with any details about our new home, I deposited *Esquire* back to its place and shouted across the store, "Barbara, we're going to Santa Fe."

"Where's that?" was all she asked.

"Somewhere in New Mexico," I answered. And that seemed to settle the matter. If there was any hesitation on her part, Barbara didn't show it. She had made an agreement with me and she meant to keep it, and so Santa Fe it would be. Even if she hadn't heard of it.

We returned to Claymont and soon began Bhante's silent meditation retreat. Seven days of sitting, watching my mind recycle the same assorted sexual images stolen from memories and fantasies almost drove me mad. It seemed there would be no end to it. Only being able to talk again would stop the vacuous bouncing around inside my head. Finally, the retreat was complete and we had a celebratory dinner—vegetarian of course. At our table people spoke of what they planned to do after Claymont. The talk came round to Santa Fe. Someone at the meal said, "Bhante says that Santa Fe has the second-highest vibratory rate on the planet."

"And the place with the highest?" I queried, no doubt asking the question everyone at the table wanted answered.

"Juno, Alaska," came the surprising reply. I felt vindicated in my choice. Second highest vibratory rate seemed pretty darn good given that it had come from a magazine article, and an unread one at that.

Leaving Claymont, off we drove westward and southward into the sunset, ending up in the "Land of Enchantment." Within a day or two we had lined up a charming guest house in Tesuque to rent and promising job prospects for the both of us.

In the 26 years since arriving in Santa Fe, I have worked as a hair cutter, construction day laborer, freelance writer, furniture and frame maker, ceramic studio production manager, playwright and producer of children's musicals, word processor, writer of sales proposals for a corporate training company, down-

Linda Braun and Gershon Siegel on their wedding day in Barbara Doern's backyard in the summer of 1991. Although no longer married, Linda and Gershon still love each other, still co-parent their 11-year-old son Ezra Sage and still co-publish their 12-year-old magazine, Sun Monthly.

town Santa Fe bus driver/tour guide, and, for the last dozen years, sales rep/business manager/reporter/writer/editor/co-publisher of *Sun Monthly,* a Santa Fe-based magazine of personal, practical and global concerns.

Almost three decades later the circle of my life continues to come around on itself. A publication first led me to a wife who altered my path and brought me to another publication that propelled me to Santa Fe, where yet one more magazine, started in partnership with my second wife, now sustains me. Was it destiny? Was it fate or karma? Is it even possible to tell where one ends and the other begins?

Whatever twisty route got me here, preordained, accidental or otherwise, most days, often as hectic as those I lived in Northern California, I'm grateful to be in New Mexico. Over the years I've been fortunate to find family, friends and a growing tribe who've connected with me and to *Sun Monthly,* whether staff, advertisers or readers. So accuse me of a pie-in-the-sky attitude if you will. But I find the heavens above Santa Fe to be bigger and bluer than almost anywhere. And if you know of a better place to practice magical thinking, please drop me a line.

I Came to Santa Fe
Linda Strong Brighton

Linda Strong Brighton *has never stopped drawing and still carries a sketch book with her at all times and fills them with the world around her. She prints her own etchings and prints combining them in her wall art. Linda sculpts, welds and creates trophies. She lives near a Zendo Im. Linda's is married to a monk and meditates as well as running a horse boarding stable and a horse motel. She rides her own horses a lot with her new knees and does her best to keep up with her large family and friends.*

I WAS BORN IN ALBUQUERQUE with the name of Matthews, raised a Stamm in Santa Fe, married a La Botz, then a Miner, then a Wickes. I found my own name, Strong, and am now married to David Brighton and have the Buddhist name of Kenji. My grandchildren call me Nina and that gives you an idea of the many lives I have lived so far.

I belong to The Santa Fe Etchers group, several drawing groups, Colored Pencil Society of America, New Mexico Sculpture Guild, The National Collage Society. I also belong to the Rio Grande Peruvian Paso Horse Club. I run a boarding stable among other things, I'm a multi-media person, as is everyone if we would stop and think about it. My wall art is based on this theme and the fact that we all have so many lives and personalities, with the different people and projects, be it families or work, are all a lot of souls wrapped up in one package we call "ourselves."

Being born in Albuquerque at St. Joseph's Hospital was fine when it happened, but now it is a hospital for the mentally challenged, so I hope I don't end up there. My dad remembered Albuquerque's first stop light, he said that it was at Forth and Central. I remember when Nob Hill came into being. It has the greatest tunnels on either side of the shopping center in which we would run down and scream into your own echo, it is so loud being concrete and all.

My dad John Mathews was in Navel Intelligence during the Second World War, and we lived in Boston where I vaguely remember black-outs and food stamps. We also lived for a time up in Anacortia, Washington where I'm told I saw my first horse at the age of two, and took off down the road for three miles before my parents caught up with me. These wonderful creatures have been in my life ever since and still are to this day, eating my roses over my backyard fence.

Back in Albuquerque my granddad O.E. Beck owned the Coca Cola Bottling Company. My granddad's big Coca Cola trucks would pick me up out on the highway in Santa Fe and take me to him and my grandmother for a visit with them in their big house with a big lawn and trees and the beautiful big chandelier with its many strings of crystal beads in the dining room which I would clean from time to time.

My granddad Stamm also lived in Albuquerque and he was the first person to have a hot air balloon. He had it tethered out at the fair grounds and would charge for a ride. He also told scary stories I still remember.

In Santa Fe I had become a Stamm and lived out at Sol y Lomas that at the time was a hard top golf course. I got my first horse at age seven who was mine alone to take care of. His name was Fiddlefoot. It turned out the girl who owned him wanted to sell him because she couldn't stay on him. Come to find out he was a cutting horse and could and would turn a fast corner. I must have fallen off 20 times on the ride home which was just a mile. I didn't have a saddle, but he never ran off. He would just stop and eat grass and wait for me to get back on. Where Quail Run is now, me and some other kids trapped three wild horses and herded them down under the highway to a box canyon we had fenced in. I remember keeping the colt and the other two were in pretty bad shape. I think my dad had them taken to the slaughter house which was at the corner of St. Francis Drive and Siringo Road. When I got my first horse I had a bet at the time with my dad Allen as to which way one would put a bridle on a horses head. I won, hee hee! Fiddlefoot lived in a 50 acre pasture. Soon several other horses and even a cow joined him. We always called the cow "Hamburger."

It was down in this pasture that my dad Allen drilled a well to fill the reservoir at Sol Y Lomas. Well it silted in and he asked what to do about it. It was suggested that he put a 50 gallon drum of Tide down it and pump the silt out. Well that sounded like a good idea at the time and fortunately he didn't put the whole drum down the well, because when he started pumping it out onto the ground the bubbles took over the piñon trees and down the pasture for several hundred feet. I remember the newspaper coming out to take pictures of the sunset on the bubbles, which were pulsating down the pasture. Needless to say all the horses and our cow stayed away from the growing throbbing blob moving ever so slowly down the pasture. It took almost a year before the bubbles quit coming up in the toilet and out into the sink or garden. I don't remember it tasting funny, but perhaps our pet bull snake Joe didn't like them in his garden. Dad put that snake into my bed one night without me knowing it. Gad what a scare I had!

Then in 1950 my life took a sudden jerk off course to where it took me a long time to come to terms with it and find my road again:

It was a nice sunny and cold afternoon. I was nine years old and was headed for the barn when I saw a car drive up to our house, which was at the end of a dirt road one which a lot of people mistook for Rodeo Road, which was also dirt. So anyone at home would go out and give directions to them.

I remember riding down Rodeo Road to the Yucca Drive-In Theater, tying my horse to the barbwire fence out in the back and climbing through to sit in front of the projection house. I remember watching the dust that showed up in its light as it went to the screen, eating popcorn and watching the movie with other kids that had also ridden their horses in to watch the movie. Then riding home in the night up Rodeo Road past the stock dam where we would take off our saddles. I had one by then, and then we'd go swimming with our horses. The pond was where the offices are now at the end of Saw Mill Road. It seems like every kid had a horse then.

On a cold afternoon there was a car with the person inside sort of lookin' familiar. They asked if my mom was home? No, I said, she is in town, just the maid is here. They said, here take this note to the maid, get a coat, it is cold and come with me. Your mom wants me to take you to town and meet her. It turned out to be eight degrees above zero that night. The request didn't seem too unlikely so I went and got a coat, gave the note to Rose, our maid and my friend, as we were room mates as I had moved in with her when the house got crowded with sisters and brothers. She read the note and tried to stop me but into the car I jumped yelling over my shoulder I'll be right back. Didn't happen! NO. We drove out onto the highway and turned as if to go to town but instead we turned onto Zia Road. The car stopped and she asked if I knew what kidnapping meant? No, was my answer. I was nine, we never even locked our house doors, the world was a safe place except for goat heads in your feet in the summers, I still don't go bare footed much.

At this point a gun was put in my face and I was told to do what was asked of me or I would be shot. I got the message even though I still didn't know what a kidnapping was. To make a long story short my Dad Allen called the FBI and I'm here to tell the tale but every time I go into town, more often than not, I look over and see the piñon trees where the ransom was put and the police got me out of the car and took me home. The kidnapper turned out to be my mother's gynecologist and I did know her. When we went to trial and she was found guilty, she was put in prison for 15 years and got out in seven on good behavior. Years later she was found dead in her home in Santa Fe by her maid. When she died that morning I was shopping for groceries. I had two kids of my own and three foster kids to feed. Three separate people told me before I ever got to the second isle that she was dead. I looked up to the sky and said "Hey I got it, she can't come get me anymore," which is something Rose our maid told me years later and I said quite frequently and quite often. Rose said that the kidnapping changed our whole family but especially my dad.

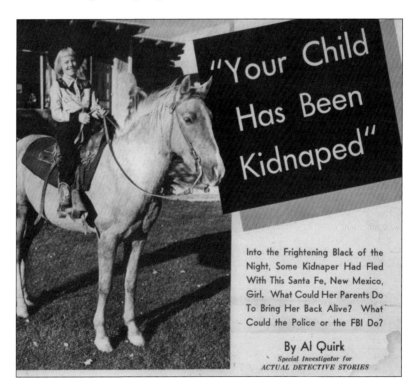

Linda on her first horse, Fiddlefoot, part of a special issue of the New Mexican *at the time of Linda's kidnapping, 1950.*

"Your Child Has Been Kidnaped"

Into the Frightening Black of the Night, Some Kidnaper Had Fled With This Santa Fe, New Mexico, Girl. What Could Her Parents Do To Bring Her Back Alive? What Could the Police or the FBI Do?

By Al Quirk
Special Investigator for
ACTUAL DETECTIVE STORIES

Still in the 50's I worked out at the Santa Fe Opera with John Crosby and with a host of characters. Now one fine day I was working down in the costume department running a power sewing machine, you know one that will sew 15 yards in a minute. Well anyway, I was sewing away when the door flew open and I was told in a very loud voice and under no uncertain terms to STOP sewing on the machine as Stravinsky could feel me in the floor and my machine was driving him crazy. O.K. So I stopped and went up into the house and sat right behind him and listened to him conduct the orchestra the rest of the afternoon. That was a day to remember.

It was about this time that a bunch of us during Fiesta rode our horses into La Fonda followed by a Model-T Ford. I went on through the bar and out into the patio, which now is the parking garage. We also used to ride our horses down to the Lensic Theater and leave them in the parking lot where the parking lot guy would watch them and our saddles. I wish I had done it more but at the time I didn't know that there wouldn't be a time I couldn't. Just a couple of years ago I could ride my horse up to the bank and go through the drive through here in El Dorado and now I can't do that any more either.

Then it was time for me to go to college. Art school was the only place I wanted to go so after much debate and sending of portfolios I went to the California College of Arts and Crafts in Oakland right near Berkeley just a quick bike ride away. It was the time of the kool aid acid test and Haight Ashbury was just starting. I was called a Beatnik. I guessed it was because I carried a tool box not a purse and that I was always drawing something and to this day I still draw a lot. Haight Street was also where my cousin lived so I went there a lot. We would go every spring to

Linda on her prize winning Stallion, Calipso at a horsemanship demo in Albuquerque, 1996.

the Japanese tea garden and drink tea, smell and see the beautiful flowers. At night I would listen to jazz at the Green Onion and for a cowgirl hick from Santa Fe it was all unreal and yet so real—not sure how I survived but glad I did. It was a time that has shaped me into the person I am as everything does. The city after my first semester was getting to me. I needed some space and air. I needed to see the sky. I found a church group going to Lake Tahoe to ski and I joined up. That is where I met my first husband. This good-looking man named Richard La Botz held the chair so I could get on the lift and that was that. We were married one year later. We made a deal that before any children we both wanted to travel so a year later off to Europe we went, leaving our dog with mom. That year would take up another book and I won't go there now. When we returned, we moved to Aspen, Colorado. I worked at a newspaper and La Botz worked in an architect's office. We bought a ranch down stream in Carbondale and had two beautiful children, but who's aren't? No

running water, a two-setter outhouse with a killer view of Mt. Sopris and the Sears Catalog; too many deer in our yard to count, wild asparagus in the spring and then La Botz took off. He says I chased him off, but from my side of the fence he just left.

I came back to Santa Fe for a visit one Christmas. The year it went to 20 degrees below zero, and my mother took me out to Shidoni Foundry to watch a bronze pour. Well I tell you the man doing the pouring, Mr. Charles Miner, got my heart right then. Another long story shortened, married, bought land next to Shidoni he

Linda smiling in her studio, 2006.

"Afternoon Gallop," by Linda Strong, a lifesize sculpture in the Westchester Mall in White Plains, New York.

started to learn how to blow glass, left the foundry where I was working now and then moved out. Then I fell in love or was it lust with an electrician. At this point Edward Wickes, Eb as we called him, helped me out when my son was hurt very badly when he fell 30 feet out of a tree in the Canyon Road Park and was in and out of hospitals for a year and he loved the kids. He left this time after I kick him out after he sent me into the toilet financially and I had had it.

At this point my kids had all left home for various parts of the planet. I was home-less living in my car with my dog Shadow housesitting when into my life an angel walked. Her name is Barbara Windom and she loved my horses and we have fun together. We have known each other now for 17, or is it 18 years, and it's "death till we part" sort of friendship. At about the time I met Barbara I also met my now-husband, David Dishin Brighton. We have a wonderful home on the south side of town, he has his art studio and I have mine. This is the kind of relationship I was always looking for timing, timing, and we too will be death till we part but I get to die first. He says no he does, that's still to be determined.

Looking back I wouldn't want any of it any different and I know that of the future.

We Came to Santa Fe
Michael & Gail Gash Taylor

Michael Romero Taylor began his career as an archaeologist working for the Bureau of Land Management in the 1970's in southern New Mexico. After moving to Santa Fe in 1983 he worked for New Mexico State Monuments, then was appointed State Preservation Officer and later returned to State Monuments as Interim Director. He currently works for the National Park Service on preservation projects along Route 66 and The Camino Real de Tierra Adentro. Michael's wife, **Gail Gash Taylor,** *has exhibited her artwork nationally and internationally since arriving in New Mexico in 1978. Her artwork is included in more than fifty museum and other public collections. She has been the recipient of an individual artist's National Endowment for the Arts Award and a United States information Agency Grant. The Taylors continue to reside in their home in La Cienega, just outside of Santa Fe.*

Michael Romero Taylor

ABOUT EVERY THREE YEARS MY FOLKS, J. Paul and Mary Taylor, would load all seven of us kids in the VW Minibus and take a summer trip up the river from Mesilla, following the old Camino Real to Santa Fe. We would rent a cabin nearby to get a little respite from the southern New Mexico summer heat and visit the many relatives of my father's mother. My grandmother, Margarita Romero Taylor, was a descendant of the great New Mexico families that came as settlers in the 16th and 17th Centuries. Everywhere we went we would run into cousins named Romero, Delgado, Baca, Ortiz or Lopez — the normal litany of family names for anyone with Hispanic blood in northern New Mexico.

Our trip north was on old State Highway 1, a two-laner that threaded its way up out of the Mesilla Valley, through the main streets of Hot Springs (now Truth or Consequences), Socorro, Belen, Los Lunas, Albuquerque,

Bernalillo, then finally, Santa Fe. The trip would take all day. We would have a cooler full of water, bologna sandwiches and watermelon, stopping under a cottonwood for occassional breaks to stretch our legs and eat.

I remember that Santa Fe was always a treat. We would breakfast at the Mayflower Café, where Pascuals is now, ordering waffles. This was very exotic to us kids, since we only ate at a restaurant about five times a year. Most of the time we would picnic near the Santa Fe River on Alameda Street. Then we would make the pilgrimage to the Palace of the Governors to learn about our roots and see the portraits of our great-great grandparents, (Trinidad Romero y Baca and Josefa Delgado Romero), hanging on the wall. They were pretty spooky looking, with penetrating eyes that followed you around the room. The portraits remained there for decades but were eventually retired from display for conservation purposes.

Dad was proud of his roots, and Mom loved to research the families, so we would get a lesson on who we were and where we came from, (something we are grateful for today). I remember visiting revered cousin Fabiola C de Baca Gilbert on San Antonio Street. She told wonderful family stories amidst a home filled with heirlooms from centuries past. We would also stop and say hi to Drew Bacigalupa, (an artist and author whose friendship we cherish), at his studio/home on Canyon Road.

I would come up to Santa Fe for Fiestas as a teenager; a big deal, since it was three nights of parties. We spent the nights sleeping on the banks of the Santa Fe River, or on the floor of some stranger's house who would invite us in off the streets. I lived in Santa Fe briefly in the '70s, doing archaeological work while renting classic adobes on streets like Delgado and San Jose for $85 a month.

In 1983 I moved to Santa Fe to work for the State Monuments Division of the Museum of New Mexico. It was a great job. I did preservation work at the historic sites of Jemez, Coronado, Lincoln, and Fort Selden

Mike and Gail with their son, Lee Romero Taylor, Christmas, 2004.

State Monuments. Later that year I met my future wife, Gail Gash, who had built a house in La Cienega. We have lived in the same house for 24 years; a house that sits on land that was once owned by my ancestors. Now I work on preservation projects for the National Park Service along Route 66, and the Camino Real de Tierra Adentro—the road my ancestors traveled north to Santa Fe.

Gail with a portrait of Lee, 14, in Spring, 2003.

Gail Gash Taylor

IT WAS 1978 AND GUACAMOLE was a relatively new food item in the diet of most mid westerners. An avocado plant I'd started from a seed accompanied me to New Mexico sitting on the passenger seat of my blue Honda Civic. Along with a yellow Datsun pickup and a red Ford, we formed a caravan of primary colors. Three of us, (friends from art school), moved west from central Illinois. Santa Fe was known for art and Mexican food, so Santa Fe seemed like a good place to start our adult lives. The food exceeded our expectations, and the art scene would eventually develop into something bigger than any of us could have imagined.

Our original plan had been to move directly to Santa Fe, but rent was cheaper for three struggling artists in Albuquerque. One of the guys got disillusioned after a year and returned to the Midwest, where he now owns a gallery in Chicago. The two of us who remained built a house, got married and divorced. I still live in that house, and building it was as formative a part of my life's education as my three art degrees.

While researching galleries, I'd met a woman who told me about a beautiful little village with spring fed ponds and acequias delivering clean, clear water to irrigated fields. The artists living there were hosting their second annual "Artist's Studio Tour." I drove north to La Cienega and fell in love with the landscape and the people I met. Fortunately, there was a five acre parcel of land for sale for $15,000. I talked my partner into the purchase with the promise that I would do the leg work to split and sell half of it within a couple of years for the price of the original parcel of land. The plan actually worked. With a small loan, our own hands and the help of new friends, we were able to build a small adobe house.

There was a community of young, idealistic artists in La Cienega. We were busy building our homes and lives in this historic village just south of the Santa Fe city limits. Whether laying adobes on one another's houses, or celebrating someone's birthday with the "free lunch on your birthday" at Horseman's Haven, we developed our friendships and with them, a sense of belonging.

The number of artist's in and around Santa Fe was relatively small in 1979. At that time only one gallery showed something other than "Western" art and most of my new friends showed there work there. Soon more galleries opened and the list of artist friends grew with the fledgling contemporary art market. Realizing the dream of being a "big fish in a small pond" became more difficult for the ever growing number of newcomers to the Santa Fe art scene.

Many big events in my life occurred in the 1980's. Tamarind Institute published six lithographs for me, (Tamarind was a lithographer's Mecca and I was a lithographer); I received a National Endowment for the Arts Fellowship; and I met my husband, Michael Romero Taylor. Mike and I spent seven months away from Santa Fe while he did a mid-career course of study in conservation at ICCROM in Rome and I traveled between Italy and Spain on a United States Information Agency grant lecturing about printmaking. Two years later, (in 1988), our son, Lee Romero Taylor was born. This last event caused me to reflect on my life's work. I gave up printmaking, started painting again and returned to realism. I'd come full circle.

Mike and I remain in our enlarged adobe home just outside of Santa Fe in the growing community of La Cienega, while Lee makes his own migration to the Northwest for college.

❖ ❖ ❖

Mike and Lee, 2006.

We Came to Santa Fe

Eugene & Clare Thaw

Eugene V. Thaw is a retired art dealer whose career began in 1950. He has given major collections of master drawings to the Morgan Library in New York; bronzes of the Asian Steppes to the Metropolitan Museum; and American Indian art to the Fenimore Art Museum in Cooperstown, New York. He is a long-time Trustee of the Morgan Library and an Honorary Trustee of the Museum of Modern Art and the Metropolitan Museum in New York.

IT WAS GEORGIA O'KEEFFE WHO CAUSED US to relocate our lives to Santa Fe. My wife Clare and I came here for a little more than a week, at the invitation of Juan Hamilton who was O'Keeffe's executor. She died in March, 1986 and we arrived in April, staying at the Bishop's Lodge.

Juan did not know me, but I had been recommended as someone with knowledge of the art market who did not have an ax to grind in the O'Keeffe world and could be neutral and unbiased.

Most of that week was spent in the basement of the large house on Old Santa Fe Trail in which O'Keeffe had died only a month earlier. There, in storage were all her remaining paintings except for a few things still out in Abiquiu.

Needless to say, it was a fascinating experience. And, Juan was happy that, although differing on individual values for some of the paintings, overall our total was only one or two percent different from his more experienced appraisal of the whole collection. Also, Juan and Anna Marie Hamilton became our very good friends.

When we weren't closeted with the art, Juan took us on long drives through the New Mexican countryside and we fell in love with it. This was a surprising reaction since I had been on the board of St. John's College of

Annapolis and Santa Fe for ten years and two meetings a year were in Santa Fe. Somehow, the rush to get home after meetings and the priority of other matters kept us from developing an appreciation of this special place, its favorable climate and its tri-cultural atmosphere.

Juan introduced us to Susan Herter whose then large property in Pojoaque we rented the next winter (including four delightful dogs we walked with every day). From that base of operations we began to look at properties for sale. I wanted to retire from art dealing and we tried several months of a winter at our farm near Cooperstown, NY. We were isolated and marooned for days at a time as the snow climbed in drifts up to the roof of our house. Santa Fe seemed ideal after that and when we found a Betty Stewart house in Tesuque with great privacy, we leapt at it. It is now 20 years later and we have added to the house (a wing which was Betty's last work) and added properties all around us, so our dog walks and our privacy are secured. Cleo is our third Great Dane in Santa Fe and Daphne our third Bull Mastiff.

We still go East once in a while but not as much as we once did. Frankly, we can't bear to leave. Fortunately Clare and I have projects to keep us interested and busy. Our modest family foundation, the Thaw Charitable Trust,

Clare and Gene on their front porch 2001.

was moved to Santa Fe about 14 years ago and has supported the arts, the environment and animal rights here in New Mexico as well as some favorite institutions in the East which still need our support.

Gene Thaw at his home in Santa Fe 2007.

Susan Herter, whose house and dogs started us off, was the first director of our Trust. Today Sherry Thompson directs our work brilliantly, guiding us to participate in discussions and actions which are as interesting and challenging as anything we have ever done.

Altogether life for us in Santa Fe has been full and satisfying. In spite of complaining about the influx of so many people coming to settle here, too much building and too little water, we cannot think of any other place we would rather be.

American Dream
Dr. Mai Ting

Dr. Mai Ting is a practicing family doctor with her MD from Boston University and has a general practice in Santa Fe. She has a small farm in the country a few miles north of Santa Fe that she farms when she is not involved in the many artistic and creative interests she shares with her friends.

WHEN I WAS A LITTLE GIRL, I lived in Hangchow, China. That was a long time ago—in the 1940s. It was after WWII, and everything was changing. I lived in a family compound with my mom, sister, my maternal grandmother, and grandfather, my aunt and uncle and their five sons. My grandmom was fat and had little feet and she didn't walk around much. She would give us sweets, pickled dried plum and watermelon seeds. She would take me to the Chinese opera. My grandfather was stern and serious, he would feed me fish cheeks as a special treat. I was praised for being able to suck the sweet fish mussels off the bone. He would practice his Tai Chi in the courtyard and demonstrate how strong and balanced he was by letting me jump all over him and swing on his outstretched arm. But my favorite treat was to go to movies. There in the dark, amidst a hall full of watermelon seed chewing and spitting crowd, I would be transported to the "Beautiful Country," where the streets were paved with gold (and if one was diligent and worked hard, anyone would be able to get rich). There were glamorous girls who wore red lipstick, had curly hair and smoked cigarettes, and gangsters making deals who were the bad guys.

But my favorite movies were always the ones with cowboys and Indians dashing across the screen on horses. Oh my, it was exciting. In 1949, when the Communist Chinese were taking over China, and it became a dangerous situation to be part of the Kuomingtang, my mother, after much persuasion, decided to leave China with her two daughters. My father had been stationed in Washington, D.C. as a Colonel in the Chinese National Air Force. My mother sewed her gold bracelets into her clothes, packed everything up into a bag, and got on a train which left Hangchow for Shanghai. We stayed with a cousin who worked for a bank and went to the airport.

Everyone was rushing around in a hustle to move. Thank goodness, at the airport, my mom met a colleague of my father's, Captain Lui, who was able to get us on a transport plane bound for Taiwan. Then we stayed at a military garrison for eight months while all the letters and permits were being processed. Then we left on a cargo ship for San Francisco. It was November, 1949. It was winter, cold and stormy. The seas were rough. There were three rooms for passengers and we "oh so lucky" to get a berth. The trip took three weeks—forever it seemed to me.

Everyone got seasick except me. I wandered through the hold of the ship. I marveled at the white skinned men with big noses and hairy arms and faces. They were kind and would feed me raw slabs of meat and pills of raw vegetables they called salad. I ate buttered toast and hard-boiled eggs. I drank milk and orange juice. Finally, on a cloudy, cold wintry morning we passed under the Golden Gate Bridge. It was actually bright orange not gold. We had finally arrived in San Francisco. The next day we flew out to meet my father in Washington, D.C., where we stayed in a small flat. There my father did the cooking—rice, steamed fish and fried cabbage was our main fare, until my mother learned to cook American style.

Mai Ting in San Francisco on her arrival in the United States in 1949.

Life was different. We moved from one apartment to another. At home, we were an isolated Chinese family. In the morning we went out to a very different American world. My father bought my mom a washing machine, a sewing machine and a black and white TV. That is when I got to learn about America and Americans. At home, my parents spoke Chinese and outside I quickly learned to speak American English with a southern accent (Maryland).

My first Halloween, I got a cowgirl outfit—a fringed vest, skirt, a cowboy hat and two guns which fitted in the holster. I was in heaven! I was a cowgirl just like in the movies. But in reality, I was still a girl with slanty black eyes and a thatch of black hair in a sea of blondes, brunettes and redheads.

We were in the United States temporarily on a visitor visa. My father did not have a green card. It was difficult to find work even though he had gotten a PhD in Engineering in Italy. But my parents persisted. The American dream was simple: If you worked hard and kept at it, you would find the dream—by saving pennies and dimes you could eventually buy a home and live the good life. My father worked as a draftsman, my mom worked as a seamstress in the sweatshops along Canal Street in New York City. Eventually they did buy their ranch style house with a brick extension and Danish American furniture.

I had other ideas. I wanted to live in the great West. I wanted to go to the University of Colorado. I wanted to be an artist. But my mom told me I would starve to death as an artist. I thought she was probably right. I decided to be practical and accepted a scholarship to Boston University to the six-year Liberal Arts and Medicine Program and graduated at the age of 23 as a medical doctor. I still had not actually seen the Rocky Mountains, but on my way to my internship in San Francisco, I drove with a friend across the United States non-stop to Rocky Mountain State Park and camped for the night. This was the vision I had dreamed of—majestic mountains, the crisp air, the towering trees, bluest skies and glorious sunshine. The next day we drove to Mesa Verde, then on to Lake Powell, where my friend Shirley went on to Los Angeles. I got on the plane with my suitcase and doctor's bag to fly to San Francisco. Somehow my doctor's bag got lost on the flight. I contacted the lost and found department at the airport. The man didn't believe me. He looked at me like, "Right, Lady! Sure." I filled out the report and went to Mt. Zion Hospital. The next day, I was paged to the front desk. There was my doctor's bag and a dozen red roses.

In 1970, I traveled by caravan to southern Colorado to a great gathering of people for summer solstice at Libre. We didn't get there until August and the folks at Libre didn't welcome us. They had enough of stray hippies looking for some free food, love and good vibes. So the caravan settled down in a circle camp on William Creek at Ordivy Farm. When it was time to move on, I decided to stay. I'd seen the East Coast and the West Coast, neither seemed to suit my needs and desires. I settled in the Huerfano Valley. There I rode a horse, lived in a teepee, and tanned deer hides. That's another story.

Santa Fe, the City Different, is where I eventually settled. It's still in the foothills of the Sangre de Cristo Mountains. I still love these craggy mountains, and the town has offered me employment. First, in 1985, I worked at the State Penitentiary. Then I became the Medical and Executive Director of Women's Health Services. I've been in solo practice since 1993. Here I've been able to practice medicine the way I choose, despite changes in medical practice and malpractice. I can be different. I can use herbs, supplements and homeopathic remedies because that's what I use to keep myself healthy.

I blend into the landscape of ethnic diversity. I no longer stand out like I did when I was a little girl. I blend into the Hispanic, Anglo and Native American cultures. I've been able to develop friendships with people who accept me. They've opened their homes and hearts. They've shown me how to set a table with table cloths, China

Mai Ting in her garden at Jacona, 2006.

Mai Ting, 2007.

and silverware. We talk about the politeness of car honking. It's not politically correct (PC) to honk your horn.

I've learned I don't need to be a workaholic to live the American dream, although I probably still tend to go at anything "gun-ho." When one arrives and works at the American dream it's not all about working hard, saving all your pennies and dimes and sitting back in front of your big screen satellite TV, drinking Cokes and eating pepperoni pizza. It's not just about how big your car is and how new, how much money you can spend, or the freedom to do whatever you want. And one thinks of the politics and democracy. Is it the best political solution for everyone and anyone on the globe? I don't know, but it works. The world has gotten a lot smaller and infinitely more intricate and complex in the past 50 years. And the American dream needs to change and evolve to meet the demands of the 21st Century, but I'm still happy I found Santa Fe and Santa Fe found me.

How I Came to Santa Fe

Anne Valley-Fox

Anne Valley-Fox *is a poet and researcher specializing in New Mexico history and literature. She is the mother of boys (now men) and the author of* Sending the Body Out *(poems, Zephyr Press, 1986);* Your Mythic Journey: Finding Meaning in Your Life through Writing and Storytelling *(co author Sam Keen, Jeremy P. Tarcher/Putnam, 1989);* Fish Drum 15 *(poems, Fish Drum Press, 1999) and* Point of No Return *(poems, La Alameda Press, 2005).*

IN 1970, **GEORGE WEISS AND ROSA VANDO** boarded a westbound Amtrak train leaving New York City. Their plan was to disembark when they came to a place with space enough to hold them. They got off the train at Lamy, New Mexico and hitchhiked north to the Lama Foundation in San Cristobal. From there they made their way north to the village of Questa. Rosa, who was Puerto Rican, felt instantly at home among the Spanish-English speakers she met in the post office and hardware store. George and Rosa settled into a tiny two-room Questa-style adobe for the duration.

Word went out by tribal drumbeat that George and Rosa had found a piece of heaven in Northern New Mexico. George set up shop as a woodworker and Rosa, soon with a baby on each hip, came to know most of the families in town. During the warm, languorous summers, friends from New York and San Francisco came to visit and some stayed on. Among the summer visitors were my sister, Nancy, her husband, Alec and Oban, their two-year old. Before returning to San Francisco they invested in a piece of land north of the Red River Road that led up to the Molybdenum Mine. Two years later, as the centerpiece of their divorce settlement, Nancy got the land and moved to New Mexico.

The summer of 1975 I sublet my apartment in San Francisco and repaired to Questa. Nancy had had her second child, Samson, and was living with Eddie, who was to become her second husband. They were renting Fidel Martinez's adobe house in an apple orchard behind the Questa Honey Farm. The house had electricity (which had finally hit town in 1954) and an outhouse in lieu of plumbing. Fidel's grazing cows rubbed their hides against the house. I arrived on the heels of a cloudburst to find Oban and his friend Serena belly down in the flooded orchard playing "alligator."

The house was bursting with visitors. Over the course of the summer a half dozen itinerant friends showed up at the Questa house for unspecified periods of time and made themselves comfortable sleeping on a pair of old couches or in sleeping bags on the floor. A tent went up in the orchard. Nancy and Eddie were breaking ground on her land and their visitors pitched in however we could, digging trenches, watching the children, cooking, kicking in money or food stamps. Most afternoons we hiked down to the Rio Grande — at Mamby Hot Springs or La Junta — with children strapped to our backs or running ahead down a trail dusty and thorned with rosehips. Without thought for the watershed we soaped and shampooed our kids and ourselves in the river; we swam to the other side and sunbathed on lava rocks open to the sky. Sometimes a golden eagle flew over, fishing the river. A lone fisherman might appear and disappear when he saw us. Local kids sometimes drove out to the rim and peered 500 feet into the gorge at the naked hippies, but most often the steep descent and ascent discouraged foot traffic.

The following summer I arrived from San Francisco with my infant son, Ezra Jack. The communal house building and river bathing and long, stoned evenings of cooking and talking and blasting music into the lovely night was very much in progress. I studied my sister's casual parenting style and attempted to copy it. We went on hikes and mushroom foraging in the mountains. We went to the hot springs and to the river. In August, we canned zucchini and apricots.

Once a week my sister and I drove 25 miles to Taos to shop for supplies. Afterwards we'd duck into the Plaza Bar to get out of the heat and toss back a beer or a shot of tequila. Our trips to town usually included a trip to the Harwood Library. Nancy was an eclectic reader and Eddie's taste for biographies featured a weird fascination with books about Adolf Hitler. That summer I read John Nichols' *The Milagro Beanfield War* (George was pals with J.C., reputedly the model for the novel's madcap hero Joe Mondragon) and *The Magic Journey,* which I especially liked. I read Frank Waters and Peggy Pond Church and Rudolfo Anaya's signature *Bless Me, Ultima.* I remember reading poetry by Frank O'Hara, Pablo Neruda, Diane di Prima, Gary Snyder, Denise Levertov, and Allen Ginsberg.

Each day was an excuse for a picnic; evenings opened into spontaneous parties with a spread prepared by my sister or campfire cooking (we fired up tofu and elk steaks, chili peppers and hot dogs). There were inevitably dogs present and children playing together and someone always had reefer to share. Every night the sky was a light show; each day shimmered in air you could see through. One afternoon my sister and I parked by the highway and walked a mile across a sagebrush mesa to visit a crooked windmill. "I love this landscape," she declared, "it makes me feel so deliciously insignificant."

The summer was a refreshing hiatus more than a solution to the quandary of my life as a single parent of minimal means in artistic San Francisco. Soon after Ezra's first birthday in February, my sister called from Questa. At last she and Eddie were in their house and connected with telephone service. I remember standing in the kitchen talking to her, gazing at a poster I'd pasted on the refrigerator, an image of Green Tara, Tibetan Buddhist Goddess of swift compassion. The dakini had answered my prayer for love by sending baby Ezra but she hadn't yet solved the problem of my existential sorrow.

"I don't like the sound of things in your letter," Nancy said. "I think it's time for you to move to New Mexico." She said that a friend of Eddie's had an empty school bus for sale for $300; Eddie would pull it onto the land behind their house and Ezra and I could live there until it got cold. "We'll help each other out, Annie." My silence on the other end resulted from stifled sobs. "Okay then," my big sister said, "I'll fly out in a few weeks with Sam. We'll do a garage sale and pack up and you and I and the kids will drive back in your Volkswagen."

The rebuilt Volkswagen broke down outside of Gallup. Eddie drove down from Questa to retrieve us and we piled my life's possessions into the back of his truck Grapes of Wrath style. A fabulous gold and red papier mâché owl that my friend Mathea had brought to me from Thailand flew out of the truck bed en route to Questa, but otherwise we arrived in tact. When I phoned Rocky, the dope-smoking, brilliant but fallible Rastafarian car mechanic who had rebuilt the VW engine and sold me the wagon to report its mechanical failure on the outskirts of Gallup, he said he'd have to think about that overnight. When I called the next day from a pay phone outside El Seville Café, Rocky told me he'd meditated long and hard and had determined that the car's throwing a rod was not his fault. He would, however, drive out and haul the carcass back to San Francisco and even though he didn't believe he was culpable he would send me $200 in exchange.

The yellow school bus didn't come through but I bought an old trailer with Rocky's settlement. Ezra and I spent the summer parked behind my sister's house with access to the back door and the bathroom replete with flush toilet and a claw-foot tub my sister had scored at Berlinda's Second Hand Store in San Luis. All summer I baked bread in my metal house, experimenting with various organic flours and nutritional seeds despite the suffocating heat. After the cold snap in late October I rented a little adobe down the road and Ezra and I spent much of the winter warming up in the bathtub. Besides the tub, the main attraction of the little house was the landlord and landlady, Moises and Juanita Rael, who were kind to us out of natural goodness. That

summer I planted a vegetable garden in a corner of their agricultural field. Though the plot was ten times larger than I could possibly handle, Moises didn't warn me off but dropped by on planting morning with a bag full of seeds. He sowed by tossing the seeds on the ground—eschewing my city-slicker method of poking them down in rows—and they grew.

Anne, Ezra and Ilmars—
Questa, August 1976.

When the pipes froze the following winter, we moved into my lover's house in Valdez, east of Taos. M's unfinished two-story house had no plumbing to freeze: it towered, ship-like, over the piñon forest. On Ezra's third birthday we were snowed in for the better part of a week; it took all day to melt enough snow for a bath. In the spring, M brought electricity to his estate. He excavated a wall of boxes stacked outside under tarps and retrieved a vast array of electric appliances—lamps, radio, clock, clock radio, hairdryer, toaster, even a black and white television—all of which sprang to an unnerving state of animation with the flip of a switch. By summer's end the strain of a mismatched alliance between M and me erupted into a single, pitched battle. An hour later, my child and I were flying through the woods over the treacherous, rutted road in my stuffed-to-the-gills white Chrysler wagon (Moby Dick) and down the highway to Santa Fe.

We came to rest at a cut-rate motel on Cerrillos Road. In the morning I called the New Mexico Arts Division to enquire about the Poets in the Schools program; the following afternoon I was sitting with arts administrators Michael Jenkinson and Stanley Noyes at a sidewalk café off the Plaza discussing the program and the marvelous paths that had brought us all to Santa Fe. To match their love of the language arts, Stan and Michael brought enormous good will to the job. I became part of a cadre of poets who traveled on interstates and blue highways to schools around the state, encouraging unsuspecting children to make the strange and beautiful things we called poems.

Anne Valley Fox, 2007.

My first rental in Santa Fe, a low-slung railroad flat with peeling linoleum floors, stood at the angular intersection of Canyon Road and Acequia Madre, Ezra started pre-school at the New School; I was glad to work off part of his tuition by washing windows and cleaning the chemistry room. I worked nights at the Hilton Hotel's then-restaurant where the waitresses were required to wear short skirts and boots in sync with the western theme. After a number of months I located a sunnier place to rent and my sister came down from Questa to lend a hand with the move. She and I were up most of the night packing and scrubbing but the landlady refused to return my $50 cleaning deposit because, she said scornfully, I hadn't dusted the vigas. Even then I realized that this was a small price to pay for having found my home on the planet.

We Came to Santa Fe

Candelora Versace

Candelora Versace is an award-winning freelance writer who started her career at The New Mexican *in 1991. She is also co-owner of Howard Goldsmiths, a custom jewelry gallery in the Railyard district, with her husband, master goldsmith Marc Howard. The family lives in a log cabin tucked in the Ponderosa pines southeast of Santa Fe, where she plans to finish her Santa Fe novel,* Traveling Light.

WHEN I MADE THE DECISION IN THE SPRING of 1989 to move to Santa Fe, I had only the vaguest notion of what it might be like. The idea of visiting the travel section of a bookstore never occurred to me, and "Santa Fe Style" was still a few years from publication. I simply imagined it would be hot, dry and desert-like, perhaps like Tucson, and very appealing to a Midwesterner who couldn't stand cold, wet, gray weather.

Not that I had any first-hand experience of Tucson, either. I was living in Seattle, had been there perhaps half a year and suffering from a typical gray Seattle winter. On this particular day, I also had attempted to tentatively enjoy what appeared to be sure signs (finally!) of spring: warmer weather, a sunny day: seems like a walk around Green Lake on a day like this would be very pleasant.

Except that as I hit the halfway mark and still had a good 20-30 minutes to go to get back to my car, a typical Seattle spring squall rose up and within minutes the temperature dropped, the wind picked up dramatically and the heavens opened. I spent the rest of my lovely spring walk with my denim jacket pulled up over the back of my head in a ridiculous attempt to keep dry (so obviously not a native Seattlite, as I was surrounded by people fully prepared for this and any other weather event at all times) and formulated a plan for escape from my misery in the form of relocating to Tucson.

I met my sister as arranged after my walk at a nearby coffeeshop. "This sucks. I'm moving to Tucson," I told her. Her husband immediately piped up, "Why don't you go to Santa Fe? I have a good friend there, you could stay with her." And with that, my move was a done deal.

I imagined Santa Fe would be populated with eccentric nonconformists such as I had found when I lived in Key West, Ann Arbor and New York City's East Village. Perhaps I had seen pictures of it? Blue gates? Flat-roofed houses? Had the big National Geographic expose of Santa Fe as a foreign culture right here in America even been published yet?

I also imagined it to be as far from Detroit (my hometown) as possible, a place where a person could be absolved of the failure to find a steady cubicle job or a nice man who wore a suit to work, a place where someone of reasonable intelligence could continue to roam on the outer edges of polite society and be not only tolerated but perhaps celebrated for the ingenuity and flair it takes to create an exotic life on few marketable skills and even less money.

Frankly, by that point in my life, I had not a clue how to reenter any sort of ordinary career path, having spent my 20s largely avoiding the issue entirely in favor of, well, let's just call it adventure. And truthfully, I just didn't know how to talk to those people in those big glass buildings anymore. I had thrown

away my last pair of pantyhose in 1981 and was struggling mightily to make something out of myself in Seattle that didn't also include making coffee and serving food.

My plan took shape almost immediately. My friend Susan, a waitress in a cafe

Candelora Versace at Tsankawi, Bandelier, in the summer of 1989, just before she moved to Santa Fe.

near my apartment, jumped on the opportunity for a road trip. We would drive to Santa Fe in June, stay with my brother-in-law's friend for a few days, and make some decisions about housing and jobs in preparation for a September relocation.

That trip would turn out to be one of the last few grand-scale roadtrips I would ever take. Because once I got to Santa Fe, I knew I'd be staying. The drive itself was one of those unforgettable slices of time, where I reveled in the intense red landscape of Utah, the sight of a streaking comet across a midnight sky in Colorado, or was it Arizona?, the endless roads of a western emptiness I had never seen before.

And Santa Fe itself, in the summer of 1989, was all it was promised to be: eccentric and funky, lively and interesting. We found ourselves driving in circles on Paseo de Peralta, watched the moonrise in La Cienega, enjoyed the silence of Tsankawi and the hippies in Madrid. I was smitten.

But I drove back in September by myself; Susan had opted out to check out Cannon Beach in Oregon instead, and it was some 10 years before I heard from her again, when she called to apologize for not making the trip with me as planned.

Whereas in June we had tried to make the most of every minute by driving the 24 hours or so almost nonstop from Seattle, this time I took the slow route. I stayed with a cousin in Portland for a few days, where I got a phone call from my dad in Michigan; my mother, 66 at the time, had fallen and was in intensive care with a broken foot and wrist, a blood clot poised dangerously to inflict serious damage. Should I come home? No, no, she'll be fine, he said, and with that, I put it out of my mind. And in a few days, she was; in fact, they relocated to Santa Fe themselves in 2000. I didn't realize until years later how perilously close her fall had come to changing the entire course of my adult life. I doubt I would have found my way back to New Mexico had I gone back to Michigan that day.

From Portland I drove down to LA where my brother lived, and stayed with him in Venice Beach for a day or so. Then I headed east; finally, while driving from Albuquerque up to Santa Fe on I-25, I passed a billboard that said, Welcome Home! and I smiled with relief.

I was 30 years old. Even though I had left Detroit years before on my quest for a life outside the cubicle, it had remained "home" in my consciousness, but only for its familiarity, certainly not for any fondness.

Candelora Versace at her studio in Santa Fe, 2006.

Eighteen years later, I am still in Santa Fe, and most of the time I am generally confident in calling it "home." I have a husband and a daughter, own a house and a business, and know secret shortcuts through quiet neighborhoods, how to make calabacitas and the name of the guy in the white truck who drives down from La Junta to sell his corn, chiles and melons.

Not that anyone actually considers me a "local" here, though, that's for sure. No, I'm still "just off the bus" to these folks who claim some 500 years of attachment to the place. For that matter, I barely claim attachment to America itself; a classic third generation American, I find myself with a genetic longing for a homeland I've never known but am less than a 100 years away from.

And perhaps underneath it all, that is Santa Fe's true appeal for me; the increasingly faint Old World feel of some of its dusty back streets; a language with ancient roots lilting out of a slightly lopsided window, the now rare sight of a bent old man in a small garden reminding me of my Nonno in his little row house garden in Washington, D.C. in the 1960s, so far from his homeland, which he left when the century was young. He would head out to the garden in the morning, pick the squash blossoms still damp with dew, and bring them in to Nonna, who would dredge them in a seasoned batter and fry them for dinner. I like to think he would feel quite at home here, too.

We Came to Santa Fe
Zenia Victor & Galen Duke

After a lifetime of traveling the world **Gaylon Duke** *and* **Zenia Victor** *settled in Santa Fe in 1981. For fun they now take eight local high school students to Bali every summer in what they call the Bali Art Project. Not many people would call being totally responsible for eight kids, 24 hours a day, seven days a week for a month on the opposite side of the world fun, but that is what makes these people different.*

I DROPPED TO ONE KNEE AND FIRED TWICE. This was my fantasy growing up on a diet of Western movies where, as the film opened, the camera scanned a torn map of the west eventually focusing on the bold words SANTA FE.

Maybe that is how I ended up here, an imprint on my brain from a darkened theatre 60 years ago, or maybe it was a conscious choice that Zenia and I made 30 years ago.

When we met in San Miguel de Allende in the early 70's we had already seen a good part of the world. Zenia, from New York City, had married and lived in Italy, San Francisco, and then San Miguel. I, from a small town in Oklahoma, married and moved to San Diego after college and a few years later in 1964, '65, and '66 took an extended trip around the world in a VW camper, settling in Japan for a year before returning to the States.

The year after meeting we traveled for a year through Central America in an old hippie school bus and soon left on a year and a half backpacking trip through SE Asia, always on the lookout for that magical place we would like to settle together. Nelson, a then lovely town on the South Island of New Zealand, tempted us for awhile but many factors combined to eliminate it.

While visiting Santa Fe for a few months we had once created a list of what we wanted in a place to live. Of the 73 things on the list, Santa Fe had everything except an ocean, a good radio station, a vibrant university, good coffee, and large deciduous trees. Now it is only missing three things.

One thing we both agreed upon was that we wanted our home to be in the United States. We had met too many people who after years in Latin America, Africa, or Asia had been forced to leave because of a change in the political climate or having everything taken away because some influential local person decided they wanted that persons property. So while Nelson was tempting for awhile we knew it would never work for us. So six months later, upon returning to the West Coast, we set out to find where we wanted to live in the United States.

In our many years of travel we had met people from all over who said that they lived in a great place. So we proceeded to visit many of them to see if what suited them might suit us. And while many places were attractive for a few days, we found most towns were missing a heart. There was nothing to bring people together, no gathering place, no common purpose, no cooperative spirit, in essence no reason for being.

In 1982 after months of traveling around the United States we returned to Santa Fe to see if it still fit most of our needs.

Galen and Zenia arriving in Santa Fe in 1992.

Other than cowboy movies we both had some past history with Santa Fe. I had passed through Santa Fe with my parents in 1943, explored for uranium in eastern New Mexico in 1954, and stopped briefly in 1966 dropping a friend off on my way back to San Diego from San Miguel. Zenia, on a long road trip across America with Romano, her Florentine husband, in the early '60s had found Santa Fe to be the only place between the two coasts that had any character other than New Orleans. Together we had visited many of our numerous friends living here that we had known in San Miguel de Allende years before.

San Miguel at that time was one of the glorious places in the world before it was discovered. Friends made there include the John Muir Publication people for it was where John wrote his *How to Keep Your VW Alive* book that launched his publishing business. Many of the people in Dixon came almost in mass from there when Mexican officials started creating flaws in legal documents in order to confiscate property. And other friends like Mike and Charlotte from Chacon, to Jane, Ted and Linda, all encouraged our move.

As many people have done, we stayed with friends when we first arrived, originally in Cerrillos, then housesat in various places in Santa Fe until renting a house on Camino Santander for a year while we searched for a permanent place. We thought we knew everything for sale within an hour of Santa Fe, but Halloween in 1982 was the pivotal point. People we had met in New Zealand came to visit and he had read of an incident involving a house being burnt down and wanted to see where it was. We found it and a few hundred feet farther on came to the edge of Arroyo Hondo. It was a magical place, a deep wide canyon with a flowing stream just minutes from downtown.

Nothing was for sale on the short road following the rim of the canyon, but we returned many times to visit and hope. And then one day a FOR SALE sign appeared: *12 acres on the rim and all the way through the bottom of the arroyo.* We bought it that day.

Soon we moved to a small rental next door and started planning our dream home. First we tried to explain to architects what we wanted and after some futile attempts to draw what they thought we had said, we gave up knowing we would have to do it ourselves to get what we wanted.

A house slowly rose out of the ground, built a handful at a time of the sand, gravel, and dirt that we dug up and of the trees that we purchased for vigas and cut ourselves from the mountains east of Pecos. It was a bygone time when someone could build a house themselves and with the encouragement of the building inspectors who understood the solar and ecological aspects of the building we poured our money, sweat, and too often blood into it for the next two years. Many dear people, some skilled, most not, some for a few days, some for months, helped out and all became and remain friends. And then, somehow, one day it was mostly finished and we moved on with our lives.

With the emphasis on the building behind us we could focus on other things, like the joy of living in Santa Fe. A horse came into our lives earlier, now dogs, and with time available travel became a top desire.

We had been into China for a week in 1979, but now it was just becoming possible to travel somewhat freely throughout China so with our backpacks we headed to China for three months in 1985. Back again for another three months in 1986 to write a guidebook on China for John Muir Publications and our desire to get to know China was temporarily sated.

Importing, which we had done a little of, became more serious as we made friends in China and started getting ancient jade and

Galen and Zenia with their Bali student tour participants at Angkor Vat, 2006.

other treasures and more trips to South America, Africa, and Asia for whatever interested us continued on until 2000.

The desire to combine travel and friends led us to begin a Travel Club which involved travelers getting together for a meal, discussion, and a slide show which went on monthly at our house for 18 years.

Volunteer work with kids continued on all the time. Having both been teachers the desire to be around young people was fulfilled in many ways. I became a Big Brother, and helped out in numerous other ways. Zenia volunteered in many youth organizations and loved doing mediation. We both were seriously involved in the early stages of the Children's Museum.

In 2000, following an inheritance, we decided to start the Bali Art Project to encourage young people from Santa Fe to get to know other cultures. Each June we take eight high school juniors, most of whom have not traveled and could not afford it, to Bali for a month. Classes are organized in Balinese dance, gamelan, painting and batik in order to use the arts to get to know the culture. So far we have taken 64 kids from Santa Fe to Bali and many of them have later gone on to study and volunteer abroad.

Santa Fe has fit our needs for a place to live that has a heart and soul and we feel that in our own little way we have helped make Santa Fe a better place to live.

Our Old Adobe Home in La Villita
José & Clare Villa

José Villa is a professor emeritus from San José State University, California. His undergraduate degree is from the School of Inter-American Affairs, University of New Mexico. He has a graduate degree in social work from Arizona State University and in education administration from San José State University. He has been an organizer and educator throughout the southwest.

Clare Cresap Villa earned her bachelor's degree in fine arts from Loretto Heights College in Denver. After marrying José, she took a 25-year sabbatical to bear and raise their eight children. Since resuming her art career in the early 80's, she has experimented in many different media and has her work in many private and corporate collections across the country. For the past ten years her passion has been for the Spanish Colonial religious art of the Santero.

WE WERE ALWAYS NEW MEXICANS....despite the many years we spent wandering the southwest in search of education and occupation, we always knew we'd be back some day. As it turned out, we were beckoned back from San José, California to the Santa Fe area by an aging, neglected, crumbling, abandoned and abused adobe ruin--for us, it was love at first sight. The once-proud home of an Apache slave woman sat next to the village church that once had been the heart of this small farming community, itself de-consecrated and also in a state of abandonment, housing only extended families of pigeons.

In the seventeen years since Manamela, the last occupant of "our" adobe ruin had left her life-long home, the house had fallen victim to a succession of misfortunes, the last of which had been a pestilence of gangs who congregated here to do their drinking and drug abuse. They used the inside of the house for a public toilet and they burned the latillas and wood from the windows and doors for warmth in winter. It was a sad sight, indeed, missing parts of its walls, vigas falling in under the weight of the sod roof, birds nesting in the remaining latillas, ant hills big as small mountains. Why we took a liking to such a sad pile of adobes is a wonder, but that we did.

It was my brother John who brought us out from Santa Fe to see this place. He had spotted it several years before, when both he and the house were in better shape. He had hunted down the owner and negotiated to buy it (for $2,500), thinking of spending quiet, cool summer nights here with his dogs and chickens, and some corn planted by the acequia nearby. Unfortunately, he had a heart attack before he could make the place liveable, and after that he didn't have the strength to do it. It was in 1980, during one of our visits with him after his illness that he brought us out to see the place of his dreams....and in the conversation, mentioned that he was going to have to sell it. My son Daniel, visiting from Alaska, asked how much he wanted for the property; my brother answered "$5,000," whereupon Daniel raised his eyebrows and retorted "I'll buy it!!" Then he turned to me with a challenge, "Dad, I want you to have it. You learned to work with adobe from your father. Let's see what you can do with this place."

It was true: my wife Clare and my eight children had often heard the stories about how my parents escaped the Mexican Revolution in 1915, and of how our family survived the Great Depression by traveling miles every day to work the fields in west Texas. In the off-seasons, my dad, Encarnacion Villa, built small adobe homes for fifty dollars...and furnished all the adobes. With eight sons and two daughters mixing mud, he could crank out hundreds of adobes a day. My mom's tasty tacos, beans, and chile along with her spirited singing of Mexican *corridos* (ballads) kept us joyfully nourished. Dirt and water were plentiful, and we gathered straw from nearby fields. I recalled the blistering summer days that baked the adobes and browned our skin. My dad always kept talking to us, encouraging us to outwork each other by pointing out how strong, how swift we were. *"La tierra es su hogar."* (The dirt is your home.) *"Por mientras tengan su salud, sus brazos y su respecto pueden cumplir con lo que quieran."* (So long as you are healthy, have strong arms, and your self-respect you can accomplish anything.)

Unwittingly, my dad was preparing us for the Fr. Conradin Stark adventure. One May day in the early 1940's, my brothers and I were walking by an empty lot near Our Lady of Guadalupe Church in Clovis. There was our Pastor, a Franciscan missionary from Ohio, in the middle of an empty lot scratching in the dirt with a hoe. "Father, what are you doing?" we asked respectfully. "Why, I'm going to make adobes to build a convent," he replied. We turned away from him to keep him from reading the surprise and disbelief in our faces. "Father, that's not the way to do it," we said. "Well, show me how it's done," he challenged. Father Conradin had just inveigled us into a huge, summer-long project that resulted in a convent for the teaching nuns. Those were lessons none of us ever forgot — the politics of getting things done, and the actual labor it took to get there.

As it turned out, we now needed a lot of both.

We arrived that first summer in our '77 Ford F-150, four-wheel-drive pickup and a trailer loaded with custom-made, thick wooden doors that my son Christopher had made from recycled wood. We also had recycled windows, old door knobs, hinges, and tools we bought at a recycling place in East San José. Our daughter Angela (then 14) and Steve (son of friends) were with us. We were really emotionally charged and eager to get started on our family project. We celebrated July 4th with twenty-three relatives. We had none of the taken-for-granted amenities…such as running water, electricity, or bathroom facilities.…just a passel of curious relatives from a 250-mile radius. We made an outhouse out of four old recycled doors.…the neighbors gave us access to their well water. It was a grand fiesta, with family musicians blessing us with their songs and our family around us to cheer us on. In those first years, we had no electricity, plumbing or water. All our work was like in the old days…hard labor done by hand.

"La Vi" (as our ongoing summer project came to be known) was a continuing delight and challenge. Since I was a professor at San José State (a profession not known to be exceedingly lucrative) and we still had five of our eight children living at home, with two of the others in college, money was scarce — but enthusiasm made up for it. We dreamed about La Vi for ten months out of the year, continuing to gather odds and ends from used building material lots, from friends who had cast-off windows and such, until summer break would finally arrive and we could be off for New Mexico and more adventure. Our stories were so infectious that we had all sorts of young people who wanted to come to be part of the scene. We never lacked for workers the eleven summers we spent here! Our children and their friends came out of curiosity about what we were doing with an old, dilapidated adobe. Once they got here they were hooked. They had to get their hands in the mud, patch cracks in the walls, put up wire for plastering, tear down the sod roof and replace it with materials that didn't leak, clean and cut latillas, repair or make door and window frames, and bathe in our improvised outdoor shower.

I didn't have to use much of my dad's or Father Conradin's psychology: Clare set the pace, and it was as torrid as the noonday sun! She turned out to be the swiftest plasterer in the bunch…and that included me and my strapping young sons. Angela, our youngest, was not far behind in keeping the cement mixer chugging along at full speed. It seemed as if everyone was swaying to the rhythm of men working on a chain gang…and liking it. Teams came together, and soon teams were competing to get their side of the wall done faster. *Mas lodo!* (More mud!)

With all of the pressures brought on me by my work at the University and the "Chicano revolution," in which I was on the forefront in northern California, I was in dire need of reconnecting with the earth—with my family, my faith, and my culture. La Villita became the catalyst to reconnect me with my Mexican and Spanish roots. Somehow our family sensed this, and resonated with their enthusiasm.

In 1982, we started with the remnants of an 1100 square foot pile of dirt. The neighbors had volunteered to bulldoze the old place, but it was our dream to restore it by using the thick adobe walls that were still standing. In 1993 we retired and moved here permanently, continuing the odyssey of building that now adds up to over 3600 feet of comfortable living space, as well as a garage and two workshops, *portales*, and *sombras* (covered and shaded areas), an adobe *tapia* (wall), and a *capilla* (chapel).

From the first moment we set foot in La Villita in 1980, we felt that we had come home. There is something spiritual about this area that called to us—continues to call to us—with a calmness and richness of culture that is unparalleled anywhere else we have lived. It is a community with many needs, one that is receptive to the volunteers that offer their hands and talents in response to those needs.

It is our philosophy that if you want to be a part of any community, you need to put in your share of sweat equity. With that in mind, in 1994 (the year after we arrived here full time), I set about helping to organize a local Habitat for Humanity group—which still is active in the area, repairing and building homes for needy families in the area. Several years ago I was the main organizer for I-LEAP, a community-wide organization of faith communities supporting each other's efforts to address the social ills of the area, specifically drug use. And for the past six or seven years, I have been one of the main proponents for garnering National Heritage Area status for the upper Río Grande valley—Santa Fe, Taos and Río Arriba counties. After years of politicking for this designation, our proposal finally passed both House and Senate and was signed into reality by President Bush earlier this year.

Clare, being an artist, joined the Española Valley Arts Festival board in the fall of 1994, and has been instrumental in putting the festival on every October since that time. In the fall of 1997 she enrolled in the NNMCC Spanish Colonial Furniture department in El Rito, and also began carving and painting santos, which she considers a true marriage of her lifelong interest in the saints and in her wide experience in producing art in many genres.

One of her first major projects, one that took several years, was to create Spanish Colonial altar furnishings for St. Anne's church in Alcalde, where we worship regularly. This included carved and painted altars and reredos, side altars, ambo, music cabinet and baptismal font.

In 2003 she was asked by Mayor Lucero to be part of a project to create an historical museum in the San Gabriel Museum reproduction on the Española Plaza. Clare designed the displays, worked with Daniel Tafoya of Peñasco who carved her projections so that she could paint them, and organized over 30 local artists whose work is displayed as part of the museum project.

Later she carved and painted another altar and reredos for the chapel at historic Los Luceros ranch, which had been restored by members of St. Anne's church in Alcalde. And currently we are building our own chapel in our front yard, in thanksgiving for God's gracious gifts.

This old adobe home brought us to La Villita. This is a holy place that comforts us and brings us peace. In the midst of a humble community, it serves as a testimonial to the endurance, strength, and faith of its original builders. We now have a safe sanctuary where our children and grandchildren can come to escape the vicissitudes of worldly tensions, and where they can share stories of how it was resurrected from a pile of dirt. Its earthen walls resonate as we chant the Salve Regina...a hymn to guide us in our final journey.

For our old casita de adobe we say, "Gracias a Dios!"

PRAYER OF THE ADOBE

Lord I am only a simple adobe
    put together with water
        and with Mother Earth

But I have a special calling
    and that is to be one in spirit
        with all who come to this abode

Of prayer and worship
    to give thanks to You
        for all of your gracious gifts.

Lord I am a simple adobe
    that praises and embraces You
        with ever wakeful love.

José and Clare Villa at the door of their first home, a broken down adobe out of which they have built their lives.

*José and Clare Villa
with their eight children.*

*José and Clare Villa
with their entire clan.*

St. John's, Santa Fe, and the Seventies
Charles L. Weber & Robin Jones Weber

*After many years of the Santa Fe Shuffle, working two and three jobs to afford to live in Santa Fe, **Charles** settled into being a Real Estate Broker in 1989. Volunteering in his beloved Casa Solana neighborhood as well as coaching and afficiating local soccer leagues brings Charles closer to this wonderful community. Married to writer **Robin Jones** with daughter Abagael, Charles continues to share the secrets and joys of Santa Fe with everyone.*

I FIRST CAME TO SANTA FE IN MARCH, 1972, on a tour of potential colleges. I arrived with all the arrogance and inexperience of a high school senior. I also carried with me the burden and baggage of my upbringing in Memphis, Tennesse, a place that saddened me with its close mindedness, upset me with its violence, and exasperated me with its pettiness (the prep school that I was fleeing had promised great academics; but what I mainly remember was the ominious promise—"No haircut, No diploma!"). Against that background, St. John's and Santa Fe shook me out of my world and opened my eyes to all the possibilities this southwestern mecca held.

I was first of all fascinated by the St. John's curriculum. I was also captivated by the physical majesty of the campus and its surroundings. Finally, the sense of community in this small mountain town intrigued me like no other and gave me a home.

The St. John's "program" focused on reading the greatest books of western civilization. Reading is the start, but talking about and writing about these archetypal ideas and people moved me, and still moves me, more than any other intellectual endeavor. There is no better measure of a world than in the writings, ideas, conversations, arguments, and histories of these great minds.

And there is no better measure of what one can become, by absorbing the past and learning from it, to achieve a future with potential and honor.

I read Aristotle and Sophocles, the plays of Stoppard and Shakespeare, the poetry of Milton and Donne. I studied science and math—from the Pythagorus theorum to Einstein's theory of relativity. I learned Greek and French (and while in Santa Fe, perfected my Spanish which I had learned as an exchange student in Costa Rica). And I expanded my ability to think, reason, and discuss in the midst of beauty. We students would talk about the past. We'd argue what was and wasn't just. We'd try to reason out our own understanding of a book against the understanding of others; we learned to listen, to be silent, to think, and to put our ideas together in order to learn more and deeper.

That first visit to St. John's, I had arrived on a Wednesday. I had no sooner checked into my dorm room, than I realized I couldn't see any sky out the window. What I saw was mountain! Monte Sol reared up and blocked that view completely. I have to admit, I didn't unpack, I didn't begin to prepare for the classes I was to visit. I felt called. I immediately trekked to the top of Sun Mountain. That was the first of countless occasions I would be stirred and awed by the view of the Galisteo Basin to the South, the Rio Grande Basin defined by the Jemez to the west, and last of all, the snowcapped Sangres. Since then, I have sought out and happened upon many other extraordinary vistas in Northern New Mexico, but that moment up on Monte Sol divided my life into before and after.

Artists have tried for centuries to capture in words and pictures the luminous beauty of Santa Fe. Each vision is different. Each day shows a different form of that beauty—light at play in the Rio Grande Valley. All of us who choose to stay in Santa Fe marvel at what each day brings.

Up on campus I found a new home. From mountain tops I

Charles Weber, 1972.

looked down on mesas and plains, houses and churches, fields of flowers and acres of snow. Sitting in the St. John's cafeteria with my friends, I watched the sunset blazing down. I'd sit in the shade of piñons at noon and watch the carp idling by water lilies in the pond at the center of campus. I'd listen to music, watch movies, and listen to great minds. I learned to waltz, swing dance, and jitterbug in the college's Great Hall (I met my wife at a St. John's waltz party!). I played pool and bridge long into the night, taking breaks from my reading and studies. And always there was talk. Talk with my fellow students, talk with my tutors, talk with the countless visitors to the College. Sometimes, it seems that for four years, all I did was to sit on campus and talk, but I know there was more. The joy and freedom of college offered the perfect opportunity to explore this formerly sleepy mountain town.

In 1972, Santa Fe was a lot different than it is today, in 2007. Back then Rodeo Road was gravel with no stop signs or stop lights; St. Francis Drive was only four years old. It didn't take me long to discover the Plaza. I could eat at Josie's Cafe, shoot pool at the Old Plaza Bar, drift over to Safeway to shop or to Zook's Pharmacy for aspirin. The glass blowers across from El Farol up on Canyon Road fascinated me. I watched the heart and soul of this town take place in casual conversations around the Plaza.

The constant spark of ideas from the great books exercised the mind incredibly. After a smoky dinner at Three Cities of Spain (now Geronimos), where it seemed everybody in town was awake, must have been inside drinking, dancing, and smoking—walking back to campus was exhilerating. If anyone had been watching, I'm sure we seemed nuts, revisiting conversations from the bar, from class, from the readings, trudging up Camino de Monte Sol. We talked loudly, gestured wildy, gloried in that starry pine scented night.

With Atalaya Peak as my backyard, the opportunity to explore was ever present.

Some weekends, when the federal government was blazing a trail for I-25, many families would converge on the work sites for that week. The machinery of construction would lay waste to the hills and arroyos southeast of town. Some of us would gather firewood for friends or tutors from the College. And that was the first time I saw anyone spread sheets underneath the piñon trees and shake them for their nuts. There was a joyous almost circus atmosphere. Pickups would park all along Old Las Vegas Highway. Different groups would hike along the path of destruction and give a big shout when

Charles Weber with wife, Robin Jones and daughter, Abagael.

they found a nut laden tree that had escaped, or several trees together that had been pushed, roots and all into a chaotic pile. There would be kids climbing, chain saws buzzing, and always a rush for lunch at Bobcat Bite.

When St. John's students would celebrate Spring with their Reality Parade, I'm sure we were outrageous and over the top with makeup, togas, and loud music in our trek from the Plaza to campus. However, no one wrote letters to the editor; no one protested from the side of Garcia Street. There was simply that indulgent smile and gentle shake of the head.

Now I realize that if the citizens of Santa Fe could put up with legislators for decades, student antics were pretty tame. The only time I saw the town get into an uproar was the time a legislator missed a turn on Acequia Madre. This narrow curving street has been around for as long as the ditch. One winter a big Lincoln missed a curve, went through the garden wall, and plowed into the dining room. When the family awoke to the crash and came out of their bedrooms, there was the legislator, leaning against the fridge, drinking milk right out of the carton.

I don't recall asking myself if I wanted to go St. John's or live in Santa Fe. I never made a conscious decision as I stood on the Mountain of the Sun more than 30 years ago and looked at my future. But at that moment, I became a Santa Fean *(Santa Fecino),* I became a *"johnnie."* I found my home.

From the Sea to the Mountains

Barbara Windom

__Barbara Windom__ owns and manages La Estancia Alegre in Alcalde, New Mexico, where she raises and trains her magnificent Peruvian Paso horses having left her former life as a noted interior designer in Southern California behind her. Showing her prizewinning horses all over the Western States, she maintains her ties to Santa Fe and all the friends she has made here in the past 20 years as well as her daughters and granddaughters in California and New York.

VICTOR AND I HAD BEEN DATING for five years; he lived in San Francisco and I lived in Malibu; one of us always had the unused portion of a round trip ticket in our pocket, and we both had the ghosts of previous lives in our homes.

The sand and sea in Malibu were so beautiful; my old Mediterranean home on the beach was fabulous, and my children and I loved it…until we tried to get out of the driveway on Monday mornings. The traffic was unbearable; the joy of entertaining on weekends became a nightmare as friends were stuck on the highway for hours trying to get home, so they stopped coming to visit. The windows corroded, the ironwork rusted, the septic tanks overflowed and the surf came into the living room. The earthquakes terrified my cats and broke all my best China. Sometimes the mountain fell onto the highway, and it took hours to go around the whole valley to get home.

When the pleasures fade, it is time to make a change. The blue skies and the cultural aspects of Santa Fe beckoned us; we rented a house for a holiday week to see if we liked it, and we fell in love. There were beautiful mountains and trails, there were all sorts of wonderful things to do and to see without getting into a traffic jam, and my love of horses and riding began to haunt me…perhaps, I thought, we could get a couple of horses to ride on the trail; we could build a swimming pool and swim without fear of undertow and sharks.

We did all that…two horses became a few more; we had friends who loved to ride, so we boarded a few horses, sold a few horses, rode into the mountains and had wonderful Sunday brunches at the Tesuque Village Market. We had pool parties on Sunday afternoons and friends brought friends; we met many wonderful people from Santa Fe and the surrounding area. We did all that…for about five years, and then I began to get really interested in breeding my wonderful Peruvian Horses. That was about the time I realized that the house was too big, and the space for the horses was too small!

We looked for a ranch…green grass and a wonderful barn and all those things… I had ideas, but everything we saw was barren with small trees and no water. One Sunday at the pool my friend surprised us with a photo of a ranch for sale…it was green and there were pastures. It had once been a stagecoach stop between Santa Fe and Taos, and it was 100 acres. Only problem was, it was 30 miles north of Santa Fe, and almost everything was broken. The good news was that it had great potential, the whole perimeter was fenced, AND there were green pastures as far as we could see and as much water as we needed to keep them green! So we changed our lives again; we sold the beautiful house in Tesuque, and we made plans to build a house in one of the fields, surrounded by horses. We see them from every window in the house …even from the shower. The few horses became 40, and now I have choices; that's what life is all about. We

*Barbara and Victor at the time
of their arrival in Tesuque 1989.*

Barbara Windom with her first Peruvian Paso, Relampago Negro — Tesuque 1991.

Barbara on LEA Poema, Multi-champion of Champions bred by Barbara at La Estancia Alegre —2007.

can ride through the arroyo, under the highway and all the way to Truchas, but most days we ride around the ranch on the trails we have made around and between the beautiful green pastures.

The drive to Santa Fe is just like the drive from my old house in Malibu to Los Angeles; it is twice as long, but it takes only half the time.... not any time at all, when it means that Santa Fe and many friends are so close by.

We Came to Santa Fe

Mark Zaplin & Richard Lampert

Mark Zaplin and Richard Lampert, born just 12 days apart, grew up in Boston only a block away from each other, created a friendship that grew over the years reinforced by their mutual interest in the arts. Each one of the two happily married and living their continuously interconnected lives contributes on a daily basis to the success of one of the premier art galleries in the Southwest. Their interest in community affairs as well as their own personal inclination have joined to make them outstanding and responsible members of Santa Fe's artistic and cultural community.

I T WAS ALMOST THIRTY YEARS AGO — September 29th, 1977, to be precise — that the U-Haul rolled up Old Pecos Trail (then, only one lane in each direction) carrying the contents of two lives displaced by — what else but broken relationships. We were 24 years old having already known each other for 24 years (more on this later). We were excited, tired and hungry. The good news is that we had already heard about the red versus the green versus the "Christmas". The bad news: it was Yom Kippur — our day of atonement, our day of fasting. The guilt is still there, although we can't remember whether we sinned at the Golden Temple, a k a The Conscious Cookery (where Pasqual's now resides), or Maria's (where Maria's *still* resides!). After confession, we needed to find a place to live — a place to unload the U-Haul. We grabbed the *New Mexican,* opened it to the Classifieds, and were led to a flat-topped adobe on Camino San Acacio. The perfect place for two bachelors to start anew.

Inside the U-Haul were the everyday items that one would expect: clothing, furniture, books, records, stereos, etc...., with one significant exception: the life works of the renowned photographer and chronicler of the Native American Indian, Edward S. Curtis.

Five years earlier, in Boston where we grew up, we had acquired the full collection of copperplates, photogravures, portfolios, along with volumes of images and writings of the Curtis magnum opus. The short version of the story is that we discovered them in the basement of an old rare book store. Self-taught as youths in the fine art of selling (lemonade, Kool Aid, Fuller Brush, AAA and the Great Books of the Western World), we had honed our entrepreneurial skills for years. And in Curtis, we recognized yet another opportunity, albeit on a much grander scale.

We somehow raised the necessary funds to acquire the collection which had been "lost" for over 40 years. At that time we were muddling through college in Boston and, much to the disappointment of our parents, we determined that there was no need to continue. The diplomas would have to wait. In fact, they are still waiting.

We opened a gallery in Harvard Square only to discover that Easterners were more interested in George Washington, John Hancock and Samuel Adams; they couldn't have cared less about Geronimo, Chief Joseph and Red Cloud. After six months, the message was clear: "Go West young men."

We charged through the West, promoting and selling the works of Edward Curtis at museums, historical societies, art and antique shows, and Native American exhibitions, constantly in search of the private collector with the big bucks who might be interested in the images of this remarkable photographer. It seemed easy at the time. It was the 70's. Back to nature was the philosophy, mother earth was the deity, turquoise jewelry the accessory, and Native Americans the torchbearers. Russell Means and Dennis Banks were raising hell. Most folks had never seen the compelling images that Curtis had created between 1900 and 1930. We lived in places such as Boulder, San Francisco and Seattle. We were criss-crossing the American West and viewing—for the first time—the Pueblos and the reservations, the unusual architecture and the striking landscape that had inspired Curtis three quarters of a century earlier. For two young men who grew up never having been west of the Mississippi, these were "Lewis and Clark times."

It is important now to go back in time—way back—to 1952. We were born 12 days apart in Newton, Massachusetts, a suburb of Boston. We lived in houses as near to one another as the Compound and El Farol restaurants. Our parents were best friends. If any of you can consciously remember the first person you knew—other than your parents and siblings—that's how we remember one another. We went to kindergarten together; we went to middle school together. We played step-ball together, we built snowmen together, we remember one another's first girl friend. We went to Fenway Park hundreds of times when we were growing up—and 50 years later we were together in St. Louis when the Red Sox finally won the World Series... a most joyous occasion. We were together for births and funerals, Bar Mitzvahs and weddings. We've mostly laughed together; we've shed a few tears.

Today, we own Zaplin-Lampert Gallery on historic Canyon Road. We have known each other for 54 years; we are 54 years old. We are both married, although our wives occasionally joke that we are married to each other. It is a unique friendship. From our first introduction to the City Different 30 years ago as a gently growing art community, to the sophisticated "small town" we've watched it become, we have embraced Santa Fe at all points along the way—and she, us.

Our love of art has evolved from the early days of representing the photographs of Edward Curtis, to the gallery and the artists whom we represent today. From the explorer artists of the American West such as George Catlin,

Mark and Richard working the phones in the early days of their Zaplin Lampert Gallery.

Mark and Richard in front of their Gallery on Canyon Road today.

Karl Bodmer, Albert Bierstadt and Thomas Moran, to the members of both the Taos Society of Artists and the Santa Fe Art Colony, among them, Joseph Henry Sharp, Ernest Blumenschein, Victor Higgins, Will Shuster, Fremont Ellis and Gustave Baumann. For us, there has been an ever-deepening admiration for those who have depicted the great region and culture that we have all come to love.

As to how we got to Santa Fe, the short answer is "by U-Haul." As for why, the short answer is, very simply, "the art." And while many of those who come west to New Mexico and Santa Fe speak of the clean air, the architecture, the food, for us it is the people. Both those who grew up here (how lucky are they!) and those who have migrated here over the years (how fortunate are we!). We are merely guests, having come here three decades ago, having added—we hope—to the uniqueness of what we Santa Feans have come to know and love.

It is a great honor to share our story and to be among the other adventurers whose stories also lie within this book. After all, isn't there a little "Lewis and Clark" in all of us?

PUBLISHER'S NOTE

Pennywhistle Press celebrates its conversion to a non-profit organization and its 22nd year of publishing brilliant poetry with an independent spirit.

Established in 1986 the Press has grown, maintaining a lively conversation between the authors it has published and their readers. It hopes to continue this conversation over the phone or on the internet at *pennywhistlepress.org* with the poets, writers, critics, reviewers and readers of the future. The Press has expanded its outreach and its books are distributed by Small Press Distribution of Emeryville, California among various other distributors and wholesalers.

Pennywhistle's latest collection of distinguished and important poetry underlines the commitment the Press has made to share a wide range of voices, presented in a responsible manner to a public seriously interested in good work and an expansion of the landscape of poetry. This book begins the expansion of the horizons of the Press that bring its approach and sensibility to prose works such as this collection of memoirs, to a collection of Women's Voices in Times of War, from Iphigenia to Cindy Sheehan and to a collection of Prison Writings from Boethius to Abu Jammal.

Hooplas! *by James Broughton*

Is a collection of festive tributes to friends and intimates of the author, who salutes their talents and personalities with song, fanfare and wit. These odes for odd occasions are offered in praise of friendship, in memory of merriment, and in awe of love. The poet died in 1999 after completing this special tribute to his many friends and his poems remain wonderfully alive today.

93 pages • $8.95 • ISBN: 0-938631-02-0

Blood Trail *by Florence McGinn; Introduction by Victor di Suvero*

The cross-cultural currents that have enriched American writing in the later part of the 20th century continue to be part of the literary scene today. Florence McGinn's work continues that cross-cultural adventure. Her poetry, crafted with care for the detail of her Chinese heritage, reaches into our consciousness with current American scenes and with language that touches our hearts.

108 pages • $12.00 • ISBN: 0-938631-34-9

Spring Again: New & Selected Poems *by Victor di Suvero*

Spring Again—a collection of Victor di Suvero's most recent work as well as a selection of poems from earlier work celebrating his life in New Mexico today. Dedicated to his children and to his extended family, this gathering of poems reaches into the poet's past as well as addressing current practical and political issues in a lyric and exciting manner. Winner of the 2007 Independent Publishers Bronze Medal Award.

170 Pages • $16.00 • ISBN: 0-938631-26-8

Moving On: New & Selected Poems *by Victor di Suvero; Introduction by Richard Brodner*

Moving On is a collection of new and selected poems published by Pennywhistle Press in the Spring of 2007. This little red book contains a striking variety of poems that confront our present political as well as our private worlds. In the spare but direct and conversational language that di Suvero chooses in his work he weaves a multicultural cloth of feelings, ideas and reactions to the everyday world we all share. Known as an "outsider" it is that point of view that has informed his work since he began writing when he was 16 years old.

120 Pages • $16.00 • ISBN: 978-0-938631-36-1

¡Saludos! Poemas de Neuvo Mexico is the first bilingual anthology of the poetry of New Mexico. Sixty six fine Native American, Hispanic and Anglo poets share their experience of the Land of Enchantment with clear and heartfelt poems that sing! Poets represented in this strong and unique collection include Miriam Sagan, Jim Sagel, Leo Romero, Charles Bell, Greg Glazner, Peggy Pond Church, Luci Tapahonso and Joy Harjo, among others.

290 pages • $15.00 • ISBN: 0-938631-33-0

The Press currently offers the following titles in its Chapbook Series:

The Blue Series

Full Turn *by Sarah Blake; Introduction by Dorianne Laux*

Her book exposes the sacred territory of domestic blood connections, of love and family demonstrating how ordinary life has a tendency to trap and bind. Blake roots herself in the present and struggles with ghosts of the past, convincingly adept at being both here and there at once.

32 pages • $6.00 • ISBN: 0-938631-05-5

The Fields *by Richard Silberg; Introduction by Joyce Jenkins*

His work is spare and complicated and speaks to the process of personal discovery. His brilliant resolutions bring one home.

32 pages • $6.00 • ISBN: 0-938631-05-5

Who is Alice? *by Phyllis Stowell; Introduction by Sandra Gilbert*

Her preoccupation with the need for a common language between the sexes generates a passionately argued sequence of poems about silence.

32 pages • $6.00 • ISBN: 0-938631-04-7

The Sum Complexities of the Humble Field *by Viola Weinberg*

She offers a poetry of the sensual that can be tasted and touched. At the same time, she presents her world with discipline and mathematical precision.

32 pages • $6.00 • ISBN: 0-938631-06-3

ℛ

The Red Series

The Width of a Vibrato *by Edith A. Jenkins; Introduction by Robert Glück*

She writes a poetry of affirmation that begins with awareness of loss and is dwelt upon until the poet is able to transmute that loss into affirmation.

32 pages • $6.00 • ISBN: 0-938631-10-1

Portal by Joyce Jenkins; Introduction by Carolyn Kizer

Her poetry offers readers a rare combination of playfulness spoken with wisdom — showing a complex nature devoid of bitterness.

32 pages • $6.00 • ISBN: 0-938631-18-7

Falling Short of Heaven *by Susan Lummis; Introduction by Austin Straus*

Her work is the quintessence of a high strung, highly sensitive and wildly intelligent woman's attempt to get along in this big, bad world. Her poetry is written with a theatrical feel that makes it seem lived in.

32 pages • $6.00 • ISBN: 0-938631-12-8

ℛ

The Green Series

Where You've Seen Her *by Grace Bauer; Introduction by Robin Becker*

She has earned her reputation for a clear and incisive use of language. Ms. Bauer illuminates her subject matter with an honesty all too rare in today's world.

32 pages • $6.00 • ISBN: 0-938631-11-X

Decoy's Desire *by Kerry Shawn Keys; Introduction by Gerald Stern*

His appreciation of the natural beauty of his world—specifically that lush hillside in Perry Co., Pennsylvania—surfaces throughout this collection.
32 pages • $6.00 • ISBN: 0-938631-14-4

What Makes a Woman Beautiful *by Joan Logghe; Introduction by Jim Sagel*

She shares a voice as ancient and wise as time. With gleaming syntax honed to perfection, Ms. Logghe's women—and men—live their everyday realities and how "beauty" abides and sustains.
32 pages • $6.00 • ISBN: 0-938631-15-2

Chaos Comics *by Jack Marshall; Introduction by Morton Marcus*

His work is sensual and intense, his supple, possibilities of perception with a philosophy that is breathtaking in its audacity and scope.
32 pages • $6.00 • ISBN: 0-938631-25-X

Between Landscapes *by Wai-Lim Yip; Introduction by Jerome Rothenberg*

He has created a magical, musical scale that enchants, soothes and lulls, rises and falls, as it simultaneously plunges us into the beauty and power of the terrible and sublime cycles of nature.
32 pages • $6.00 • ISBN: 0-938631-24-1

Still The Sirens *by Dennis Brutus; Introduction by Lamont B. Steptoe*

His poems take us from the rigors of apartheid to the bestiality of imprisonment and from the desolation of exile to those moments of recognition and acknowledgement that make the struggle worthwhile.
32 pages • $6.00 • ISBN: 0-938631-09-8

Sextet One

The first anthology in Pennywhistle's new series. This volume presents the work of six separate and distinct poets with each presentation containing an introduction by a noted critic or poet, a photo of the author and a collection of the poet's most recent work—a wonderful way to bring six new friends into one's life! This volume presents Kim Addonizio, Tom Fitzsimmons, Harry Lawton, Annamaria Napolitano, Doren Robbins and Ruth Stone, with introductions by Dorianne Laux, Victor di Suvero, Maurya Simon, Pierre Saint-Amand, Philip Levine and Rebecca Seiferle.
226 pages • $17.50 • ISBN: 0-938631-27-6

ORDERING INFORMATION

Call your order to 505-982-0066
or fax it to 505-982-6858

OR WRITE TO

PENNYWHISTLE PRESS

Post Office Box 734
Tesuque, NM 87574

email: *pennywhistle@newmexico.com*
website: *www.pennywhistlepress.org*

OR

SPD/Small Press Distribution, Inc.
1341 Seventh Street, Berkeley, CA 94710-1409
tel: 510-524-1668   fax: 510-524-0852
www.spdbooks.org